BREAKING OPEN THE WORD OF GOD

*Resources for Using the Lectionary
for Catechesis in the RCIA
Cycle B*

Edited by
Karen Hinman Powell
Joseph P. Sinwell

PAULIST PRESS
New York / Mahwah

Quotations from Psalms 15, 23, 30, 34, 78, 84, 123, 146 are taken from "The Psalms: A New Translation" by Wm Collins Sons & Co Ltd. The publisher wishes to acknowledge the permission of A.P. Watt Ltd. on behalf of The Grail, England for the use of this material.

Library of Congress Cataloging-in-Publication Data

Breaking open the word of God.

    Bibliography: p.
    1.   Bible—Study.   2.   Lectionaries
3.   Christian education.   I.   Powell, Karen Hinman,
1953-   II.   Sinwell, Joseph P.
BS592.B75   1987   268   87-6946
ISBN 0-8091-2894-2 (pbk.)

Published by Paulist Press
997 Macarthur Boulevard
Mahwah, New Jersey 07430

Printed and bound in the
United States of America

CONTENTS

Preface

By Most Reverend Patrick F. Flores, D.D.
Archbishop of San Antonio

For over thirty years I have had a great interest in helping people on their journey to the Catholic Church. I have given convert instructions and received many into the fold. However, I always felt that the converts had not been adequately exposed to the Gospel, to Jesus, and to the Church. I have participated in seminars on the Rite of Christian Initiation of Adults. I have heard from workers as well as from the neophytes, and I have become convinced that the RCIA is really the answer to my prayers. This book is a powerful tool to help us in this most delicate task.

Like its companion piece, *Breaking Open the Word of God*, for use with Cycle A, this book lays before us options for the use of Scripture-based catechesis with the lectionary. Of course, this lectionary catechesis occurs in the midst of our liturgical year. The Catholic experience—exemplified in feasts like Epiphany, All Saints, Assumption, Immaculate Conception, Trinity, Corpus Christi—is also celebrated in the liturgical year. This book provides models for catechists to use in "breaking open the word" in a parish so that our cate-chesis is pastoral formation at its best. It is a practical tool which offers *many* samples—one for each week of the liturgical year as well as for major feasts and celebrations.

A credit to the editors and to the book itself is the fact that it has been written by priests, nuns, and lay people from throughout the United States and Canada. Each writer, in a unique style, emphasizes that each catechist throughout the United States and Canada is to reflect upon the Scriptures, the tradition, the particular persons with whom he or she works. The richness of the book is that it points out clearly that there is more than one way to do this type of catechesis. The gifts and talents of each catechist are enchanced.

I heartily recommend this book to you as one among many resources, for it is just that—a resource, a guidebook. Used wisely, it will enable your catechumens and candidates to grow in their spiritual lives as Catholic Christians. Truly this is a tool for the "pastoral formation" of their lives.

Introduction

As more dioceses and parishes implement the *Rite of Christian Initiation of Adults (RCIA)*, how to use the lectionary in catechesis becomes a pastoral concern. *Breaking Open The Word: Resources Using the Lectionary for Catechesis in the RCIA* for Cycle A readings published by Paulist Press provided a resource tool for using the lectionary. This volume focuses on the readings in Cycle B and demonstrates how the lectionary can be a source of catechesis.

The use of the lectionary can incorporate catechesis with the vibrant faith of a celebrating Christian community. This book emphasizes using the lectionary in catechesis throughout the entire year. Articles focus on doctrine and catechesis, the formation of a process, the development of small groups and the integration of music as prayer. It contains outlines of catechetical sessions on themes found in the Sunday and holy day readings of Cycle B. A Scripture commentary on the readings precedes each liturgical season.

Experienced ministers in the adult catechumenate have authored the session outlines which utilize a variety of models. Catechumenate teams can use these sessions as resources for adapting the lectionary to local needs. Flexibility and adaptability are key ingredients to an effective and creative use of the lectionary in catechesis.

The use of the outlines presumes:

1. That the parish offers on-going catechesis for catechumens throughout the liturgical year.

2. That the parish has extended the period of catechesis with adult catechumens for one to three years. (Rite of Christian Initiation of Adults No. 19 & 20)

3. That the parish celebrates the rite of dismissal for catechumens in a Eucharistic liturgy. (Rite of Christian Initiation of Adults No. 19)

4. That the parish catechumenate teams promote the principles of adult religious education in the catechumenate.

5. That catechumens and team members have available their own copy of the Sacred Scriptures during catechetical sessions.

Although this volume is primarily intended for use in parish catechumenates, a variety of pastoral ministers could easily adapt it for personal reflection, Scripture sharing, post-RENEW processes and other adult religious education activities.

We wish to acknowledge the contributing authors for their cooperation and creativity: Mr. Robert Hamma of Paulist Press for his support and Mrs. Marie White and Ms. Michele Kelly for their diligent assistance.

This resource can be another pastoral tool for all adults who are breaking open the word of God. Using the lectionary in catechesis can help each adult to continue to grow in faith and respond to the challenge of living God's word in community.

Dedicated
to
David L. Powell
Elizabeth H. Sinwell

IN APPRECIATION OF
THEIR LOVE AND SUPPORT

INTRODUCTORY ARTICLES

Catechesis through the Lectionary: Soft on Doctrine or Strong on Faith?

By James Dunning

Bishop Robert Morneau tells a story about a fifteen year old boy accosted on the ski slopes with the question, "Are you saved?" Not intimidated, he shot back, "Sure, I'm saved!" "How do you know?" was the surprised reply. The quick retort: "Because my mom knows two priests and the bishop."

Some moms of the recent past felt "saved" if they knew the catechism taught by those priests and bishops. Born-again Christians feel "saved" only if they personally know the Lord Jesus. It seems basic questions about salvation include: Whom do you know, what do you know, how do you know, and what do you mean by knowing?

I share concerns of moms, dads, and some priests that children today at times know more fluff than stuff about religion. At confirmation time I once met a boy who wasn't sure if Moses or Jesus led Israel into the Red Sea. I taught college for a while and was dismayed by the religious ignorance of students. But can we not be equally dismayed by moms, dads, and some priests who know a lot of religious stuff and theology (new or old) but fall mute when called to voice their relationship with Jesus Christ? A study of priests claimed two-thirds were underdeveloped in their ability to articulate a personal faith.

The Catholic version of fundamentalism is a literalist approach to doctrine and law with scant insight into meaning and truth behind doctrine or experience and values behind law. One priest said to me about doctrine: "Who cares what it means? Just believe it!" My own seminary training gave short shrift to biblical and historical exegesis allowing non-fundamentalist insights into Scripture and creed. Not until I taught a course on the creeds fifteen years later and studied the history of councils which gave us creeds did those formulae explode into meaning.

I also share concerns of born-again Christians about religion without relationship, facts without feeling, Church without community, just works without Jesus. But there can be relationship without reason, feelings without faith, community without commitment, Jesus without justice. Some privatistic "saved" Christians need a healthy dose of Matthew 25 about

banishment with goats for those who don't see Jesus in the hungry, naked, prisoner, and stranger. And the Protestant version of fundamentalism is more often a non-historical, literalist reading of Bible texts which limits meaning to words and twentieth century understandings of those words. After arguing with a Catholic, one fundamentalist retorted, "Well, if the King James Bible was good enough for St. Paul, it's good enough for me!"

Let us explore how we might connect lectionary with doctrine in catechesis in ways that avoid both biblical and doctrinal fundamentalism but also ease concerns about being soft on doctrine, more fluff than stuff. Before doing that, I shall name some of my own assumptions about basic issues and terms. There is disagreement about the meaning of these terms. I shall not resolve that disagreement here but simply adopt a stance which you may accept or reject.

Assumption: Faith is not theology, is not doctrine.

When the centurion tells Jesus to only say the word and his servant will be healed, Jesus exclaims, "I have not found such *faith* in Israel" (cf. Mt 8:5–13). He was telling Israelites who knew doctrine and law that faith is not doctrine and law. Faith is not "the faith," statements about God. Faith is personal relationship with God, surrender of not just the mind but the whole person to the God who surrenders himself to us in Jesus. Faith is our basic stance before the God of grace who gives life and healing and reconciliation as sheer gift. In response to the gift of love, faith is our response of love. Credo comes from the Latin, "cor dare": to give the heart. Believe in German means to "be-love." Faith is expressed in words (and music, art, ritual, drama, stained glass, etc.). Faith is wedded to some expression, or there would be no faith. But faith is not words but being in love.

In the strict sense, *theology* is "faith seeking understanding" (St. Anselm) in a systematic way by teasing out the meaning of people's experience of God through the use of philosophy and other disciplines. In the broad sense, whenever we express faith we begin to do theology, in stone, glass, dance, and especially words. Out of their relationship with Jesus, writers gave us great words in biblical stories and doctrines. But while there can be no faith which is unexpressed, there can be words without faith. That is the fundamentalist danger. Later generations can mouth others' words and become what E. M. Forster calls "poor little talkative Christianity." Literally, they don't *know* what (whom) they're talking about. The challenge is to let the theologies of others generate, express and deepen our faith-relationship to God.

Doctrines (dogmas) are one-liners or brief paragraphs approved by the universal Church as official theological expressions of the faith of the entire Church, helpful for clarity but never exhausting the meaning and usually not adapted to all cultures. Doctrines are few. When people complain about catechesis being soft on doctrine, they often mean the popularized theological commentaries on doctrine found in most catechisms. Here is the key question: What invites most people to deeper faith—the more abstract words of theological commentary (like this chapter) or words closer to people's experience, the concrete language of narrative and story (like the parables of Jesus)?

Assumption: Religious education is not evangelization, is not catechesis.

I use the term *religious education* in its broadest and least Catholic sense. It includes the study and communication of the Scriptures, rituals, images and symbols, theologies and ethical teachings of any religious tradition, including the Catholic Christian tradition.

Evangelization is sharing the good news of the Judaeo-Christian tradition (in our case, in its Catholic forms), aimed at faith (as understood above), initial conversion, the first hearing of the good news (cf. *RCIA*, 9, 10).

Catechesis in Greek comes from "to echo." After initial conversion, catechesis echoes the good news, unfolds its meaning, deepens on-going conversion, interprets and applies for action.

With this perspective, religious education embraces evangelization and catechesis; evangelization and catechesis do not include religious education. For example, colleges might offer religious education courses which compare the writings of the major religious traditions, not to convert students to any tradition but to create freedom so students can explore different visions of the meaning of life. The principal purpose is information, not transformation. But when a student chooses to seek membership, for example, in the Catholic Christian tradition, evangelization and catechesis begin. Evangelizers and catechists are unabashedly biased. Their principal purpose is not information but transformation. Religious education is not always aimed at con-

version; the grist of evangelization and catechesis is conversion: *turn* to God, in Christ, through the Spirit, in the Church.

The point is this: fundamentalist catechists who know not the meaning of doctrine can offer interesting religious information which titillates the cortex but in no way summons to conversion. That plays right into the hands of fundamentalist inquirers who desire information about the Catholic Church, not deeper transformation into God. Some inquiry classes, with all their paraphernalia of classes, lectures, instruction, and programs, offer not catechesis but religious education. Catechesis, indeed, offers information but always for the purpose of transformation. We hope that catechesis offered in the context of worship and based on the transforming power of the word of God in the lectionary will situate doctrine where it belongs—anchored in the conversion journey of following Jesus through death to life.

Finally, evangelization and catechesis are two sides of the same coin. Evangelization means beginnings, initial conversion, first hearing of good news *for me*. Catechesis means growing up, on-going conversion, echoing good news. In the precatechumenate, we do not presume that people with Bible quotes, theologies and doctrines have personally heard good news. Wondrous words can mask feeble faith.

Inquirers, either catechumens or baptized candidates, are gloriously unique; the time of precatechumenate for each may be gloriously unique. With each person the goal is initial conversion. Then they join catechumenate, on any Sunday of the year, since they can choose to follow Jesus more deeply on their schedule, not ours. With the good news of the lectionary, catechumenate simply echoes what has been happening in precatechumenate, with the goal of deepening on-going conversion. Catechumenate never becomes religious study; its focus remains not information but transformation.

Assumption: Catechesis is more than words.

John's Gospel proclaims, "The Word became flesh and lived among us" (Jn 1:14). That Word in Hebrew is "dabar" which means not just verbiage but word-deed, word in action, speaking-acting, doing what we say, practicing what we preach, a sacramental word which effects what it signifies. That Word is not primarily Jesus' words but his life. That Word *is* Jesus. Therefore, John can add, "Something which has existed since the beginning, that we have heard, and we have seen with our own eyes; that we have watched and touched with our hands: the Word, who is life . . . " (I Jn 1:1).

We who are Church receive and become that Word. "Everybody who believes in the Son of God has this testimony inside them" (I Jn 5:9). We become words of the Word. To be God's Word, however, empowered by God's Spirit, we are called to be "dabar"— not words tripping off the tongue signifying nothing, but word-deeds, who, like Jesus, "do the truth in love" by serving the hungry, the naked, the prisoner, and the stranger (cf. Mt 25). A "Catholic difference" that sets us off from some Protestants is that the Church is not just a help and support for faith in God's Word. To paraphrase John, the Word has become Church and lives among us. Faith comes through hearing the message (cf. Rom 10:17); and the Catholic vision is that this message is always incarnate, becoming flesh in Jesus and through his Spirit in us.

The good news: in this perspective, the Church *is* the message. The bad news: unlike Jesus, we have other spirits, demons, evil spirits. No matter what we say, our deeds proclaim who we are. We can wax eloquent in catechetical sessions about scriptural images of Church as the salt of the earth and the light of the world; but if the local church is infested with dark demons of violence, apathy, prejudice, greed, those words signify nothing. "This little light of ours" isn't shining. We can gush panegyrics about Vatican II doctrine of Church as people of God; but if the local church is dominated by clerics and this missionary people is more "navel-observatory" than launching pad, doctrines die. We can rhapsodize about a reconciling, warm, welcoming Church; but if the parish assembly watches their watches during catechumenal rites of welcome, those rites aren't much of a gala homecoming. Words of neither lectionary nor doctrine alone can bear the weight of "dabar."

That is why our national catechetical directory, *Sharing the Light of Faith*, takes a broad view of catechesis (cf. #213). It affirms that catechesis certainly happens in proclaiming that Word in words (in Greek, "kerygma"), but also in the life of the community ("koinonia"), in worship ("leiturgia"), and in service and witness ("diakonia"). Certainly, formal catechesis happens in proclaiming the message in lectionary and doctrine. But there are catechetical dimensions to the life of the community, its worship, and especially its service and witness that speak louder than words. Once again, as with Jesus, *the* Word of God as "dabar" is the Church's life. Catechesis during the catechumenate period taps and echoes all incarnations of that Word which is life.

That is why the RCIA also has a broad view of what happens during that period. It mentions celebrations of the word leading to suitable knowledge of dogma, living with the community its life of prayer and moral values, liturgical celebrations, and apostolic witness and service (cf. RCIA, 19). We hear much concern about being soft on doctrine. Might we be equally concerned about being soft on service? Might we cease surprising new Christians by delaying the call to mission until mystago-

gia? Might we do catechesis in the catechumenate period by inviting them into ministries to meet God's Word where he said he would be, in the hungry, naked, prisoner and stranger?

With these assumptions as background, let's explore the meaning of doctrine and its relationships to catechesis with the lectionary.

How Doctrine?

How does doctrine happen? It happens not as first word or last word. The first "word" is life: our experience of life as gift, grace, God's gift of love, enfleshed in Jesus and still enfleshed in life touched by his Spirit. That experience at times can be created, generated by the words of others. For example, when people hear Jesus' prodigal son story, that can unveil times when reconciliation came to their lives as absolute gift. They learn the language of grace. But those words cannot replace experience. Faith is about personal relationship to God. Conversion is about that. The conversion most wounded, bored, lonely, guilt-ridden, self-sufficient people need is not to doctrine about Pope, penance, or purgatory but to experience their very lives as sacramental: visible signs of invisible grace.

Then we stammer and stutter to find words to voice that gift, that grace, that love. Enter Scripture and doctrine. In a Catholic understanding, there is not Scripture *and* tradition. There is only tradition (in Latin, "traditio," the "handing on" of our experience of God's love through Jesus in our Spirit-touched lives). We do so especially through words. When the Church accepts words from the first generation of Christians to express its common faith and experience of Jesus, that becomes Bible. When it accepts words of later generations, that becomes doctrine. But the roots are the same: words grounded in personal and communal experience of God in Christ Jesus.

Implications. First, whenever we echo those words today in catechesis, we invite people to discover their experience of God. If we do not, we fall into fundamentalism.

Second, historically *development of doctrine* happened partly because people struggled to express experience of God in the context of the language and search for meaning of their own culture. Someone has said that one's faith is given by God, one's doctrines by one's century. That language does not contradict the biblical words but goes beyond Scripture to find words that speak to other cultures. The Bible never says Jesus has one Person and two natures. But reflecting on the biblical experience and their own experience of Jesus, Greeks of a later generation spoke in those philosophical terms of the time, both for their own understanding and to preach Jesus to others in words which they might hear. The Catholic understanding is that the

Spirit continues to guide the Church in finding such words.

Third, every generation is challenged to find words which help people experience Jesus in their times. Much of Scripture uses words of an agrarian culture closer to Boise than Boston. Most great doctrines were formulated in philosophical words of the first six centuries and may not speak to people today. For example, the Greeks could say Jesus is not a human person but only a divine Person, Son of God. They understood "Person" philosophically; we understand "person" psychologically. In popular parlance, if we preach that Jesus is not a human person, people hear that he does not have a personality. That is heresy, even for the Greeks. Jesus would not "be like us in everything but sin." We have to change the words to honor the faith.

Fourth, in developing doctrine and theology for different cultures, including our own, we do not deduce doctrine from Scripture. We don't claim that everything is already in Scripture, and that it simply took us a while to find it. Catholics believe that when guided by the Spirit, we shall discover nothing contradictory to Scripture, but we shall find "something new under the sun" about a God who cannot be captured in any words, biblical or modern. New experiences of death and life, seen in light of the creative power of biblical words, generate new understandings of the heights and depths of the wisdom and knowledge of God (cf. Rom 11:33–36). The point is this: when using the lectionary, we do not "pull" doctrine out of Scripture. Rather, the stories of Jesus healing the sick, for example, give us occasion to explore how the Church in later times celebrated healing in sacraments and how we might experience healing in a broken and wounded world today. Catechists need to know and make those connections.

Finally, when finding words for our own times, the pioneer English catechist, Canon Drinkwater, said in the 1930's: Keep it simple. He suggests four kinds of religious language: scientific difficult (Thomas Aquinas, Karl Rahner); scientific simple (Baltimore Catechism); poetic difficult (Gerard Manley Hopkins); poetic simple (the parables of Jesus). He insists most catechesis should be poetic simple, story and narrative, with a bit of scientific simple (doctrinal summaries of meaning).

Translated that means: a lot of lectionary, a lot of contemporary story and poetry in dialogue with the lectionary, and a bit of doctrinal and theological commentary, for most people. For example, when the lectionary proclaims the story of the Emmaus journey, might we put that in dialogue with our own journey stories, with the help of the following journey story from Anne Sexton, penned when she was dying of cancer? Then might we name our common experience with the doctrine, paschal mystery, "rowing" through death to life?

A story, a story!
(Let it go. Let it come.) . . .
And God was there like an island I had not
　　rowed to,
still ignorant of Him, my arms and my legs
　　worked,
and I grew, I grew.
I wore rubies and bought tomatoes
and now, in my middle age,
about 19 in the head I'd say,
I am rowing, I am rowing
though the oarlocks stick and are rusty
and the sea blinks and rolls
like a worried eyeball,
but I am rowing, I am rowing,
though the wind pushes me back
and I know that that island will not be perfect,
it will have the flaws of life,
the absurdities of the dinner table,
but there will be a door
and I will open it
and I will get rid of that rat inside of me,
the gnawing pestilential rat.
God will take it with His two hands
and embrace it.
As the African says:
This is my tale which I have told,
if it be sweet, if it be not sweet,
take somewhere else and let some return to
　　me.
The story ends with me still rowing.
("Rowing," *The Awful Rowing Toward God*,
　　Houghton Mifflin, pp. 1–2)

Why Doctrine?

Humans are meaning-making mammals. We love to say, "Aha! Now I see what it means." In the play *Equus*, the psychologist discovers he needs to see more than his patients: "I need—more desperately than my children need me—a way of seeing in the dark." Elizabeth Barrett Browning speaks of our crying need to see:

Earth's crammed with heaven,
And every common bush afire with God:
But only he who sees, takes off his shoes . . .
("Aurora Leigh," *The Poetical Words of Elizabeth Barrett Browning*, Macmillan, 1897, p. 466)

For example, humans stand on that earth crammed with heaven and ask, "What can a meal be?" Those who see take off their shoes and see the possibilities: "Aha! Birthdays, anniversaries, Thanksgiving, Passover, Eucharist!" Bible words come from those who saw those possibilities, like Jesus. John Shea writes:

The stories of Scripture were remembered and today remain memorable because they are similar enough to our lives for us to see ourselves, yet different enough from our lives for us to see new possibilities. They tell us what we want to know and more. (*Stories of Faith*, Thomas More Press, 1980, p. 114)

Official doctrine and unofficial theologies reflect the human passion to unpack meaning from the stories of people who see. We attempt to get beyond the details of those stories to name the common denominators. For example, after two thousand years of official and unofficial theologies, the Catholic-Christian common denominator which discloses the "why" of many of those stories is the doctrine of incarnation—God in the flesh. The Catholic experience is that grace (God's presence) is mediated, incarnate in the persons and events of Judaeo-Christian biblical history and in the subsequent history of God's people, including us.

Theological reflection on lectionary stories and on our personal story, launched by our experience of incarnation that sees earth crammed with heaven, connects the stories. We move beyond differences of the Hebrews' exodus from Egypt, Jesus' exodus through death to life, and our exodus from slavery as blacks, women, native Americans, refugees, alcoholics or addicts. Aha! We see. That which connects all these stories is incarnation: God, enfleshed especially in his people, is present at the center of all journeys through death to life, precisely when we feel most abandoned, when we surrender ourselves to liberating love.

The Catholic experience and doctrine of incarnation also connects and gives meaning to apparently diverse aspects of contemporary life. If we unpack the meaning of incarnation (God in human flesh), we explode into "aha's." Aha! about ecumenism (God enfleshed in Protestants and Hindus). Aha! about sex (I am like God when I enflesh love). Aha! about justice (God lives in streets, not just sanctuaries).

Exegesis is the discipline which helps catechists in the search for the meaning of both biblical and doctrinal texts. Catechists will turn to commentaries by exegetes who critically examine texts and draw upon history, archaeology, and literature to elicit meaning. The task is like that of homilists. However, too often both homilists and catechists present exegesis without connections, interesting historical information without any "so what's" for life today, data without "aha's," words without "a way of seeing in the dark." Exegesis leads homilist and catechist into the world of texts; homily and catechesis after the dismissal reverse direction—from texts back to life and culture. Homilies exegete lives, not just texts. That calls for cooperation between homilists and catechists who bring lives to texts and texts to life for *these catechumens in this parish.*

Words which light up both biblical and doctrinal texts in homily and catechesis are usually words of simple poetry of people on the search for meaning. For example, in her "rowing toward God," in a body racked by cancer, in contemporary language Anne Sexton raises questions of death and life. Her language sends us to raise questions and to mine our tradition for meanings found by those who rowed before us. Listen to part of Sexton's final poem. Might these words lead us toward the dock where Jesus is moored?

> I'm mooring my rowboat
> at the dock of the island called God . . .
> I empty myself from my wooden boat
> and onto the flesh of The Island.
>
> "On with it!" He says and thus
> we squat on the rocks by the sea
> and play—can it be true—
> a game of poker.
> He calls me.
> I win because I hold a royal straight flush
> He wins because He holds five aces.
> A wild card had been announced
> but I had not heard it
> being in such a state of awe
> when He took out the cards and dealt.
>
> As he plunks down His five aces
> and I sit grinning at my royal flush,
> He starts to laugh,
> the laughter rolling like a hoop out of His
>   mouth
> and into mine . . .
> Dearest dealer,
> I with my royal straight flush,
> love you so for your wild card,
> that untamable, eternal gut-driven *ha-ha*
> and lucky love
> ("The Rowing Endeth," *op. cit.*, pp. 85–86)

What Doctrine?

"What is learned is no more and no less than the love *of* God *through* Jesus Christ and *in* the Holy Spirit. All the doctrines of Christianity are but explications of that one statement" (*Why Doctrines?* Charles Hefling, Cowley Press, 1984, p. 69). Catechumenates are about that love, the *experience and meaning of grace.* Doctrine in the catechumenate is for transformation, not just information, catechesis not just religious education, conversion to God not data about God.

Therefore, when speaking of doctrine the RCIA uses adjectives pointing to *quality* not quantity: the catechumens are led to "suitable knowledge" of dogmas and "intimate understanding" of the mystery of salvation (cf. #19). The RCIA suggests three gifts for catechumens: Bible, Creed, and Our Father. It does not suggest treatises of Aquinas, but hints that we stick to the basics. Therefore, the catechumenate team determine what is suitable and intimate doctrine about the love *of* God *through* Jesus *in* the Spirit, and make a checklist of the principal Catholic-Christian meanings which reveal, celebrate, and witness to that love. Praying the lectionary during the Church year, in an atmosphere in which homilists and catechists prompt catechumens' questions of meaning, should cover that checklist. If that does not happen, the team should deliberately raise those questions and issues.

Some complain this does not get at "the Catholic difference." People want to know about Mary and Popes, purgatory, and penance, Catholic sexual ethics and increasingly about a Catholic vision of justice and peace. Fine. Take all questions. Some of that will happen during the precatechumenate. The lectionary will tease out other issues, e.g., when the Gospel proclaims fidelity in marriage until death, certainly questions will arise.

But Greeley/Durkin claim the real Catholic difference is at the level of experience of God's love. They claim that Catholics (and some Protestants) normally experience that love in a "sacramental" world of not just seven but seventy-times-seven incarnations of God in the persons and events of our world. Ultimately, that gives birth to other Catholic differences: the presence of God in Mary and Popes, seven sacraments not just two, reconciliation in community not just to God, incense and holy water, "smells and bells." If doctrine is situated in the midst of that sacramental world, through the lectionary in the midst of a catechumenal community of two or three gathered in Christ's name, it will be grounded precisely in the faith, the relationships, the experience of God enfleshed which gives birth to doctrine in the first place.

If that happens, our creeds would "give our hearts," our beliefs would "be-love," and we might not just say but pray our doctrine not about but into God:

> We believe that where people are gathered
> together in love
> God is present
> and good things happen
> and life is full.
> We believe that we are immersed in mystery
> that our lives are more than they seem
> that we belong to each other
> and to a universe of great creative energies
> whose source and destiny is God.
> We believe that God is after us
> that he is calling to us
> from the depth of human life.
> We believe that God has risked himself
> and become man in Jesus.

> In and with Jesus we believe that each of us
> is situated in the love of God
> and the pattern of our life
> will be the pattern of Jesus—
> through death to resurrection.
> We believe that the Spirit of Peace
> is present with us, the Church,
> as we gather to celebrate
> our common existence,
> the resurrection of Jesus,
> and the fidelity of God.
> And most deeply we believe that in our struggle
> to love
> we incarnate God in the world.
> And so aware of mystery and wonder,
> caught in friendship and laughter
> we become speechless before the joy in our
> hearts
> and celebrate the sacredness of life
> in the Eucharist.

(John Shea, "The Prayer of Belief," *The Hour of the Unexpected*, Argus Communications, 1977, pp. 36–37).

Small Groups: Resources for Christian Initiation

By Joseph P. Sinwell

After the period of catechesis in the Rite of Christian Initiation of Adults (RCIA), a catechumen stated, "The sharing and reflections in the small group really made the word of God and the faith come alive for me and helped me to deeply examine what I believe and how I live it. I felt cared for by each member of the group and encouraged to serve others."

This statement points to some distinct advantages of small group interaction when using the lectionary in catechesis. Group interaction can encourage deeper reflection, conversion and a sense of Christian community. Catechesis in the adult catechumenate focuses on Christian growth and conversion. The Rite of Christian Initiation of Adults explicitly states in paragraph 19:

> Familiar with living the Christian way of life and helped by the example and support of sponsors and godparents and the whole community of the faithful, the catechumens will learn to pray more fervently, to witness to the faith, to be constant in the expectation of Christ in all things, to follow the supernatural inspiration in their deeds and to exercise charity toward neighbors to the point of self-renunciation.

Catechesis in the catechumenate must respect how adults learn and grow. The formation and building of group interaction can aid in how adults learn and grow in faith with one another. This article will examine advantages and disadvantages of small group learning and ways to promote skillful facilitation of groups in the catechumenate.

I. Advantages

Small groups can promote adult religious education in the catechumenate in several ways. Small groups promote a comfortable atmosphere. They enable individuals to know one another gradually and build a level of trust. This level of trust can lead to deeper sharing of faith and the development of supportive relationships within a Christian community.

Small groups can encourage individuals to participate. Catechumens learn in different ways and as responsible adults they can contribute to their own learning about the Gospel and growth in Christian living. A small group can allow for each catechumen to reflect and respond from his or her perspective and to raise appropriate questions or to provide unique contributions to the process of journeying in faith together.

Small groups can support flexibility in a variety of learning experiences. A key adult religious education principle is that each adult learns in unique ways. The small group experience can provide the atmosphere and time for a diversity of processes that appeal to either the left or right brain. It can create ample opportunity for pursuing critical analysis or explanation of doctrinal or pastoral concerns, for reflecting imaginatively on key Scripture themes and their implications or pursuing a meditative process.

If a particular process, activity or presentation is not working with particular individuals because of the group size and atmosphere of trust, the process can be adjusted to the group more readily. Individuals can be encouraged to pursue another method.

A small group can promote on-going conversion. Due to the development of trusting relationships and the level of communication, individuals in small groups can become freer to raise and focus on critical life issues of living out the Catholic faith. At times it becomes difficult to highlight the need for on-going conversion. A small group may also resist change. Adult catechists must be aware that adults often seek practical solutions to what are perceived as crises or problems. By personal sharing and prayer, individuals can help others to examine critically their own way of living out their faith. This personal interaction will provide encouragement and offer practical insights for Christian living.

II. Disadvantages

The disadvantages of small groups in the catechumenate is that they can become self-centered, produce unrealistic expectations and become dominated by a few individuals.

As catechumens, sponsors, and catechists grow to know each other, the group could have the tendency to examine only their own needs and become satisfied or closed. The challenge of the catechist would be to raise broader questions and issues that the lectionary highlights.

To avoid self-centeredness, catechumenate groups should be encouraged to be in contact with parish leadership and issues. Parish leadership can be invited to discuss or share on specific issues and ministries. An emphasis on a global view of Church and world will decrease any focus on self-centeredness and elitism.

In the experience of catechetical sessions, individuals often say, "What a wonderful experience of community," or "This group offers me so much." The experience of growing deeper in faith together, feeling mutual support and drawing close to others can create unrealistic expectations for catechumens and ministers. They may become discouraged because what happens in the smaller catechetical group does not happen in the larger parish community. Realistically, the smaller community may be a sign and witness of what is beginning to emerge in the parish.

Catechumens and others may also begin to demand that all their needs be responded to and fulfilled by the catechetical group. The development of a mature Christian demands relationships to a variety of individuals and emphasizes that spiritual growth is ongoing life process. This group does not exist for self-fulfillment, but as an integral part of the process of an individual's initiation into the Christian community.

A few people can dominate a small group by a lot of interacting and emotional expression. These behaviors can lead to conflict and annoyance. Catechists must allow time for reflection and emphasize that silence is not wasted time. They must encourage the interaction of all members and create a healthy respect for those who do not wish to respond verbally or prefer inner reflection. Silence must be fostered as a meaningful religious value.

III. Skills

Both catechumens and catechumenal ministers are involved in the process of deepening faith through ongoing conversion. Catechists who are facilitating this process must acquire some basic skills when working with adults.

Catechists must establish a warm, respectful and trusting relationship with catechumens and sponsors. A climate of hospitality will encourage these relationships. Welcoming individuals fosters trust and openness. It also means that catechists must be confident within themselves and willing to admit their own weaknesses and strengths within the group.

In using the lectionary as a basis for catechesis the expectation is not that the catechist be a Scripture scholar or eminent teacher, but rather that he or she be a person who profoundly respects the insights and faith journey of others and understands the uniqueness of responding to God's call. Implicitly, he or she too must continue to respond to God's call in his or her own life.

The catechist has the responsibility of preparing and leading sessions; these sessions need to be adapted to respond to the needs of the catechumens within their own parish setting. Simply following an outline from a book will not suffice; the catechist through listening and observation can adjust processes to the faith journey of the catechumens.

The catechetical process with adults will demand that the catechists be trained in group dynamics and skills of communication. They must be attentive to the content of a person's message or story and the feeling with which it is expressed. Without awareness of both, the catechetical group will become mired in personal conflict and tension. Creative listening is an essential skill of the adult catechist.

Group interaction and process will demand patience. When an activity or reflection questions are begun, catechists do not need to be the first to respond. In many situations, they must be able to refrain from expressing their own opinions and feelings and encourage others to respond. They do not have to prove that they are an expert to lead the group. They must be able to communicate a support for individuals' growth and respect for a diversity of opinions.

In dealing with small groups the catechist must become aware of behaviors that aid and hinder the catechetical process. A catechumen may consistently interrupt discussion by citing personal experiences or opinions that have nothing to do with readings, discussion or reflections. This is behavior known as blocking and can harm communication. Another person may try to discern differences in points of view and present weaknesses and strengths of each. This is known as harmonizing and it often enables the group to move deeper into the subject. The more skilled a catechist can become at identifying behaviors, the more he or she can aid in the process of delving deeper into the word of God within Catholic tradition.

Critical evaluation of the catechumenate session is a necessity for developing small group interaction and growth. Catechumenate team members must review sessions to assess whether they are facilitating the growth of catechumens and exploring understanding and implications of the lectionary. Some helpful questions to aid this process are: What were the strengths and weaknesses of the sessions? How did the participants and groups interact and react to the process? How did the session aid or hinder the faith journey of the catechumens? How did the session enable catechumens to learn and change? Routine evaluation will enhance the catechetical process and the skills of team members in developing the use of small groups.

Primarily, catechists must be persons of faith who are involved in a personal process of on-going conversion. They cannot offer what they do not have. They must be persons of prayer who continue to develop an ever deepening relationship with the Lord and God's people. Without personal and communal prayer and reflection, their ministry will become arid.

Hopefully, the catechists will meet with other catechists and catechumenal ministers for support and to evaluate the catechetical sessions and process. Support, frank observation and encouragement will only enhance the growth of catechesis.

The key to small groups is support and formation of adult catechesis. Small groups should not be exclusively used. However, they can become resources in which adults can delve deeper into an understanding of God's word, experience Christian community, recommit themselves to Christian growth and become a stunning witness of process of Christian initiation to the entire parish community.

The Lectionary as a Source Book for Catechesis in the Catechumenate

By Karen Hinman Powell

The catechumenate is "an extended period during which the candidates are given pastoral formation and are trained by suitable discipline." Paragraph 19 of the Rite of Christian Initiation of Adults (RCIA) provides insight into the formation of candidates for membership in the Roman Catholic Church. The formation of these women and men is to be "pastoral." This formation is achieved through four elements: catechesis, community, liturgy, apostolic works. This article will unfold these elements of the formation process pointing to the fact that the Sunday morning dismissal and the use of the lectionary is the way to achieve this pastoral formation.

Catechesis is "given in stages and presented integrally, accommodated to the liturgical year enriched by celebrations of the word," which leads catechumens to a "suitable knowledge of dogmas and precepts and also to an intimate understanding of the mystery of salvation in which they already share" (RCIA #19). This catechesis is rooted in the celebrations of the word of God. The lectionary is one way to open men and women to this word of God. I propose the lectionary as "the way" for the catechumenate.

Human experience in dialogue with the word and our living tradition (as we do celebrate this word each week) leads catechumens to a rich understanding of dogmas and Church teachings. Using the lectionary as sourcebok for catechesis, more than one catechumen has said: "I have learned a great deal about the Catholic Church—its teachings and way of life—but I have also walked a way of faith where I have been given the tools to live and continue learning and growing as a Catholic Christian the rest of my life." Catechumens learn dogmas and precepts, Church teachings using the lectionary as sourcebook for catechesis. Catechesis accommodated to our liturgical year means living and reflecting on the word in the midst of our major celebrations and feasts—our Catholic celebrations: Christmas, Assumption, Easter, Ascension Thursday, Advent, Lent, All Saints Day, Immmaculate Conception, Corpus Christi, Trinity Sunday, Epiphany, to name a few of the major celebrations to say nothing of other daily feasts which can be found in our lectionary and liturgical year. It is the use of the lectionary *in the midst* of the liturgical year! What better way to learn our Catholic truths than to experience them with us. Do we not learn more about a community by what they do and who they are than what they say! This applies to our Catholic truths as well. Catechumens learn about our major truths as they are dismissed each week from the Sunday celebration to reflect upon these truths to make them their own.

The lectionary is the best tool for catechesis because it provides for the fact that catechesis can then be given in stages and the "unique spiritual journey of candidates" (RCIA #5) can be reverenced. As Catholics we have three years of readings. This means we have three years of catechetical material—liturgical Year A, Year B, Year C—with enough material for three years of different sessions in the journeys of the men and women who seek membership with us. Men and women can respond to the word of God uniquely and can then be called to the sacraments of initiation some Easter as they are ready. The three year cycle allows for time, for change. This cycle opens up a variety of Christian truths in our Catholic way of life providing time to the catechumens to integrate these truths and to respond uniquely to the call of God in their life as they live it with us.

Community: Pastoral formation is achieved by catechumens "becoming familiar with the Christian way of life" (RCIA #19). This means that catechumens are formed as Catholics by being in relationship with other Catholic Christians. Through these relationships catechumens learn about the Christian way of life. They will "learn to pray to God more easily, to witness to the faith, to expect Christ in all things, to follow God's inspiration in all their life deeds, and to exercise charity toward all" (RCIA #19). Sunday mornings when the community assembles together is the primary time for the community as a whole to share in this formation process. On Sunday mornings the community hands on our tradition of liturgical prayer where catechumens can be drawn to pray to God more easily by our praying together. Sponsors, spouses, other members of the Christian community are readily available on Sunday morning as witnesses of faith. This is *the* community gathering of the week, a very appropriate time for pastoral formation. This is not to say that Sunday mornings are the only times the catechumen is formed by the community but to point to the fact that it is the primary time.

Implied in the community as a dimension of pastoral formation are hints at who the catechists and members of the catechumenate team may be. Women and men in our parish who can break open the word are the best catechists. Catechists will be skilled in sharing faith, in listening to others, in enabling the faith of the community to be handed on to the catechumens. Catechists are, as one person in Texas said, "the BLP's: The Basic Lay People." Pastors, catechumenate directors, pastoral ministers, directors/coordinators of religious education, are enablers of the community, are model catechists; however, they are the ones who need to let go and enable the community to be the primary catechist in this formation process. The best catechists with whom I have worked in three parishes directly and around the United States and Canada are women and men who are serious about their faith, have *no* degree in religious education or ministry, and who are persons of prayer and commitment to their own conversion journey. These women and men hand on a faith they have lived for many years. Selection and training of these catechists is essential; however it is not the topic of this article. There are other resources available for assistance here.

Liturgy: "Catechumens are cleansed and strengthened through celebrations of the word with the faithful" (RCIA #19). The pastoral formation of catechumens occurs in liturgy. Throughout the Rite the importance of catechumens gathering with the assembly of the faithful for the liturgy of the word is repeated. Likewise it is repeated that catechumens, except in *extreme* situations, are dismissed. The liturgy of the word, once known as the Mass of catechumens, is essential to their pastoral formation. Many catechumenate directors and pastors throughout the United States and Canada say: "But we can't dismiss because. . . ." Why can't you? What are you afraid of? The rite points to its importance. Pastoral practice of dismissal indicates that they are dismissed to be nourished by the word, that this experience of dismissal is a rich experience for both the candidate (who deepens in hunger for the Eucharist and who in the meantime is nourished by the "real presence of Jesus in the word") and a valuable experience for the community (who begins to question why the process takes as long as it does, what Eucharist means for them if they are able to stay, and what being a Catholic means today). Dismissal is not a negative experience as most people fear it will be. Rather it is an enriching moment for all involved. What better catechetical moment for

both candidate and the faithful when questions begin to emerge about the process as it becomes visible on each and every Sunday! Pastoral formation in the liturgy on Sundays especially with dismissal also better prepares the catechumens to celebrate, to receive and become Eucharist. Sunday dismissal after the liturgy of the word is *the* time for catechesis.

Apostolic Works: Pastoral formation in this area is to assist the candidates to live and spread the Gospel in family, neighborhood, work, church and all areas of their life and world. This formation does not necessarily include extra service projects or "churchy" ministries such as those involved in religious education, liturgy, etc. Rather this formation develops an apostolic way of life. Apostles are formed in the breaking open of the word.

Summary: Paragraph #19 of the Rite points to the fact that catechumens are to confront their human experiences in order to discover in that experience divisions, contradictions of values, and anything in themselves and in their world that separates them from life with God. Thus, the bottom line of this pastoral formation is conversion—a continually changing person: someone who is passing as a catechumen from an old self to a new self; someone who is learning that to live as a Catholic Christian is to live in response to a Gospel each and every day of his or her life confronting divisions and contradictions in values, in relationships, in beliefs which separate one from God and from other women and men; someone who can celebrate the changes that have already occurred—the signs of new life—the ways that he or she has already grown close to God and others. The pastoral formation pointed to in paragraph #19 is one of conversion of the whole person. The way to conversion is through the Gospel. Catechesis during the catechumenate is thus conversion catechesis. Such catechesis can be built on our Sunday lectionary. The tradition which we hand on to catechumens is a "living" tradition—experienced in word and community celebration on Sunday. The lectionary and homily in the midst of our liturgical year will raise issues of life, issues of doctrine significant to our Catholic Christian tradition. These issues can and will be dealt with throughout the catechumenate period. The agenda, however, is set by the lectionary and the experience and searching of catechumens in response to this lectionary agenda. In using the lectionary where conversion is the norm, catechumens may not learn "everything *we* always wanted them to know about the Catholic Church." However, if we believe that growth in faith, understanding and knowledge of our faith is a lifelong process, then by using the lectionary we are giving catechumens the skills they need to live this life the rest of their life. Is this not the goal of all Christian formation?

Sample Method for Sunday Morning Catechumenal Session Following Dismissal

Sunday morning arrives! What does it look like when we have our catechumenate sessions on Sunday mornings? A typical Sunday agenda is provided below. The structure provided is a sample; it is not "Gospel." It is the agenda on an average week in any parish.

9:00 a.m.	Gather with the assembly for liturgy of word
	Dismissal after the homily
9:30 a.m.	Coffee/rolls as catechumens and catechist(s) gather
9:40 a.m.	Time for prayer with catechumens only
10:00 a.m.	Sponsors and spouses join catechumens (Mass is over)
	Catechetical session
11:20 a.m.	Closing prayer and dismissal

Allow me to elaborate on the various elements of this schedule.

The gathering of the assembly for the liturgy of the word and dismissal of candidates is self-explanatory. This happens *every Sunday* as long as there are catechumens! After the homily the candidates are sent forth by the assembly with the words: "Go in peace to reflect upon the word and to make it your own."

Once settled in the gathering place a catechist reads the Scriptures of the day (one or all three). It is best to select the word upon which your catechetical session is built. Following the rereading of that text one of several activities may be done: a guided meditation (whereby catechumens are invited to place themselves in the text or in a similar situation); a journal exercise recalling a life event similar to the readings; a time of spontaneous prayer or prayer based on the psalm response; quiet meditation; reflection and/or discussion of some point of the homily. Vicky Tufano's article in this book gives some helpful guidelines for this prayer time with catechumens.

When sponsors and spouses arrive there are as many options for catechetical sessions as there are persons and Scriptures. This book is filled with sample sessions and methods so I need not deliberate more about this here.

The closing prayer and dismissal can be as simple or as complicated as you would like. Again samples are provided in this book. Some parishes I know ask a sponsor/candidate team to prepare the closing prayer for each week based on that week's readings. Creativity leaves open all sorts of possibilities here.

In general the structure of Sunday morning is simple. The process is simple when the lectionary is used as the basis. The sessions in this book are good guide-lines for creating a process which will work best for your people.

Method for Catechist to Prepare for Sunday Morning Dismissal Session

Preparation for the Sunday morning session is essential for effective use of time and materials. There are many ways a team member may prepare to be the facilitator for Sunday morning. The method I present is the one I have used and have shared with team members for their use. There are seven steps to this method. ALL seven are essential!

First, find the readings for the given Sunday in the lectionary. Read all three readings slowly and thoughtfully at least three times, preferably one time aloud. Underline thought patterns, significant words and phrases in all the readings. Jot down connections you notice between the readings. The purpose of this step is to become familiar with the texts for the given Sunday.

Second, work with the Gospel. Read the Gospel slowly and deliberately one more time. Visualize the Gospel. Where is this text taking place? At what time of day or night? What season of the year? Ask yourself: Do time and place make any difference in the reading? Name all the characters. With whom do you identify? Of these characters, who is the principal person in the Gospel? What is their problem? Find a passage from the text which articulates the problem of the principal person—from his or her perspective. Finding the problem in the text of the Gospel is essential. What is Jesus' response? How does Jesus deal with the problem? Again find the answer in the text. How do the other characters respond to the situation? Situate the text by visualizing it—sensing it (feeling, seeing, smelling, hearing that passage). Place yourself in the text.

Third, once you have done the work of visualizing the text (and only then), read commentaries about the passage. Helpful resources are *Unfinished Images* available through Wm. H. Sadlier Company and *Share the Word* from the Paulist Evangelization Center. Commentaries assist in stretching beyond our own images, understandings, and interpretations of this passage. Note any connections between the commentaries, your reflections, and readings. How do commentaries enlighten, challenge, affirm your understanding of this passage?

Fourth, set all readings, visualizations, commentaries aside and go before God to pray with this Gospel. Questions you may sit with are: What meaning do these readings offer for my life? for the life of the catechumens? for the Church? for the world? Where do you find yourself in the Gospel (e.g., are you the man born blind, the family, his neighbors, the Pharisees, Jesus)? What similarities and/or differences do you find in your world and the world of the principal character? Does this passage recall for you a concrete example or situation in your life? If so describe that time in detail. In what ways do the readings call you to growth? to new awareness? How do you meet this challenge? What is the hard word that the Gospel calls you to hear? How do you or will you respond? These are just some ways of being with the Gospel. There are many ways to pray with the word. Methods of praying with the Scripture are left to your creativity.

Fifth after reading texts, visualizing, attending to commentaries, and praying with the Gospel, call the pastor/presider for the liturgy at which the catechumens will be present. Ask him to share with you briefly the focus of his homily. The catechumenal session builds upon the word and upon how that Word is broken open by the homilist. Therefore, it is helpful to speak with the presider in the planning stages.

Sixth, with all of the data gathered, list the questions about the Catholic Christian tradition which could emerge. For example from the Feast of the Baptism of Our Lord questions about baptism could emerge. Readings on the call of the disciples could lead to questions about the origin of the Catholic Church and/or what it means that Peter is the rock of the Church. On Sundays when a letter is read (e.g., from the bishop, about reconciliation, peace pastoral, economic pastoral), questions could emerge about these issues. The issues raised about our tradition emerge as candidates live this tradition with us on each and every Sunday of the year. These issues and concerns emerge from our living and being together.

Seventh and last, realizing the wealth of information in word, in experiences, in homily, the team member sets aside preparation materials and designs a process to be used with catechumens on Sunday morning. The team member decides how to use the Gospel, what other texts of the day will be used, what symbols can be used effectively from the Scriptures for prayer or reflection, what context needs to be addressed, and what catechetical issues may emerge based on his or her experience with the catechumens.

With all this in mind the team member designs a process to be used on Sunday. This process will vary as do the readings from Sunday to Sunday.

Concluding Image: Alcoholics Anonymous

James Dunning and others have recently been making analogies between RCIA and Alcoholics Anonymous (AA) or any twelve-step program: Overeaters Anonymous, Gamblers Anonymous, Adult Children of Alcoholics, etc. The analogy is as follows: AA is peer to peer recovery. RCIA is Church handing on tradition: adult to adult. The Big Book is the guide for the Re-

covering Alcoholic. The Big Book is a book of stories of the lives of other alcoholics. The lectionary is the sourcebook and guide for RCIA containing the many stories of our tradition. AA members attend weekly and sometimes daily meetings. RCIA attends our Sunday morning dismissal. Both groups gather to share stories, strength, hope. In AA the recovering alcoholic selects a sponsor to help him or her work the program. RCIA provides each catechumen with a sponsor to support him or her through the journey: "to work the program!" "Let Go and Let God" is a theme of the twelve-step programs. Conversion is the heart of the catechumenate—is that not "letting go and letting God?" Twelve-step programs have for the fourth step a moral inventory of their life and later in the steps they make amends to all they have hurt. In RCIA we have scrutinies, major and minor exorcisms, sacrament of reconciliation, blessings. AA claims to be a way of life forever! In RCIA we are led to profess vows—to make a commitment forever! The promise of AA is life! The promise of RCIA is eternal life!! The final step of AA is to "share the message with all who still suffer." The final stage of RCIA: is to proclaim the good news. The unique parallel about RCIA and AA is that twelve-step programs are meetings of peers with each sharing strength, weakness, changes, growth in his or her life. It's a spiritual program with no leader. The marvelous mystery is that it works. If it works with AA, why not with RCIA? I suggest that AA offers us a model for our Sunday morning dismissal sessions, for the structure of our catechumenates. The mystery, I believe for us, is that it will work!

(This article has been reprinted from BREAKING OPEN THE WORD OF GOD, CYCLE A)

Music and Prayer in the Catechumenate

By John T. Butler

One could hardly conceive of life without music. So integral to living, music is a manifestation of the deepest recesses of our heart, soul and mind. It lifts us to greater heights and consoles us in the depths of our longings. Music is a basic substance of our very existence. So too is our communication with God. Prayer in its varied and fluid expressions elevates us, consoles us, shapes us and humbles us. We see the sun rise or set and are reminded of God. The changing seasons, the hills and valleys of nature and those of our very lives cause us to turn to God in prayers of praise, thanksgiving, petition and contrition.

St. Augustine is reputed to have said, "When we sing we pray twice." Obviously in touch with a fundamental connection here, St. Augustine put his finger on a mystery that is so central it almost passes without notice, especially for us who strive to echo the word. Song, with its many tempos, rhythms and idioms, has the potential to multiply our expressions of joy, sadness, expectation, awe and wonder, and it serves to connect us while forming the mosaic out of which we communicate more intensely with God.

The Rite of Christian Initiation of Adults presumes a process that is woven with music and prayer. Throughout the catechumenate, prayer and song bind the rest together. Beginning in the precatechumenate with our focus on "story," inquirers are encouraged to sing and pray out of their own experience of God's activity in their lives. The catechumenate period is a time for more intentional catechesis and therefore a time when we might hand on our Catholic tradition of music and prayer. As we enter Lent and our period of retreat and preparation for the sacraments, the elect are invited to pray more earnestly. Prayers of deliverance and minor exorcisms are introduced. After the vigil celebration of the resurrection we sing to the glory of God and pray for constant growth, while reflecting on the sacraments and the journey that has brought us to this place.

Our celebration of the movements from one period to the next is the bridge which supports us in all that we have become and leads us to the next phase. Care should always be taken to ensure that when we celebrate we are faithful to the rite and responsive to the catechumens and candidates we gather with. The prayers and songs we use must speak intimately to those celebrating and all those assembled.

This was illustrated clearly for me at a parish celebration of the rite of election a few years ago. After moving testimony presented by sponsors and assembly, the catechumens and candidates were being called by name to come forward and sign the book of life (book of the elect). One by one they approached the book with sponsors and put pen to paper. In the background could be heard a quiet melody slowly giving way to a familiar song. The melody began to stir within me and, I realized, within others as well. Slowly from the midst of the choir emerged a vocalist with a humble but assured voice singing, "I told Jesus it would be all right if he changed my name." Repeating the same verse, his voice rising intensely, "I told Jesus it would be all right if he changed my name," tears began to swell in the eyes of the catechumens, candidates and sponsors still approaching and signing the book. It was obvious that some connections were being made, not only in the minds and hearts of those celebrating but in the entire assembly as well. The ritual gestures, stories shared along the journey, and election by the assembly somehow were all brought together with this prayer in song. The catechumens celebrating the rite could clearly resonate with the heartfelt belief that God had called and chosen each of them and had given them a new name that would forever be inscribed in the book of life.

Having journeyed for many months with these catechumens and candidates, I knew of their stories and the struggles that had been shared. The soloist continued: "I told Jesus it would be all right if he changed my name." In fact, one candidate celebrating this adapted rite was the first of a long line of Baptists to convert to Catholicism and thus was met with some resentment and challenge from family and friends. This song was surely a prayer of her journey. "Still I told Jesus it would be all right, be all right, be all right . . . I told Jesus it would be all right if he changed my name."

In the catechetical session that followed this rite, catechumens, candidates and sponsors were invited to share their reflections on the celebration. As the dialogue began, we found ourselves being taken more deeply into the faith life of those who had celebrated. Recalling the various aspects of the ritual, music, prayer, gesture, word, assembly, the reflection led catechumens, candidates and sponsors alike to see more fully their particular journey in light of the larger story of our faith tradition. Having been both affirmed and challenged in these reflections, we ended our session praying that we would be made ready for the celebration of the resurrection and sang together "Amazing Grace."

Considering the possibilities of what the catechumenate journey can be for both those in the process and the entire parish, do we sometimes miss the point because we as catechist, liturgist or presider are not adequately prepared for the celebration or session? Are we relying on the tried and what we perceive to be true? It worked last year so why not this year? Or are we so focused on the rubric that we neglect the lived experience of those standing before us? Still further we might find ourselves wanting to be so creative and adaptable that we introduce too many variations and adapt for adaptation's sake rather than out of a need to respond more adequately to the faith journey of those in the process?

Might there be some principles that guide us in our use of music and prayer in the catechumenate? Allow me to suggest a few:

- *Start with the experience of those in the process*—Inquirers come to us often with some manner of communicating with God (prayer) and some orientation to a particular idiom of music. The challenge is to discover, name and share this in light of the journey on which they now embark.

- *Be faithful to the Rite*—There is no substitute for a good fundamental understanding of the Rite of Christian Initiation of Adults. Particular attention must be given to the celebration at each stage.

- *Be sensitive to the culture of those on the journey*— An obvious danger for us is that we tend to negate particular cultural experience that in fact has helped form this mosaic of culture we call American. Our Spanish-speaking, black, African, Caribbean and Asian brothers and sisters have a richness that is uniquely theirs—one that can enrich us if we only invite their sharing. Too often we expect all others, regardless of ethnicity, to be able to resonate fully with what is primarily an Anglo and European culture.

- *Planning*—Given the points already discussed, adequate planning needs to occur. Advance planning allows us to adjust catechetical sessions and celebrations so that attention is given to specific needs. Good catechetical sessions do not just happen. Good liturgy does not just occur. Even those who are gifted and skilled in these areas know that planning enhances one's effectiveness.

- *Be persons of prayer and song*—We ourselves must be persons who pray daily with some appreciation for the variety of prayer forms that might speak to others, specifically spontaneous prayer as it can capture present moments and experiences. We need also to be persons not afraid to sing. God did not gift us all with an eloquent voice. Then again God did not ask that we all sing eloquently, but rather that we make a joyful noise.

- *Be flexible*—After all else is said, we need to realize that it is the action of the Holy Spirit that in fact has priority throughout this process. We must leave space for the Spirit to work. Our planning and concern for detail must not be so rigid that we miss the work of God in the natural, unplanned events and responses of those whom God is calling.

- Finally, our openness to the Spirit requires of us, to some degree, to be *spontaneous* in our echoing God's word, prayer and song. Our response does not always have to be planned and oftentimes connects more intimately when we have listened carefully and respond with prayers and songs that embody another's sharing.

The catechumenate journey has the potential to release myriad activity that can capture an entire parish. Many parishes might view the weight of a RCIA process as one more burden. Catechumenate, we know, is not just one more thing to do; rather, when done well, we realize it might epitomize the way to do all other things. Still much time, attention, care and reliance on the Spirit should occur as we grow to a fuller experience of the Rite. Catechists, liturgists and presiders can do much to help the parish grow in the vision of the catechumenate. Given all that needs attention throughout the process, let prayer and song be the glue that binds the rest together.

St. Paul tells us: "At every opportunity pray in the Spirit, using prayers and petitions of every sort. Pray constantly and attentively for all in the holy company" (Eph 6:18).

> Sing to the Lord a new song . . .
> Sing joyfully to the Lord, all you lands;
>   break into song.
> Sing praise (Ps 98:1–4).

Resources

Behind Closed Doors: A Handbook on How To Pray,
    Joseph Champlain, Paulist Press, New York, 1984.
Glory and Praise, Vols. 1–3, North American Liturgy
    Resources, Phoenix, Arizona, 1977, 1980.
Lead Me, Guide Me, The African-American Catholic

Hymnal, G.I.A. Publications, Chicago, Illinois,
    1986.
Sadhana: A Way to God, Anthony de Mello, S. J.,
    Doubleday, New York, 1984.
Songs of Zion, Supplemental Worship, Resources 12,
    Abingdon, Nashville, 1981.

ADVENT AND CHRISTMAS

The History of Salvation

By Eugene A. LaVerdiere

The Gospel readings for Advent and Christmastime outline the history of salvation and develop its dramatic tensions: the absence and presence of God, sin and divine love, the promise and fulfillment of salvation, yearning for the Lord and rejoicing in his presence. Even as the Gospel proclaims Jesus' birth, it announces his passion and death. These too are part of the beginning of the Gospel of Jesus Christ, the Son of God (Mk 1:1).

Salvation history is universal. It begins in the life of God with God's own inner word but then enters the world to give life and shed light by dwelling among us as the Word become flesh (Jn 1:1–18). For a time its history coincides with that of the Hebrew, Israelite and Jewish people (Mt 1:1–17), but then in Jesus it opens up to all nations (Lk 2:22–40), to climax in the Lord's final coming (Mk 13:33–37). Most of the readings explore the life and mission of Jesus, of his disciples, and of the Christians who share in Christ's life and continue his mission in every time and place.

Vigilance at the Lord's Approach

The First Sunday of Advent and of the new liturgical year (Mk 13:33–37) continues the theme introduced on the last Sunday of the previous year (Mt 24:37–44). We had been brought face to face with Christ's full and final manifestation in glory. On the first Sunday, we take Mark as our guide and look at the attitudes required of all who await the coming of the Lord.

The reading is the conclusion of a longer discourse (13:5–37) addressed to a community of Christians troubled by the destruction of Jerusalem and the temple. It seemed to them that the end announced in prophetic and apocalyptic literature was at hand. They consequently saw little point in pursuing the Christian mission. It was enough to remain faithful to the end. The Gospel's response was that what appeared to be the end was but the beginning, in the same way that Jesus' death had not been the end of his life but a passage into new life. Even so, Christians must always live with the end in mind. The vision of the end gives meaning and seriousness to every other moment of life and history. For each and for all, the Lord is indeed coming.

A Herald's Voice in the Desert

Christians also have a role in preparing the way of the Lord. And in this, as we see on the Second Sunday of Advent (Mk 1:1–8), John the Baptizer is our model. All four Gospels trace the origins of Jesus' ministry to the prophetic circle of John the Baptizer. It is with John's story that Mark opens the account of "the beginning of the Gospel of Jesus Christ, the Son of God" (1:1). Mark's account is but the beginning of a story which continues down to our own time. It started with John the Baptizer. Today it continues with us.

Mark presents John as a prophetic reformer who called people to baptismal repentance for the remission of sins. This is the way he prepared others for the coming of one who came after him, that is, one of his followers, who far surpassed him in greatness. John was the Lord's messenger (see Mal 3:1), a new Elijah (Mal 3:23) and his garments were those of Elijah (2 Kgs 1:8). In his mission as a herald in the desert, he readied the way of the Lord and fulfilled Isaiah 40:3.

Preaching the Good News

John the Baptizer, who prepared the way for Jesus' first advent, is our model as we prepare the way for Jesus' definitive advent. The Third Sunday of Advent shows us how John's mission made him confront injustice on all sides (Lk 3:10–14). In turn he spoke to the crowds, to the tax collectors, and to the soldiers, and his message was tailored to the context of each. The crowds, that is, everyone, had to share with the needy. Tax collectors were not to insist on more than was strictly required. Soldiers were not to extort money from the people to supplement their income.

John also had to direct attention away from himself to the life and mission of Jesus (Lk 3:15–18). John was not the Messiah. He merely prepared the way for his coming. Neither are we the Messiah as we prepare the way for his full coming.

The Servant of the Lord

The Gospel for the Fourth Sunday of Advent (Lk 1:26–38) is the story of the annunciation, when God's messenger came to Mary and announced to her that she would be the Mother of Jesus, the Son of the Most High. Like John the Baptizer, Mary's call to motherhood is about a unique personage in religious history, but it is also the story of us all. Every Christian is called to conceive the life of God within himself or herself and bring it forth into the world. Such is the heart of the Christian vocation. Like Mary we cannot do this on our own or through any human relationship. The life of God does not spring from human creativity but from the presence of the Holy Spirit. So it was with Mary at the annunciation. So also at Pentecost. And like Mary we are asked to respond with trust. We too are the servants of the Lord, eager that all be done according to his word.

Jesus Christ, Son of David, Son of Abraham

At the Christmas vigil, we read the entire first chapter of Matthew (1:1–25), which begins by recapitulating the biblical history of salvation in the form of a genealogy of Jesus (1:1–17). This genealogy (see also Lk 3:23–38) is a theological statement. It emphasizes Jesus' identity as the Christ and his relationship to King David and Abraham. As the Son of David, Jesus is a messianic king. As the Son of Abraham, he fulfills the promise that in Abraham's seed all nations would be blessed (see Gen 22:18). So it is that in the Gospel's conclusion Jesus commissions the eleven remaining disciples to "make disciples of all the nations" (28:18–20).

The second part of the chapter tells the story of how the birth of Jesus took place (1:18–25). Its central personage is Joseph, son of David, the husband of Mary, to whom the angel of the Lord appeared in a dream. His wife's child was conceived by the Holy Spirit. In him the prophecy of Isaiah 7:14 would be fulfilled. He would be called Emmanuel, which means "God is with us." In him God would be present among his people.

Tidings of Great Joy

Matthew helped us see Jesus' relationship to the biblical history of salvation (vigil). At the Midnight Mass of Christmas, Luke helps us see his relationship to Caesar Augustus and the Roman Empire. It is through Caesar's decree that Jesus came to be born in David's city of Bethlehem, which did not provide hospitality at the time of his birth. Even the Roman emperor could be God's instrument in the unfolding of salvation history (2:1–7).

The shepherds were the first to hear the Gospel, the tidings of great joy that a Savior has been born to them, the Messiah and Lord. Here was the good news of salvation. It came from heaven, from God through an angelic messenger, just as Jesus himself was born Son

of God through the power of the Holy Spirit. After they were given a sign in which they would be able to see the good news, a chorus of angels responded with a hymn of praise (2:8–14).

Seeing and Understanding

The shepherds had been given a sign: "in a manger you will find an infant wrapped in swaddling clothes" (Lk 2:12). In the Christmas Mass at Dawn, we read of how they went to Bethlehem, saw the baby lying in the manger and believed (2:15–20). A manger is a place where nourishment is given to the flock. The shepherds, who evoke the leaders of the early Church, saw how Jesus' life and person was offered as nourishment to the little flock (see Lk 12:32) of the Church. They saw, and on the basis of this concrete experience, they understood the Gospel they had heard. The story ends with a series of reactions to the event and its Gospel.

Much of the same text, but without 2:15 and with the addition of 2:21, is read on January 1, the Solemnity of Mary, Mother of God. This second reading invites us to focus on how "Mary treasured all these things and reflected on them in her heart." Here is how we are to hear the Gospel. At the end of the passage, the circumcision is mentioned to introduce the naming of Jesus (2:21). Just as his very life came from God and the Gospel of salvation came from heaven through God's messenger, so also did his name, Jesus, which expressed his very identity (see Lk 1:31).

The Word Became Flesh

At Christmas Mass during the Day and on the second Sunday after Christmas, the magnificent prologue of St. John (1:1–18) is our Gospel reading. The basic form of this prologue is a hymn, which most likely was written independently of the Gospel. It sings the story of the Word, a term which gathers up much of the biblical reflection on God's self-expression and communication from creation, and even before, to the sharing of divine life. Although the Greek term used for this, *logos*, came from popular Greek philosophy, its meaning is closer to wisdom, *sophia*, as developed in works such as the Book of Wisdom.

The hymn opens with the first words of Genesis, "In the beginning," to introduce the Word in God's own life prior to creation (vv. 1–2). It then shows how the Word burst into creation (vv. 3–5), entered the world, the cosmos, a human reality (vv. 10–12), and even became flesh, taking on our human condition (vv. 14–16).

Several prose passages were added to the hymn when it became John's prologue. These verses speak of the person and role of John the Baptizer (vv. 6–9, 15), explain the meaning of "children of God" in terms of virginal conception (vv. 12b–13), and comment on God's enduring love which came through Jesus Christ (vv. 17–18). The hymn had referred to the Father's only Son without actually naming Jesus. The prologue's editor named him directly. Jesus Christ, the only Son, is the revelation of the Father.

Light to the Gentiles, the Glory of Israel

The history of salvation is a story of God's presence first to Israel but then through Israel to all nations. Already this is true in the Old Testament—in Isaiah for example, and in several other prophets. In the New Testament, it constituted a major theme in the infancy narratives of both Matthew and Luke. For Matthew, God's revelation to the Gentiles is one of the main points of the story of the magi. In Luke, we find it in the presentation of Jesus in the temple (2:22–40), which we read on the Sunday in the Octave of Christmas, the feast of the Holy Family.

The presentation in the temple highlights Jesus' fulfillment of the law of the Lord (2:22, 39). It is in the course of that fulfillment that Simeon, a living voice of prophecy in Jerusalem, announces in a canticle that God's offer of salvation to all had been realized in Jesus. Jesus was a revealing light to the Gentiles, the glory of his people Israel. A prophetess named Anna also came forward to thank God and address all who yearned for the deliverance of Jerusalem.

Magi from the East

On the feast of Epiphany, we celebrate the manifestation of Jesus to the magi, who alone see the special star of Jesus at its rising among all the lesser personal stars in the heavens. King Herod and all Jerusalem, including the chief priests and the scribes, failed to see the star of Jesus.

The magi, religious Gentiles from the East, prefigure the eventual proclamation of the Gospel to the Gentiles, all the nations, after Israel's rejection of Jesus. Prostrating themselves before Jesus in homage, as they would before God himself, they offered the two gifts mentioned in Isaiah 60:5–6, gold and frankincense, and they added myrrh, an aromatic substance used in anointing a body for burial (see Jn 19:39). In Matthew 2:11, the myrrh may well symbolize the passion and death of Jesus. Jesus was offered gifts worthy of a king, but his kingdom was not of this world.

You Are My Beloved Son

Jesus was baptized by John (Mk 1:7–11), an event we celebrate on the Sunday after Epiphany, which closes the Christmas season and at the same time is the first Sunday in Ordinary time. In Mark's Gospel, the baptism of Jesus is even more important than in the other Gospels. Matthew, Luke and John each has a prologue which has already introduced the divinity as well as the humanity of Jesus. The baptism of Jesus comes later. In Mark, the baptism is the highpoint of the prologue itself, and nothing about Jesus can be presupposed.

The reading focuses on two kinds of witness. John the Baptizer announces that one of his followers was more powerful than he was and would baptize in the Holy Spirit. Then the Spirit in which Jesus would baptize descends on him and a heavenly voice addresses him: "You are my beloved Son." Jesus, the man from Nazareth in Galilee and one of John's followers, is God's beloved Son.

Introduction to Advent and the Christmas Season

The format for the dismissal sessions of the catechumenate is divided into opening prayer, reflections, and closing prayer.

The prayer sessions give examples of a variety of styles of prayer. Some of the blessings are adapted from the blessings for the catechumens from the Rite or blessings from the sacramentary. Another type is the litany of petition or of thanksgiving. A third example is the "Gloria," a classic prayer of the Church. A fourth type is song. On occasion, specific songs are suggested. These are meant to be from the repertoire of the parish. In the Christmas season, a few carols are suggested. Most of the songs reinforce the theme of praying and rejoicing constantly.

In anticipation of the presentation of the Creed and the Lord's Prayer after the rite of election, a nice copy of the Gloria could be given to each person to keep in a folder of prayers of the Church.

The setting of the room for the breaking open of the word should correspond to the arrangement and environment of the assembly. The dramatic change from Advent to Christmas in color, texture, light, and plants should be repeated or at least echoed. Planning and coordination with those responsible for the decoration of the church is important. There should be a place of honor for the lectionary. The space should be prepared.

The reflection section is divided into a couple of themes, each of which is divided into paragraph "a" and paragraph "b." The first part, "a," is a statement of the theme. The catechist or leader should introduce the theme in similar words. Several themes predominate the readings of the Advent/Christmas season. Forgiveness, incarnation, conversion, prayer, and mission will be woven throughout the statements and reflections.

The second part, "b," suggests several ways to begin the discussion and sharing. One of the leaders can begin by relating a personal experience and then asking for stories of similar situations, or the questions can be asked of anyone in the group. A significant amount of time should be spent in this sharing. Adults come to faith by integrating their personal story with the experience of God. No one can do this for them. The catechist is the guide. The catechist can make connections and can relate the catechumens and candidates to the immediate experience of the local church, the immediate neighborhood, or the people who are known to the catechumens and candidates.

After the sharing and questioning by members of the group, the catechist could summarize the theme. Sometimes the catechist will be able to move the discussion to a deeper or broader level. For example, after exploring the theme in terms of personal experience, examples from an historical context or situations of the contemporary Church outside the immediate experience of the parish could be introduced. The catechist or leader should research these examples prior to the Sunday.

At the end of each closing prayer two or three pastoral or doctrinal issues are listed. These can serve as guides, as pivotal or hinge points for the catechist during preparation. These should not be presented in an academic manner, but rather should always be grounded in the reflections based on experience.

First Sunday of Advent

Isaiah 63:16b–17, 19b; 64:2–7
1 Corinthians 1:3–9
Mark 13:33–37

OPENING PRAYER

Leader: Let us pray. (Invite all to open hands.)
God, Creator of life,
open our eyes that we might see you.

All: (Touch eyes and then open hands saying:)
We pray.

Leader: Open our ears that we will hear your life-giving word.

All: (Touch ears and then open hands saying:)
We pray.

Leader: Open our hearts that we might recognize you.

All: (Touch breast and then open hands saying:)
We pray.

Leader: We ask all this so that we will follow your way.
We ask this in the name of Jesus.

All: Amen.

REFLECTION

1.a. God is present and faithful. Sometimes we become aware of that presence through an experience of absence, despair, or when there seems to be no justice or peace. Beginning the period of Advent, we are still mindful that we are living in the light of Easter and we have the death/resurrection of Jesus before us. Death is related to the experience of loss and absence. Resurrection is related to the fullness of life with God. Our story is full of ups and downs, death and life.

b. Identify some time of grief or longing. This could be personal or relational. (Take some time in silence if needed. Invite the group to share after a few minutes.)

Out of these experiences, what can we now see, looking back, that was hopeful? Were there any clues or glimpses of hope earlier that we realized at the time?

2.a. Can we train ourselves to be watchful for God's presence in our lives? God is constant—that is hard to grasp. We say: "Nothing lasts forever." Believing in God's constancy is a learned attitude and practice. Paul says: "I continually thank God." Christian prayer is a continual thanks. To be thankful we are challenged to broaden our experience of God—not only in crisis, but all the time. We are challenged to "look, listen."

b. Remember the signing of your senses when you entered the catechumenate period. Reflect on eyes, ears, hands, shoulders, heart and feet. Consider and ask yourself how in each or any of these areas you have become more aware of God in the past week. Reflections could be written in a journal.

CLOSING PRAYER

Leader: Let us pray.
Almighty God, we are growing in trust of your goodness and give thanks for your faithfulness.

(Name one new way that awareness of God's presence is becoming known—even in painful as well as in happy circumstances. Invite others to do the same.)

We thank you in the name of Jesus, the Christ, who taught us to know you as Father, Abba.

(Introduce the song "Abba! Father!" (Rev. Carey Landry, *Glory and Praise*, Vol. 1, North American Liturgy Resources) with song book, or recording. If all will be listening, or if the song is familiar, invite all to pray with open hands.)

Doctrinal and Pastoral Issues: God's initiative, God's faithfulness, Prayer–thanksgiving, Hope, Advent

Elizabeth S. Lilly

Second Sunday of Advent

Isaiah 40:1–5, 9–11
2 Peter 3:8–14
Mark 1:1–8

OPENING PRAYER

Leader: God of forgiveness and endless goodness,
we thank you for calling us together,
for giving us your word, and for the time to
    know you.
We pray for candidates,
    that the spirit of their baptism will fill
    them;
for catechumens,
    that they will be strengthened by the
    faith of the Church;
for all, that together with Jesus the Christ,
    we will reveal the kingdom of God in
    our world.

All: Amen.

REFLECTION

1.a. God, always present to us, is gift. And yet, we look around the world and sense the absence of God. To bring the gift of God present to us in our world, we need to move into the experience of absence and create the experience of forgiveness. In forgiveness we return to the sense of awareness of God's presence. We must ask for God, for-gift-ness.

b. Name some gifts that would make a new earth a reality. Name some part of your life that needs the gift of God, and needs the experience of forgiveness.

2.a. There is such a tension between wanting something and waiting for it. Children ask, "How many days until Christmas?" This is the plea of all of us. When we become aware of our need for God, then we want to experience forgiveness immediately. This does not happen automatically. Patience. Why is waiting so difficult? What do we learn in our waiting?

b. What have you waited for—a birth, a job, a reunion? Share stories of waiting. Relate them to the present situation of waiting for full communion in the Church.

3.a. If we are to move toward the kingdom of God, we have to confront the way we live in the present moment. Judgment, confrontation and conscious choice are the painful seedbeds of change. Most of us will not change until we recognize the need to change.
Picture a highway. In California, the El Camino Real, King's Way, is filled with things: car dealers and lots, fast food places, discount stores . . .Is this the way of the Lord? Are we not tempted away from looking for God by our consumer values, our need to find happiness and security in the accumulation of things?

b. What needs changing—forgiving—renewing? Name a situation that needs changing (in the world, in your life). What specific change could each one make in preparations for Christmas that would move us from gifts to Gift? What can be done to change? Catechist can give an example from the local church/community of an outreach project. Personal conversion will show forth in new actions and interests.

CLOSING PRAYER

Leader: Let us pray.
Lord, we ask you to forgive us when we
    are distracted in our search for you.
Help us to change.

(Name something that you want to change, and invite others to do the same, from their own experience.)

Almighty God, you have opened our
    hearts,
and we long for you;
you have opened our eyes, and we begin
    to see you.
Continue to teach us of your love.
We ask this in the name of Jesus.

All: Amen.

Leader: (Introduce the song "Though the Mountains May Fall," Dan Schutte, S.J., Glory and Praise, Vol. 1, North American Liturgy Resources.)

Doctrinal and Pastoral Issues: Justice—Corporal Works of Mercy, Forgiveness, Giftedness and Waiting, Patience

Elizabeth S. Lilly

Third Sunday of Advent

Isaiah 61:1–2a, 10–11
1 Thessalonians 5:16–24
John 1:6–8, 19–28

OPENING PRAYER

Leader: God of peace,
thanks for opening our eyes, and ears,
and hearts to your goodness and forgiveness.

All: (All who wish can give thanks in a word or
sentence.)

Leader: Form us in your image, show us the way to
peace.
We ask this in the name of Jesus, the
Christ.

All: Amen.

REFLECTION

1.a. Change always goes in stages. First we see the
need for change, then we must want to change,
and finally we set about making the change. As
with our other experiences of waiting, we experience the time and tension between the now and
the not yet, between God present and yet not visible, between anticipation and celebration.

b. Remember the image of the highway, the business
route, the El Camino Real. What needs to be
straightened before this can become the king's
highway, the road to peace? How are consumption, justice and peace related? Are we tempted to
consume without being aware of issues of justice?
How is this life my life? Share or write some specific needs for peace and justice in your life.

2.a. A prophet is one who can see the extraordinary in
the ordinary. Often we are prophet for each other.

Often we need prophets to teach us to watch and
listen. Discerning God's presence is not done
alone—the first reading says that we are clothed
and wrapped. In the Church we are wrapped in
the community of believers, some of whom are
prophets. Discovering God's presence and will is a
continuing process of the Church.

b. Name some prophets in your Church. These may
be members of your community, members of the
Church in the world . . .Catechist could be prepared to share one story of a contemporary
prophet. The catechist should also reflect to the
members of the catechumenate that they are
prophet to the assembly in their faithfulness to the
presence of God in the Scripture.

CLOSING PRAYER

Leader: God of perfect peace,
help us to work without ceasing
for that justice which brings true and lasting peace.

(Invite petitions for peace and justice; name what needs
healing and forgiveness, reflecting the sharing that had
gone on earlier.)

We ask this through our Lord Jesus Christ
who is in peace and harmony with you and
the Holy Spirit,
one God, for ever and ever.

All: Amen.

(A song expressing hope and joy would be appropriate.)

*Doctrinal and Pastoral Issues: Prophet, Church, Dis-
cerning Community, Conversion, Justice and Peace,
Hope*

Elizabeth S. Lilly

Fourth Sunday of Advent

2 Samuel 7:1–5, 8b–11, 16
Romans 16:25–27
Luke 1:26–38

OPENING PRAYER

(The following is an adaptation of the blessing of cate-chumens, from *Rite of Christian Initiation of Adults,* #123.)

Leader: Let us pray.
    All-powerful God,
    help our brothers and sisters, as you help
      us all,
    to deepen our knowledge of the Gospel of
      Christ.
    Guide us in faith,
    and open us to your word.
    May we continue to know and trust you
    and do your will with generous hearts and
      willing spirits.
    We ask this through Christ our Lord.

All: Amen.

REFLECTION

1.a. Revelation is the action and being of God in com-munication with all of creation. We believe in a God who communicates, who is in relationship. One way we describe this communication is word. This essence of relationship we call Trinity—crea-tion, redemption, salvation, or God who creates us, who calls us to unity, and who enables us to re-spond to that call. In the readings today, there are examples of these dimensions of God's being. God communicates in and through men and women of faith. The message of creation and salvation is heard in the context of a family or community of faith (David and Nathan, Mary and Elizabeth).

b. Where do we sense the presence of God—in a person, an event? How can we be certain that this sense is of God? With whom do we carry out a dis-cerning process?

2.a. In practicing faith and awareness of God's pres-ence we learn a response, an attitude: accept God's will. Mary is the prime example of one who is open to God's communication, presence, and is transformed in the process, becoming something more than she was. This requires trust.

b. We have been petitioning God for forgiveness. Do we expect a response? Are we ready for God's in-tervention in our lives? Are we thankful for new roads, new ways, new roles in our lives, new chal-lenges?

CLOSING PRAYER

(Copies of the Hail Mary prayer could be given to each candidate and catechumen for their prayer folders.)

Leader: (Introduce the prayer and invite all to say
    it aloud together.)

All: Hail Mary, full of grace,
    the Lord is with you.
    Blessed are you among women,
    and blessed is the fruit of your womb, Je-
      sus.
    Holy Mary, mother of God,
    pray for us sinners, now,
    and at the hour of our death. Amen.

Doctrinal and Pastoral Issues: Trinity, Revelation, Church—Discerning Community, Mary—Model Disci-ple

Elizabeth S. Lilly

Christmas Day

Isaiah 52:7–10
Hebrews 1:1–6
John 1:1–18

OPENING PRAYER

Leader invites all to join in the Gloria. Copies could be made for each for the prayer booklets.

REFLECTION

1.a. Today the Church celebrates the mystery of God's self-revelation in Jesus. The context is human birthing. The Church ponders the event of Jesus' birth much the way each of us reflects on our own birth. That is, we look back with the eyes of our experience. The Church looks at the birth of Jesus in light of all that his life showed and revealed the mystery of God.

b. How do you know of the events of your own birthing? How have these stories been influenced by the rest of your life to now? Describe the family into which you were born, and describe how that family has changed over time. How much of who you are today is influenced by the story of your birth?

2.a. Jesus is sacrament because Jesus reveals God.

b.1) What story or event of the life of Jesus gives you a glimpse of God? Each one can tell of one example of God's saving power made concrete and visible in Jesus. Listen for examples of compassion, justice, healing.

2) What story of Jesus is your story today?

3.a. The Church continues to be the sacrament of Jesus in the world today. The Church should reveal the signs of the kingdom. The Church is always birthing, becoming.

b.1) What does the Church need to do today to make the presence of God visible in our world? How is the Church compassionate, working for justice, making whole what is broken?

2) Each catechumen and candidate is in a birthing process—becoming the Church. How does the birthing story of faith of each one relate to the Church and to this birthing season? What is new in each one's life in terms of the love of God made present?

CLOSING PRAYER

Leader: Let us pray.
Lord God, your Word lives among us.
Help us to bring your peace and good will to light in our lives.
We ask this in the name of Jesus the Lord.

All: Amen.

Leader: (Invite all to sing a carol of praise such as "Angels We Have Heard On High.")

Doctrinal and Pastoral Issues: Incarnation, Christmas, Salvation, Church as Sacrament

Elizabeth S. Lilly

Holy Family

Sirach 3:2–6, 12–14
Colossians 3:12–21
Luke 2:22–40

OPENING PRAYER

The following is an adaptation of the alternate opening prayer of the liturgy:

Leader: Let us pray. (pause)
God, Creator of all life,
you have formed each of us
and given us each other to become family.
Into our story you revealed yourself in Jesus.
Teach us the sanctity of human love,
show us the value of our interrelatedness
    in family life,
and help us to live in peace with all people
that we may share in your life forever.

All: Amen.

REFLECTION

1.a. Simeon and Anna are examples of men and women who seek the truth. They are found, in this story, in Jerusalem and in the temple. These are the revered places of God's presence with the people in the time of the birth of Jesus. The parents of Jesus follow the tradition of the time in the temple rites. Today the whole of creation reveals God, and the Church is the community of men and women who seek the truth of God revealed in Jesus and celebrate together in rituals of praise and thanksgiving.

   b.1) Which person in today's Gospel tells our story best? Each one can reflect upon Simeon and Anna, Mary and Joseph. Are we looking and seeking in the Church? Do we already have the truth within us and need others and time to ponder it and bring it to life? As each one shares, perhaps we will hear that we have parts of both—looking outward and looking inward for the presence of God.

2) What aspects of the tradition of worship of the Church do we begin to take on? How is the pattern of Sunday Mass changing our life? What part of the prayer touches each one—praising God, recognizing the need for and asking for forgiveness, seeking direction and instruction in the way of the kingdom?

2.a. The Church is described as a family and the first two readings tell of the interrelationships within a family. The primary governing factor is forgiveness and love.

   b. As members of the Church, as catechumens and candidates, relate some of your experiences as members of the family. When do you feel "at home" and when do you feel like a visitor or distant cousin? What does the local church, the parish need to do for you? What can you do for the family? Have there been instances of forgiveness and love? Where does this process have to continue to work for you now?

CLOSING PRAYER

Leader: Let us pray.
Eternal God,
you reveal your love in the midst of family
    relationships.
We pray for all the members of our family,
that we will be filled with the Spirit,
and become more forgiving and loving.
(pause)
We pray that we will grow in peace,
    through Jesus,
who lives and reigns with you and the
    Holy Spirit.

All: Amen.

Leader: (Invite all to sing a carol, such as the Kentucky ballad "The Cherry Tree Carol," which ponders the mystery of the relationships of Jesus, Mary, and Joseph.)

(If this is the day of a parish Christmas party, the sponsors should be encouraged to invite the catechumens and candidates to participate. This could be a day of visiting and caroling together.)

Doctrinal and Pastoral Issues: Liturgy—Prayer of the Church, Virtues—Forgiveness and Love, Trinity, Family—Christian Family

Elizabeth S. Lilly

Mary, Mother of God

Numbers 6:22–27
Galatians 4:4–7
Luke 2:16–21

OPENING PRAYER

Following the instructions of the first reading, the leader should invite all to give and receive the blessings of the Lord. This could be done in pairs, or, if the group is not too large, each one in turn could be blessed by all the others, repeating the three blessings. Those giving the blessing should raise their hands toward the other or touch the other on the head or shoulder.

> The Lord bless you and keep you!
> The Lord let his face shine upon you,
>   and be gracious to you!
> The Lord look upon you kindly and give you
>   peace!

REFLECTION

1.a. Word is a powerful symbol. We use words in blessing. Jesus is the Word. Word communicates. Word calls for and invites response. Word must be received. In today's Gospel both the shepherds and Mary hear the word of God. The shepherds respond immediately, and yet we do not hear of them or those with whom they spoke in the Gospel again. Mary, on the other hand, heard, reflected, and remained faithful to the life of Jesus and the Church. Mary, Mother of God, is also called Bearer of God. This is the model for us. We hear the word and then must hold the word within us.

b. Today, the new year of our calendar, let us concentrate on one word of Jesus, one word of blessing—peace. The Old Testament image of the Lord's favor was peace. Jesus greeted with peace. What do you think of, what comes to mind, when you hear the word "peace"? Where have you found peace? Where do we need peace?

2.a. In our ritual we have many responses to greetings, prayers, and word that are acclamations of praise—opening song, Gloria, psalm, alleluia. A few weeks ago (Third Sunday of Advent) we heard "Render constant thanks." The shepherds in today's Gospel were "glorifying and praising God."

It is usual to give thanks for a gift—this is the season of thank you notes. But gift times, birthdays, Christmas, are usually times marked off from the ordinary—indeed the feast of Christmas is not Ordinary Time. How can we grasp the idea—again—of God's constancy? The birthing of God's presence into our lives is now. Can we accept life—all life, death, pain, joy, illness, loneliness, fellowship—as gift? Only as we move toward this can we consider giving constant thanks and glorifying God.

b. Think for a few moments of a time, or situation, or relationship, that did not seem to be gift. Looking back can you now see it as gift? Can you accept it as gift? Can you thank God for it? Catechist could give an example. These stories could be shared, or could be written in a journal in the form of a litany of thanks.

CLOSING PRAYER

Leader: Let us give thanks for today, for where we are now,
and let us pray for peace.
For the gift of my friends, I give thanks.
For peace in my relationship with my colleagues at work, I pray.

All: (Each one is invited to pray for specific gifts and needs.)

Leader: Lord,
We thank you for your gift of Jesus and your constant blessings.
Hear our prayers and grant us your peace.
We ask this in the name of Jesus.

All: Amen.

Doctrinal and Pastoral Issues: Mary—Model of Church, Mother of God, Peace, "Word"

Elizabeth S. Lilly

Epiphany

Isaiah 60:1–6
Ephesians 3:2–3, 5–6
Matthew 2:1–12

OPENING PRAYER

The verses of "We Three Kings of Orient Are" will be read by alternating sides. The words should be available in a parish hymnal or book of carols. All five verses should be used. The leader should divide the two groups.

Leader: Let us pray.
Lord, you are the light in our darkness.
We turn as travelers to follow you.

Side one: verse 1

Side two: verse 2

Side one: verse 3

Side two: verse 4

Side one: verse 5

Leader: Guide us to your perfect light!

All: Amen.

REFLECTION

1.a. The Gospel continues to put before us different models of those who had the opportunities in Jesus' early life to see God's revelation and act upon it. The contrast today is dramatic. One response is to ignore the signs and to depend on human power. The other is to change one's life dramatically, to journey into unknown territory and to follow unfamiliar routes.

b. We have spoken of the highway image before (Second Sunday of Advent). Then the emphasis was on noticing the things in our life, along the road, that needed changing. Today's image might be of a new and unfamiliar way. How do these images illustrate your life of the last few weeks or months? Give specific examples of changes that you have made. What have the changes cost you? What have you gained?

2.a. Gold, frankincense, and myrrh—king, God, and sacrifice. The carol already reflects on the Chris-

tian understanding of the nature of Jesus. Gifts often tell something of both the giver and the receiver. The gift of God's love, of God's presence is wholly unearned on our part.

b.1) Reflect on your own giving and receiving this season. What gift did you really enjoy giving? Why? What gift did you enjoy receiving and why? Is it more difficult to give or receive? Is there something new that you received this Christmas?

2) Is the Gospel becoming a gift to you? In what way have you received the presence of God in the Scripture this Christmas? What difference has this made for you in your relationship to Church?

CLOSING PRAYER

The following is an adaptation of the prayer over the people for this day (found in the sacramentary). Copies should be prepared so that each one can read the appropriate part.

Leader: Let us pray.

Reader 1: God has called us out of darkness into wonderful light.

All: May we experience the Lord's kindness and blessings and be strong in faith, in hope, and in love.

Reader 2: Christ appeared on this day as light shining in darkness.

All: May each follower of Christ be a light to all who seek the light.

Reader 3: The wise men followed the star, and found Christ who is light from light.

All: May we all find the Lord at our journey's end.

Leader: We ask this prayer in the name of the Father, and of the Son, and of the Holy Spirit.

All: Amen.

Doctrinal and Pastoral Issues: Journey, Epiphany, Magi, Gift, Conversion

Elizabeth S. Lilly

Baptism of the Lord

Isaiah 42:1–4, 6–7
Acts 10:34–38
Mark 1:7–11

OPENING PRAYER

Leader: Let us pray.
Lord God, we pray in the name of the Creator
who formed each of us
and calls us to form the community that reflects his image.
(pause)
We pray in the name of Jesus, true God
and true man,
light in the darkness,
who announced the presence of the kingdom.
(pause)
We pray in the name of the Spirit of God,
the breath of the Word,
who enables all to build the kingdom on earth.
(pause)
Fill us with your peace and empower us with your life.
We ask this in the name of Jesus.

All: Amen.

REFLECTION

1.a. Jesus began his public ministry, the public life recorded in the Gospels with the authority of the presence of God. His baptism by John became a significant watershed in his life. When Mark was written, it is from this time on that the disciple can look back and recognize signs of the kingdom.

    If we look at the three selections in the lectionary in reverse we find a complete picture of the ministry of Jesus. Following the baptism, Jesus "went about doing good works." The first reading gives us a list of the "good works."

  b. Baptism commits one to a life of service, a life of "good works." Where is this evident in the Church? Catechist could be prepared to share some of the more structured avenues of service (organizations, missions . . .). All could share some individual responses. Where is the Christian challenged to be more responsive? What can and should the Church be doing to "open the eyes of the blind?"

2.a. The spirit of God is described as the power of God. Power is usually associated with control, wealth, and status. The power of God in our lives calls us to let go, identify with the poor, and serve others.

  b. What are some examples of the power of God in our lives? How do these compare and contrast with other examples of power? How is justice related to God's power?

CLOSING PRAYER

(The following is an adaptation of the blessing of the catechumens, from the *Rite of Christian Initiation of Adults*, #122.)

Leader: Let us pray.
God, through your holy prophets
you have told all who draw near to you:
"Wash and be cleansed."
And through Christ you have chosen to give us
a birth in the Spirit.

Bless our brothers and sisters
as they earnestly prepare themselves for baptism.

Renew in the baptized the power of your Spirit.
Strengthen all of us in the fellowship of your Church.

We ask this through Christ our Lord.

All: Amen.

Doctrinal and Pastoral Issues: Trinity, Baptism, Mission/Service, Power, Authority

Elizabeth S. Lilly

LENT

The Work of Redemption

By Eugene A. LaVerdiere

Lent is a very special season in which we look at Jesus' teaching and all of his activities in the light of his passion and death. We also see what his passion and death meant for our redemption and how by learning from the example of his life and by following his teaching we fulfill our baptismal commitment and progress toward salvation.

The Gospel readings begin on Ash Wednesday with a call to enter into the season devoutly and generously as people willing to translate the first century demands of the Gospel into those of the twentieth (Mt 6:1–6, 16–18). On the First and Second Sundays of Lent, we approach first the life and mission of Jesus (Mk 1:12–15) and second his ultimate glorification (Mk 9:2–10). Both of these are presented in summary form or at least in a story which sums up the whole of Jesus' existence.

From the Third to the Fifth Sundays, we turn to John's Gospel. With the cleansing of the temple our attention is drawn away from the temple built of stone to the person of Jesus (Jn 2:13–25). We then explore the dynamics of entering into eternal life as presented in one of Jesus' discourses (Jn 3:14–21). Finally, we join a number of Greeks who want to see Jesus, and we discover what this implies (Jn 12:20–33). Finally, on Passion Sunday, we accompany Jesus into Jerusalem (Mk 11:1–10) for the unfolding of the passion (Mk 14:1–15:47).

Almsgiving, Prayer and Fasting

The Lenten season begins on Ash Wednesday with a Gospel reading on the three practices characteristic of a good religious person in the cultural world of the New Testament. The passage is taken from Jesus' Sermon on the Mount (Mt 5–7). It includes a general principle (v. 1) and its application to almsgiving (vv. 2–4), prayer (vv. 5–6) and fasting (vv. 16–18). The close parallel structure of each of these sub-units indicates that they formed a rhetorical whole before they were included in Matthew's Gospel, when 6:7–15 was inserted, with the result that the parallel pattern is now less obvious. The same three practices are referred to in the Old Testament's Book of Tobit (12:8–10).

The purpose of the passage is to warn against inappropriate attitudes and behavior in each of these areas, where public display and self-aggrandizement are a danger. Alms should be given discreetly, not in order to be applauded by others. Prayer should be done quietly or privately, not in order to be noticed. Finally, one's fasting should not be advertised to draw attention to oneself.

Wild Beasts and Angels

The Gospel reading for the First Sunday of Lent includes the conclusion of Mark's prologue (1:12–13) and the introductory summary which opens Jesus' ministry (1:14–15). For this summary, see the Gospel for the Third Sunday in Ordinary Time.

The conclusion of Mark's prologue, commonly referred to as the temptation of Jesus, is deceptively simple. The scene follows the baptism of Jesus. Although it is presented in the form of a particular event in which the Spirit sends Jesus out toward the desert where he stays for forty days, what Mark gives is actually a summary of Jesus' entire life. Jesus' story is that of one sent by the Spirit which descended on him in his baptism. His life unfolds in the desert like a new exodus. His entire life was a time of testing by Satan, who once approached Jesus even in the form of Simon Peter (Mk 8:31–33). The passage also refers to wild beasts and angels. Who and what were the wild beasts which surrounded Jesus in the course of his lifetime? Who were the angels which waited on him? Are the wild beasts of the Gospel still with us today?

The Reign of God in Power

In Mark 9:1, Jesus tells the crowd and his disciples that some of those present would not know death until they had seen the reign of God established in power. The Gospel story then continues with a vision of that reign in which Jesus is accompanied by Peter, James and John. The transfiguration (Mk 9:2–8) and its sequel (Mk 9:9–10), which constitute the reading for the Second Sunday of Lent, point to the final coming of Jesus when as Son of Man he would appear in full glory. Moses, that is, the law, and Elijah, the prophets, witnessed to this great manifestation. The disciples of Jesus must also do the same, but after he had risen from the dead. For us that time is now.

Cleansing the Temple

For many, the account of the cleansing of the temple (Jn 2:13–25) indicates how human Jesus really was. Like us, he could get very angry, but in his case anger always was righteous and called for. Actually the story, which we read on the Third Sunday of Lent, is about the passing of an era. There was no longer need for money changers, because the time for sacrifices in the temple had passed. Unfortunately, there were those who clung tenaciously to the past and could not recognize that the ultimate sacrifice was taking place in the life of Jesus. Nor was there need for a temple built of stone, since the Father had made his home in the person of Jesus, his Son, the new and definitive temple about to be raised up.

Eternal Life

We all know the story of Nicodemus and how Jesus challenged him to accept a new kind of birth, one which was from above and from the Spirit. Human birth makes one a member of a particular family. The new birth of which Jesus spoke makes one a member of the family of God and introduces one to his kingdom. Jesus continues that teaching with a short discourse on the dynamics of rebirth, the process of entering into eternal life. On the Fourth Sunday of Lent, we read John 3:14–21, and see how for his part God gave his only Son that we might have life. Our response to that is belief, the kind of belief which flows into life. Those who believe walk in the light, not in darkness, as they journey to eternal life.

In Search of Jesus

On the Fifth Sunday of Lent (Jn. 12:20–33), we follow a group of Greeks who approach Philip and ask to see Jesus. We then listen to Jesus speak of what it means to really see him. As the Son of Man, Jesus is to be glorified. First he will die, as a grain of wheat must die if it is to produce fruit. Those who want to see Jesus must be willing to do the same. They must be willing to follow him as servants. It is in this way that God's name, his personal presence and self-communication, is gloried. Jesus' life is the revelation of the Father's life, and his glorification is the glorification of the Father's name. That revelation and glorification continue in and through the life of all who are servants of Jesus and join him in his glory.

Triumph of the Son of David

As Jesus enters Jerusalem, the crowds chant, "Blessed is the reign of our father David to come!" We read those words on Passion Sunday as we prepare our own procession with palms to commemorate Jesus' triumphal entry into Jerusalem (Mk 11:1–10). In Mark's Gospel we had already been told what that journey to Jerusalem meant. More than any other Gospel, Mark had emphasized that it was a journey to suffering and death, a way to the cross (see Mk 10:32–34). We had also heard people reach out to Jesus with the title "Son of David" (see Mk 10:46–52). We are consequently well prepared for Jesus' triumph. Unknowing, the crowd was chanting the triumph of the cross. Jesus' reign was not an earthly reign. His rule would be without end.

The Passion and Death of Jesus

The Gospel reading for our Passion Sunday liturgy is Mark's account of the passion, death and burial of Jesus (14:1–15:47). Jesus' life as one baptized by the Spirit (see First Sunday of Lent) has come to its climax, and the final events of the redemption are being played out. We can read the story from the point of view of Jesus' enemies. The plan to destroy him, already underway since Mark 3:6, when the Pharisees joined the Herodians in an evil alliance, was carried out. We can also read it from the point of view of Jesus. It is not that he was the hapless victim of a deadly plot. His whole life had been for others, and he had followed through to the end. His life was not taken away from him. On the contrary, he had offered it and he gave it for our salvation. Or again we can read the story of the passion from the point of view of the disciples, who made great promises and pledged solidarity with Jesus, but who proved less than heroic. Each of these three readings of the passion is a Lenten challenge to us as we begin the celebrations of Holy Week.

Introduction to Lent and the Triduum

Each session for the Lenten season and the triduum contains the following elements: gathering prayer, reflections/response and closing prayer.

It is anticipated that there is more material provided for each session than can be used. The catechist should select especially from the reflections according to the needs of the group, planning the time allotted to include gathering prayer, response and closing prayer. The response is the question or activity that relates to a practice or change in attitude for daily living. If it happens that a section of the reflections takes more time than planned, the catchist will need to be flexible. It is important, however, not to cut the prayer exercises or response. It is in these elements that the word takes effect in daily life.

These sessions are intended for catechumens, not the elect. Hence, the reflections based on the rites for the elect ask that the participants share as members of the assembly rather than as those celebrating the rites.

Some reference is made to writing in a journal. If this form of prayer has not been previously mentioned, some introduction of journal writing could be made at this time.

During the triduum the symbols of the rites as well as the Scripture readings provide much food for reflection and sharing. In a focused way these celebrations witness to the connection between our belief and our prayer (*lex orandi—lex-credendi*). Let the shared reflections be an "unpacking" of the experience of the rites as much as possible. Hopefully in your parish they are celebrated well, with generous use of symbols. Familiarize yourself with some background on the paschal mystery, the triduum, the sacraments of initiation. Use the suggested questions only as needed. Let the richness of these days speak to and through the catechumens. (It is assumed that the catechumens will be dismissed during the triduum.)

Note: The sessions for the triduum are found in the next section, Easter.

First Sunday of Lent

Genesis 9:8–15
1 Peter 3:18–22
Mark 1:12–15

GATHERING PRAYER

Sing: "Believe and Repent," Ken Meltz (*Until He Comes,* World Library)
or, "Turn to Me," John Foley, S.J. (*Glory and Praise,* NALR)
or, "I Lift Up My Soul," Tim Manion (*Glory and Praise,* NALR)
(option: sing only the antiphon)

Read the following reflection slowly:

In today's Gospel Jesus calls us to repent, reform our lives and believe in the good news. Repentance is more profound than being sorry for having done something wrong or hurting someone. Repentance is not simply putting bandages on the wounds we have caused. In true repentance we try to move behind all our sins to the sinful condition itself.

What makes us act to hurt people?
What prevents us from forgiving others?
Why are we afraid to love?
We are not concerned so much with healing the various wounds we have acquired or inflicted. Rather we want to move to the heart of the matter; we want to discover our integrated self as it was and still is in the mind of God.

Pause for some moments of reflection. Repeat song or antiphon.

REFLECTIONS/RESPONSE

1. Discuss what repentance means to you in the light of Jesus' proclamation in today's Gospel and the reflection used in the gathering prayer. Discuss the questions included in that reflection.

2. Mark's account of the temptation in the desert is the shortest of all the Gospels for the First Sunday of Lent telling of this event. He merely says that Jesus went into the wilderness where he was tempted. Jesus was sent by the Spirit who had descended on him at baptism and in whom he would baptize oth-ers. The desert was a preparation for Jesus' mission. His whole life from the beginning of his ministry to the passion is presented as a time of testing. It is in this context that Jesus proclaimed the good news of God in Galilee and called everyone to faith and conversion.

How did Jesus encounter temptation and resist it?
How do we encounter temptation?
How can we see temptations for what they are?
Discuss the following statement: Temptations do not merely happen to individuals like Jesus or ourselves; they can grab hold of entire nations and peoples as well.
In what ways do you experience this?

3. Lent is a special time of preparation for baptism. It is also a special time for all Christians to renew their decision to follow Jesus. This decision is never made once-for-all. Instead of allowing the ego to continue to determine our habitual patterns of living, we now search for the real meaning of our lives, the meaning of our jobs and professions, the meaning of our relationships. Some form of self-denial may help us realign our priorities according to the vision of the kingdom of God. The penance we undertake for Lent can create conflict in our lives. To allow the different aspects of ourselves to emerge will not happen without a struggle but through this struggle we can learn to rely more on God.

Fasting has been a traditional Lenten practice. It clears the way in our body and our psyche to look at the meaning of our life and our priorities. By fasting we also come to share in the experience of the poor and hungry of the world. We come to feel solidarity with our brothers and sisters and hopefully join with them in their fight for survival.

In addition to lessening food intake, fasting can include cutting back on alcohol consumption, smoking, television or habitual overwork. Discuss how you might practice fasting during Lent in ways which will lead you to consider the meaning of your life. Summarize in your journal your resolutions about fasting.

4. As recounted in the reading from Genesis, Noah and his family begin an entirely new life after the flood. This account is the first expression in the Old Testament of God's covenant with all humankind. God promises never again to destroy the earth by a flood.

The sign given is a rainbow in the clouds. The ancient sign of war, the bow, is turned upside down in the heavens, the rainbow. Thus God reconciles and does not destroy. This is a turning point in the history of the world. God has always initiated the covenants he makes. The key attitude held by the Hebrews about the covenant was that it was Yahweh's free gift of love to them.

Did anyone ever make a free gift of friendship and helpfulness to you?

Think especially of anyone who was under absolutely no obligation to you.

How did you respond?

If you accepted the gift of relationship, did you remain loyal to that person, seeking to return some of his or her goodness?

What response does God's initiative call for from us?

If you were given a free choice right now, would you accept this covenant relationship?

6. The reading from Peter points out that the flood was a prefiguration of baptism. Just as the flood washed the world clean and allowed us a new beginning ratified by the rainbow covenant, so our baptism will wash us clean and we will emerge shining with the resurrection of Christ.

Why is water used in baptism as a symbol of covenant?

References

Basic Beliefs in Genesis and Exodus, Emil A. Wcela, New York: Pueblo Pub. Co., 1976

Conversion and the Catechumenate, ed. Robert Duggan, Mahwah, N.J.: Paulist Press, 1984

A *Lenten Pilgrimage—Dying and Rising in the Lord*, Richard Chilson, C.S.P., Mahwah, N.J.: Paulist Press, 1983

Of Fast and Festival, Barbara O'Dea, Mahwah, N.J.: Paulist Press, 1982

Parish Path Through Lent and Eastertime, ed. Mary Ann Simcoe, Chicago: Liturgy Training Publications, 1985

The Sinai Myth, Andrew Greeley, New York: Doubleday and Co., Inc., 1972

Turning, Emilie Griffin, New York: Doubleday, Image Books, 1982

Doctrinal/Pastoral Issues: Fasting, Election, Covenant, Baptism, Repentance, Lent.

Ellen Bush

CLOSING PRAYER

Sing: "Anthem," Tom Conry (Oregon Press)
            or, "Believe and Repent," Ken Meltz
            (World Library)
            or, pray Psalm 51:

Have mercy on me, God, in your kindness,
In your compassion blot out my offense.
Oh wash me more and more from my guilt
and cleanse me from my sin.
My offenses, truly I know them:
my sin is always before me.
Against you, you alone, have I sinned;
what is evil in your sight I have done.
A pure heart create for me, O God,
put a steadfast spirit within me.
Do not cast me away from your presence,
nor deprive me of your holy spirit.
Give me again the joy of your help,
with a spirit of fervor sustain me.
O Lord, open my lips
and my mouth shall declare your praise.

Second Sunday of Lent

Genesis 22:1–2, 9, 10–13, 15–18
Romans 8:31–34
Mark 9:2–9

GATHERING PRAYER

One way to enter into the story of the Gospel is to use the method of meditation outlined by St. Ignatius. Following is an outline of this approach and a suggestion for applying it to today's Gospel.

Ignatian prayer outline:

1. Set a mood of prayer; recall God's presence. (Relaxation breathing exercises may be helpful) Read reflectively the Gospel I wish to contemplate.

2. Picture briefly the place where the Gospel event takes place.

3. Ask for one grace related to the Gospel event.
   I imagine I am one of the characters in the story.
   What do I smell?
   What do I feel?
   What do I taste?
   What do I hear?

Conclusion: What thoughts go through my mind as I . . .? (Do whatever the character is doing.)

I remain there just looking at Jesus and he at me.

I end by speaking to Jesus in my own words.

Follow through with this outline using today's Gospel. After a centering exercise, the leader reads the Gospel slowly, inviting participants to put themselves into the story with the disciples. Invite them to picture the scene, imagining the climb up the mountain and the experience of seeing Jesus' transfiguration. Imagine the radiance in Jesus' body, the light, the clarity, the peace. To conclude, speak to the Father. Ask him for guidance on the journey to baptism, bringing fears as well as hopes for transformation.

REFLECTIONS/RESPONSE

1. Take some minutes to reflect on experiences when you felt "beyond" the limits of the moment, such as the most joyous, happiest, most blessed moment of your life, the moment you know you are in love, some instance of sudden silence in the summer woods when there seems nothing beyond the trees but eternity, meeting someone whose life story reveals possibilities that split one's ideas wide open. It might be helpful to record these times. Those who wish may want to share with the group one of these experiences.
   Reflect on how you felt differently about yourself at those times.
   What were your impulses?
   How did you change (if you did)?

2. We may want to hold on to such experiences. Like Peter we try to sustain the event by staying there and building a tent. But Jesus takes his disciples down from the mountain and back to the business office.
   Why did Jesus go on?
   Why must we go on?
   The story of the transfiguration can be seen as a foreshadowing of baptism. Just like the mountain top, baptism is not an end in itself. We may be tempted to look at it as the climax of our journey; in a sense it is, but in another sense baptism is a turning point.
   Discuss the following statement: "In becoming Christian we have decided to commit ourselves to live by certain values, to give public witness to our belief in the Lord. We are undertaking God's continuing mission in the world on behalf of the poor, the blind, the suffering. After our baptism our Christian lives will turn more and more in this direction of service" (Chilson, *A Lenten Pilgrimage*, p. 57).
   Discuss ways you can more fully participate in the life of service called for by the Christian life. Discuss with your sponsor one practical way you can begin during Lent.

3. Love sacrifices to the life of a relationship. Real love offers, not a portion, but all. It is total. It is radical. But so are the rewards. This is true with all persons; with God it is more so. Since he is life, the living God, so is his gift. God's response to the offering of Abraham is life, abundant and blessed descendants for countless generations. Jesus' loving obedience transfigured him to what he truly is, the image of God, glorified and beautiful. So full is he of love for

the Father and all of us that the inner source of his very being becomes transparent to the apostles. Love radiates the fullness of life.

What is being transfigured by the Christ-love within us?

Where do we see this love transfiguring the world?

Why do we get the good news of the transfiguration during Lent?

4. Faith, which is acceptance of a living relationship with God, helps us bring wholeness into our lives so that faith is expressed in what we do and say. Faith enabled Abraham to say yes to the test of being asked to sacrifice his only son. The story of Abraham is not that of a last-minute escape, but an affirmation of life. It is the story of a Creator who keeps his promises.

What is faith?

How does faith lend wholeness to our lives?

What are some characteristics of a faith-full person?

Describe some characteristics to be found in a faith-full community.

5. "With God on our side who can be against us?"

How is God on our side?

What could the phrase "God will not refuse us anything he can give" mean for us about our journey?

6. Glory is one of the great themes of Scripture. Glory means more than a joy or radiance. When the glory of God appears in the Bible it is a sign that God is present and revealed to us. God's presence is not merely for show; when God is present with his people he is liberating and saving them.

Discuss the various ways that different characters in today's readings discovered the "glory of God."

Discuss what glory meant to each character.

Do you identify with any of them in their discoveries?

Where do you experience the glory of God most powerfully?

CLOSING PRAYER

"Posture of openness" prayer. Sit centered and quiet. Leader reads statements at each breath.

Exhale: "Lord, fill my mind with your light."

Inhale: picture light filling the mind

Exhale: "Fill my heart with your love."

Inhale: sense love filling the heart

Exhale: "Fill my body with your presence."

Inhale: feel the presence filling the body

Repeat prayerfully four to five times. Do not hurry.

References

From Ashes to Easter, Washington, D.C.: The Liturgical Conference, 1979

A Lenten Pilgrimage—Dying and Rising in the Lord, Richard Chilson, C.S.P., Mahwah, N.J.: Paulist Press, 1983

Paschal Mission 1982, Chicago: Liturgy Training Publications, 1981

You, Mark Link, S.J., Allen, TX.: Argus Communications, 1976

Doctrinal/Pastoral Issues: Faith, Glory of God, Transformation, Love, Religious Experience, Service

Ellen Bush

Third Sunday of Lent

Exodus 20:1–17
1 Corinthians 1:22–25
John 2:13–25

GATHERING PRAYER

God of mystery, whose folly is wiser than human wisdom, and whose weakness is more powerful than mortal strength, we praise this power and wisdom made flesh for us in Jesus your Son.

Let your Spirit search our hearts and lead us away from the comfortable slavery that snares us.

Give us the courage to make the Gospel our lives, that we may at last begin to take our stand with the world's rejected, to embrace our enemies in peace, to glory in the cross of Jesus in whose name we pray. Amen.

(Option: Begin with film, "Up Is Down" (Pyramid Films 6 min.)

REFLECTIONS/RESPONSE

1. Paul tells us that as Christians we preach Christ crucified, the power and wisdom of God. This is a stumbling block for some and an absurdity for others. Weakness as power does not fit the traditional image of the Messiah who would be expected to be a glorious being, not someone rejected and crucified.

   How is a crucified Christ seen as a stumbling block?

   How is this paradox God's folly?

   How have you experienced God's folly in your own life, for example, in finding unexpected insights emerging from ordinary events?

2. John sees many levels of meaning in relation to the themes of the temple. The Jewish leaders take Jesus' words about rebuilding the temple in three days literally and scoff at its impossibility. After all, they objected, it took forty-six years to construct it. But Jesus was talking about the temple of his body when he said, "I will rebuild it," or "I will raise it." In looking back after the resurrection the disciples could see that Jesus had foretold his death and resurrection although they had not realized it at the time.

John, written later circa 90 A.D., sees several things that were not clear to the original witnesses:

   a. The real meaning of Jesus' protest is that Jesus had replaced the temple as the place of encounter and worship with God.
   b. Jesus' zeal for the house of his Father did consume him literally, that is, it did eventually lead to his death.
   c. The temple which Jesus promised to rebuild was that of his crucified body.

In today's Gospel story God's wrath drives the merchants out not because they are evil but because they take up the room in the Father's house where he urgently wants to be at home with us.

   Is my practice of fasting helping to clear the way?

3. In reading and reflecting on the passage from Exodus it is important to set these verses in their context. God has freed his people. God is drawing his people to himself. On the basis of what God has done, i.e., bringing them out of Egypt, the people understand that the Lord is serious about wanting to make them his people. If they obey his voice and hold fast to the covenant, that is, if they accept and live out his proposal, then God promises to make them great in the future as he promised to Abraham and his descendants. God promises to make the people his very special possession.

   The Lord steps into Israel's history. He asks the people to remember how he led them out of Egypt and brought them to himself and promised to make them truly great. Their personal experience of the exodus should fill them with confidence in his love for them and in the Lord's ability to make good his promises. Remembrance inspires gratitude, confidence and hope. These become the motivators for love and submission to the Lord. To express awareness of the special relationship between itself and Yahweh, Israel used the ideas of that time; the word "covenant" (*berith* in Hebrew) seemed to suit the situation.

   The form of the covenant followed that of treaties made between kings. In the covenant with Yahweh, however, some features were unique. God expended loving kindness, or mercy, called *hesed*. It designates God's own commitment to the relationship that he had established with his people. The people's response, holiness, was not a matter of keeping rules but directing their lives and worship to Yahweh.

How does the covenant bind God?

How does the covenant bind each person?

Does the term "covenant" as used in this reflection express your relationship with God?

4. The actual ten commandments or ten words are only one section of the covenant form. Moreover, their wording, an apodictic law form, reflects only one kind of law common in the Near East. The decalogue or ten commandments must be seen in this context, being not so much an ethical document as a religious document, a testimony to the unbreakable bond between God and Israel.

The commands pertaining to one's "neighbor" were similar in outlook to other laws of the period, though there is a certain deeper humaneness, a more profound respect for life contained in them. There is more pervasive equality; for example, judgment of crimes is not influenced by the status of the criminal or victim.

The relationship with Yahweh is unique in the laws of the Near East in that Israel worshiped Yahweh only because of his concern and presence to them.

In later Christianity the decalogue acquired a more set form and importance as a charter of individual morality. It is important to note that it was not intended as the ultimate norm of all morality. The ten commandments and all the laws developed over the centuries were really a spelling out of the first commandment which was unique in itself.

The statements about God and humankind are inseparable. There is not true relationship to God without a special kind of relationship to one's brothers and sisters. The commandments need to be made alive and pertinent to changing times and situations. Each society has a responsibility to try to determine what a single-minded commitment to the one true God means in each day and age. There must be a contact with the living God to hear his word for the here and now.

Reflect on the meanings of the three God-commandments and select the one you think is in most need of being reiterated in our culture and times. Give your reasons.

The ten commandments make a basic statement about God and humankind. What do they tell you of God?

What do they tell you of humankind?

What further insights does Jesus give into their meaning as to the relationship between God and his people?

Mention at least one new insight you received from this reflection about the ten commandments.

Select the commandment with which you have the greatest personal difficulty. Change it to the opposite or a positive focus, when the statement is negative, and make it the basis for your personal action during the week ahead.

CLOSING PRAYER

"God in My Breath"

Invite participants to be quiet, close their eyes, practice awareness of body sensations or do relaxation breathing exercises. (See *Sadhana* by Anthony de Mello)

Leader reads the following, slowly:

Concentrate on breathing. Become aware of the air as it comes in and goes out through your nostrils. (Pause. Do not control your breathing. Do not attempt to deepen it.) Reflect now that this air that you are breathing in is charged with the power and presence of God.

Think of the air as of an immense ocean that surrounds you, an ocean colored with God's presence and God's being; while you draw the air into your lungs you are drawing God in. Be aware that you are drawing in the power and presence of God each time you breathe in. Notice what you feel when you become conscious that you are drawing God in with each breath you take. Give several minutes for this exercise.

References

Basic Beliefs in Genesis and Exodus, Emil Wcela, New York: Pueblo Pub. Co., 1976

A Commentary on the Gospel of John, Robert E. Obach & Albert Kirk, Mahwah, N.J.: Paulist Press, 1981

Sadhana, Anthony de Mello, New York: Doubleday, Image Books, 1978

The Sinai Myth, Andrew M. Greeley, New York: Doubleday and Co., Inc., 1972

Doctrinal/Pastoral Issues: Covenant, Image of Messiah, Paradox of Strength in Weakness, Temple, Ten Commandments

Ellen Bush

Fourth Sunday of Lent

2 Chronicles 36:14–16, 19–23
Ephesians 2:4–10
John 3:14–21

GATHERING PRAYER

Sing: "Glory and Praise to Our God," Dan
Schutte, S.J. (*Glory and Praise*,
NALR)

or, "You Are Near," Dan Schutte, S.J.
(*Glory and Praise*, NALR)

(This form of meditation includes listening to God
speaking to us in a scriptural passage and speaking to
God about what he says.) Read the following reflection
slowly:

Being loved is always a surprise. The love of another
thrills and excites us. It supports us in all that we do. It
enables us to value ourselves, and even when we recognize our own self-worth, being loved is still a startling
experience. Are we worthy of this devotion? We wonder even as we are continually recreated by the experience.

The realization that we are really loved by God is difficult to grasp. Yet the signs of God's love are all around
us. The incarnation, the becoming human of the Son, is
the Father's fullest sign of his love for us. It is a startling sign. If we believe it, this sign should support,
thrill, excite and recreate us.

Lord, help me to become more aware of your presence
within me. Open my mind to your truth and my heart
to your love.

Pause briefly and open yourself to God's presence.
Then listen prayerfully as God speaks to you.

Someone should read Ephesians 2:4–10 slowly.

Conclude with some moments of silence to allow each
person to speak to God about St. Paul's words concerning God's mercy, God's free gift of salvation and being
God's handiwork.

REFLECTIONS/RESPONSE

1. Consider together some ways in which being loved
   gives life to people. Give examples of how this life is

given in friendship, marriage, family, the community.

How does love transform people?

Can we really change someone by loving him or
her?

Are we really changed by being loved?

Do you think persons can feel the embrace of
God's love, care and concern, if they are strangers to
the experience of human love, care and concern?

Invite participants to spend some minutes reflecting and writing about relationships in their own
lives. Write a prayer of gratitude for a relationship
that is transforming; note ways that a relationship
could be made to be more life-giving.

2. Reflect on Paul's words to the Ephesians:
   Salvation is a free gift from a loving God. It is not
   a reward for work accomplished. It is not our own
   doing.

   Paul emphasizes that God's love is freely given
   and does not depend on the person's acceptance of
   that love.

   Do we really believe that we are loved by God?

   Does that make a difference in our lives, here and
   now?

   Celebrate the great gift of God's love by using
   symbol or words, individually, or as a group.

3. All through history various people and groups of
   people have emphasized different aspects of the
   reality of the gift of salvation and its relationship to
   human freedom. Official Church statements on the
   topic resulted from two extreme distortions: Pelagi-
   anism, a fifth century heresy which held that human
   beings can, without the grace of God, achieve salvation; Protestantism, which emphasized the radical
   unworthiness of the person, even after God's redemption.

   How one perceives the gift of salvation is related
   to one's view of human nature, human freedom, and
   one's relationship to the world.

   Discuss the following statements:

   "There are not in the human person two separate
   finalities, the one oriented toward the vision of God,
   and the other oriented toward human fulfillment
   apart from the vision of God. . . . This means, too,
   that the whole universe is oriented to the glory of
   God. The history of the world is, at the same time,
   the history of salvation. It means that authentic hu-

man progress in the struggle for justice, peace, freedom, human rights, is part of the movement of, and toward, the Kingdom of God" (*Catholicism*, p. 161).

"The spirit of transformation, which is bigger than all of us, works through us to righten human and social relationships. We become vehicles of divine salvation" (*Original Blessing*, p. 298).

How do I see myself as a participant in the work of salvation?

4. Typology is the technique of taking an incident or person from the Old Testament and using it as a prefigurement of a person or event recorded in the Christian Scriptures. In the Gospel the hanging up of the serpent is used as an image that prefigures the crucifixion. John uses this obscure incident from the Old Testament to make three points:

   a. As the snake was lifted up, so must Jesus be lifted up on the cross.
   b. God's salvific will is involved in both exaltations.
   c. Natural life was restored to those fatally bitten Hebrews when they looked at the bronze snake; but eternal life is given to all those who come in faith to gaze upon Jesus hanging on the cross.

As the lifted serpent in the desert freed and saved Israel, so the Son of Man by the act of being lifted on the cross shall communicate life. Baptism is believing that Jesus won life for us through the cross and is thus exalted by his Father. In baptism we are each called upon to recommit ourselves to the acceptance of God's love as it is symbolized in the cross.

What does this mean?
What can this mean in our daily lives?

CLOSING PRAYER

A good-sized cross should be available and could have been on display during the session. Some form of veneration could accompany the closing prayer.

We give you thanks, O God, for the holy cross
  of Jesus.
This instrument of death became a tree of life
  and healing, a sign of your faithful love.
May we who are preparing for baptism know
  the wonder and the glory of our unity
  with Jesus
And the freedom we have in his Holy Spirit,
  alive among us, now and forever and
  ever. Amen.

References

Becoming Catholic Even If You Happen To Be One, J. Killgallen, M. O'Shaughnessy, G. Weber, Chicago: ACTA Foundation, 1980

Catholicism, Richard McBrien, Minneapolis: Winston Press, 1980

A Commentary on the Gospel of John, Robert E. Obach and Albert Kirk, Mahwah, N.J.: Paulist Press, 1981

From Ashes to Easter, Washington, D.C.: The Liturgical Conference, 1979

Original Blessing, Matthew Fox, Santa Fe: Bear and Co., Inc., 1983

Doctrinal/Pastoral Issues: Unconditional Love, Salvation as a Free Gift, Cross as Exaltation, Typology

Ellen Bush

Fifth Sunday of Lent

Jeremiah 31:31–34
Hebrews 5:7–9
John 12:20–33

GATHERING PRAYER

Sing: "The Song of All Seed" (H. Oosterhuis, NALR)

O loving God, whose new and everlasting covenant is sealed in the blood of an obedient Son, look with mercy upon us and upon the men and women who approach the Easter sacraments. Give us the courage to live by your word alone, with your law written on our hearts. Let the fasting we have embraced bring us a paschal feast of joy. For you are good and generous and the lover of all, our one God, forever and ever. Amen.

REFLECTIONS/RESPONSE

1. The part of the new covenant described in the first reading which I value the most is

   a. having the Lord's wishes within my heart
   b. God agreeing to be our God
   c. God calling us "my people"
   d. knowing God is teaching everyone in different ways
   e. God offering forgiveness

   Discuss the following reflection: In the first reading for this week, Jeremiah preaches a new covenant. Both parties, God and the people, remain the same as in the old covenant. Though the terms of the covenant are the same, obedience to God's law, yet Jeremiah preaches that God is making a new covenant. The new covenant is unlike the old in that the new will be written on the heart. Here is a new and unparalleled intimacy between God and the people.
   How does God covenant with people today?

2. Jesus had come to know that he could not bring freedom without laying down his life. He knows he cannot avoid his approaching death by being more conciliatory toward people in power. He knows that through his hour an opening will be created where God's power can break through in a new way. Just as a seed dies in the earth to produce an abundance, he would crack open from within the shell of fear and selfishness around the human heart. It would not be a matter of imposing better rules of conduct from outside, but rather the divine love present in the human heart would appear as a shoot, weak, vulnerable, but truly the glory of God shining forth.
   Have I ever experienced a breakthrough, a time which felt as though the truth of life was written on my heart?
   How often do we resort to force and strength in the hope of bettering things?
   How might it be possible to create the space for God's power to break through in the world from within the human heart?

3. Jesus laid down his life that others might have life, just as a seed of grain is worthless unless it dies to bring forth fruit. Those who believe in him must do the same; in giving life they too will find it.
   "Loving" and "hating" one's life is a Semitic expression that indicates one's priorities. To prefer oneself to all else or to refuse to become any more than what one already is a choice to remain only a single grain. "Hating" one's life expresses a willingness to change, that is, being willing to die to self-centeredness. In this way one keeps life for "life eternal."
   In what ways are you called to "lose your life"?
   In what ways are you fearful or reluctant to follow Jesus to give your life?
   In the light of this reflection, the quotation, "Unless a grain of wheat falls into the ground and dies, it remains only a single grain," means . . .(Spend some quiet moments summarizing in your journal.)

4. Jesus answers the inquiry of the Greeks, "We should like to see Jesus," by stating, "The hour has come for the Son of Man to be glorified." The title "Son of Man" is common to all the Gospels but the author of John used it in a distinctive way. In John, Son of Man emphasizes the divinity of Jesus in the concept of pre-existence although the Fourth Gospel is well known for its words with more than one level of meaning. Son of Man can also mean "everyman" or "anyone." Possibly the author also had this meaning in mind. The title would then imply an emphasis on the human and what John seems to imply is the divinity present within a true humanity.

How do you relate the humanity and divinity of Jesus in your own life?

5. We cannot grow by ourselves in understanding and appreciating the meaning of God's word. We need one another and one another's gifts to comprehend the depth of God's relating with us. Christian faith is not a private faith but a public, common, community faith. The faith of the Christian is the faith of the Church. We experience God's covenant, God's great deed, Jesus, and the meaning of his death and resurrection in the Church as the community of believers.

The community of faith must be like Jesus in being a ministering community, ministering particularly to those who are most in need, those whom society has neglected, ignored, despised, cast out, imprisoned, oppressed, exiled or simply relegated to the fringes of social life, such as the sick and aged.

Discuss how we are called, as followers of Jesus, both to full individual development and to membership in community.

How do you see the community of believers incorporating those who are most in need?

How have you shared in ministry in the parish community?

6. In bread-making each element dies so a new creation can come into being. The wheat is crushed, combined with other ingredients and finally baked. Human energy is expended at each step along the way from planting to milling and baking. Bread symbolizes the life of the many who work together to produce that which feeds and gives life to all.

The Christian community gathers to eat that bread which symbolizes our life, Christ's body. We are all fed by the same holy bread. We all become that which we eat, the body of Christ. When we eat we destroy the food that gives life. Reflect on food as a part of the human being as it sustains life.

What parallel can be seen with the bread of the Eucharist as sustainer of life?

How can we share food with our hungry brothers and sisters this week?

CLOSING PRAYER

Gather around a table on which is placed a loaf of unleavened bread. Sing "Song of All Seed" or listen to meditative music.

The leader invites each participant to come to the table and break off a piece of bread from the loaf and put it on the plate. Ask each person, as he or she breaks the bread, to name one place in the world where people are suffering from hunger. After all have broken the bread, pray:

> We give you thanks, O God,
> for food and drink and all your gifts to us.
> You have made the many wheat grains one.
> In this broken bread, nurture our oneness.
> Nurture our concern and support for one another
> and for those who have no food.
> Strengthen us on our freedom journey
> with all who share this earth.
> Glory and praise to you, God of unity and joy,
> this Lenten day and forever and ever.

The leader passes the plate of bread for all to eat. Invite all to share a place greeting.

References

Catholicism, Richard E. McBrien, Minneapolis: Winston Press, 1980

A Commentary on the Gospel of John, Robert E. Obach and Albert Kirk, Mahwah, N.J.: Paulist Press, 1981

The Eucharist and Human Liberation, Tissa Balasuriya, Maryknoll, N.Y.: Orbis Books, 1979

The Eucharist and the Hungers of the World, Monica Hellwig, Mahwah, N.J.: Paulist Press, 1976

From Ashes to Easter, Washington, D.C.: The Liturgical Conference, 1979

The Gospel of John, John O'Grady, New York: Pueblo Publishing Co., 1982

Original Blessing, Matthew Fox, Santa Fe: Bear and Co., Inc., 1983

Paschal Mission 1982, Chicago: Liturgy Training Publications

Doctrinal/Pastoral Issues: Covenant, Divinity/Humanity of Jesus, Discipleship, Community, Ministry as Sharing of Food, Eucharist

Ellen Bush

Passion Sunday

Isaiah 50:4–7
Philippians 2:6–11
Mark 15:1–39

GATHERING PRAYER

Background Note: Today's liturgy is one of contrasts. The triumphal procession of palms is combined with the tragedy of the passion reading, the account of Jesus' trial and death. But this celebration of triumph in tragedy is just what the Church is about during Holy Week. Jesus' one act of redemption in his passion, death and resurrection is the action we celebrate. We do not retrace the steps as they were that first Holy Week. As we commemorate Jesus' passion and death we do it not to relive it but to enter into it and give thanks for our redemption in it.

Today's prayer is an adaption of the Hindu practice of memorizing and reciting the thousand names of God lovingly in prayer. Each name is full of meaning and reveals some aspect of the divinity. As a means of entering into the celebration of the coming week, each participant is invited to invent a "thousand names" for Jesus. The creativity and feelings of the catechumens will enable them to invent their own names, i.e., Jesus, my joy; Jesus, my strength; Jesus, my love; Jesus, my peace.

Encourage the participants to relax and prepare for the reflective prayer. Introduce the prayer, inviting the catechumens to recite one of the names they have chosen each time they breathe out. If one or another name appeals particularly, ask them to repeat it again and again, or to recite it once and rest lovingly in it for a while, saying nothing, and then to take up another name, rest in it, and so on. The key to the reflection is the pace and atmosphere of relaxation. Encourage the catechumens to pray at their own pace.

The next step in the prayer is to imagine you hear Jesus inventing names for you. After a time invite the participants to try to hear Jesus call them by names. What names does he invent for them? Ask them to express their feelings when they hear Jesus call them by these names. Encourage them to listen. Many people turn away from God's loving words; they are too good to be true. Some people have a hard time allowing themselves to feel God's love. Encourage them to let go of negative images of themselves and be open to hear his names for them today.

The last step is to hear Jesus applying to you the very same names that you invented for him—all the names except those that directly express divinity. Do not be frightened; expose yourself to the intensity of his love. Encourage the participants not to worry about whether what they hear is a figment of their imagination. They will know if they let their hearts be truly open to the Lord's word for them. The love of Jesus is so great that no words we invent and place on his lips will ever prove adequate to express his love for us. (Adapted from *Sadhana* by Anthony de Mello)

REFLECTIONS/RESPONSE

1. Discuss how the various members of the group experienced the celebration of the commemoration of the Lord's entrance into Jerusalem (the procession with palms).

   Discuss the parish celebration in light of the following: "In the story of Jesus' entry into Jerusalem we can see the different elements of the week (Holy Week). First there is the joy and celebration. In a sense Jesus is coming into his kingdom and being acclaimed as king. But he is a different king. He comes humbly riding on an ass. Here is a king who will give his life for his people. And underneath the festive mood there is tragedy. Jesus knows quite soon these very people will deny and denounce him. He has no illusions; he is traveling toward his death" (Chilson, *Lenten Pilgrimage*, p. 107).

   The procession is the important aspect of the opening rite of today's liturgy. In the procession we are to see the ascent of God's people, and our own ascent with Jesus to the sacrifice. The procession is Christ's journey, together with his people, to Calvary and the central act of redemption.

   Each year the whole Church enters into the celebration of the paschal mystery, proclaiming the life-giving death of Jesus, dying with him in order to lay hold of life at a deeper level, especially in those who will enter the death-resurrection waters of baptism at the vigil. Palm Sunday images that experience; we go up to Jerusalem to suffer and die that we may also rise with him. The palm symbol of victory is also a Christian's sign of hope in the face of death.

2. The first reading (Isaiah 50:4–7) speaks of the suffering servant. In this reading we find the pattern of Jesus' life and ministry. There is the same rejection and misunderstanding as that of the servant. In our own life and following of Jesus we may find this same rejection and misunderstanding. We may even feel it as a result of choosing to become a Catholic Christian. Many people have prejudices about Christianity and Catholicism. It is difficult for them to understand what this means to you. Other hardships may also come our way since there is no promise that by becoming a Christian things will be easy. In fact, our faith may plunge us deeper than before into the pain of the world. Allow Isaiah's words to open that world of pain for you. But as the conclusion of the reading makes clear, we will not be alone, for God is with us even through the rejection, pain and dying. We know that Jesus has been there before us and because of his victory we can all take heart.

Read over the words of Isaiah slowly, if helpful for the group. Ask the participants to reflect about the hard times in their lives and/or their experiences of rejection and misunderstanding. Ask the question: From your present vantage point can you see that God was there with you all along?

Reflect on ways that we may find the way this week to be faithful servants like the servant in the reading. Also reflect on the times of joy we have had in learning about the life of the servant Jesus. Remember the help we have been given to grow in the Lord. Recall times of serving. Share an experience of visiting the sick, helping to feed the hungry, working to improve the community. Let the opening words of Isaiah recall to us our discipleship and ministry.

I find the most significant part of the first reading to be:

a. speaking to the weary
b. the emphasis on listening
c. offering no resistance
d. the assurance that God will help

I find that the first reading:

a. describes me when I'm in a tough spot
b. is too passive to describe me
c. describes what I would like to be
d. is hard for me to understand

3. This Sunday's second reading is an early Christian hymn quoted by Paul in his Letter to the Philippians. In this hymn Jesus is shown emptying himself of all that is divine so that he may become a human being, even a slave, and subject to death. As we meditate upon this great hymn let us begin by putting ourselves into a situation of emptying.

Recall and share recent times, perhaps in your Lenten journey, when you have been called upon to empty yourself.

Have you been able to do so or did you cling to your position, your pride, what you felt was rightfully yours?

How did you feel about this?

If you were able to let go and be emptied, how did you feel?

Were there any fears associated with it?

Have you ever experienced being raised up?

Can we believe what Jesus reveals to us—that emptying does not lead to destruction but that through dying we are raised to new life?

The idea from the second reading which most impresses me is:

a. Jesus putting aside his position as God
b. the willingness of Jesus to accept death
c. Jesus being raised up after his death
d. the honor given Jesus because of his willingness to die for us
e. Jesus Christ is Lord

CLOSING PRAYER

In concluding, ask that you will be able to enter deeply into the spirit of Holy Week. Ask God to keep your mind on the passover of Christ. Ask to realize more deeply God's great love for us in taking on death and blazing a path through to new life and give thanks to him for showing the way. Ask that as we journey through Jesus' last days on earth we too may gain understanding for the place of suffering in our own lives. We can ask that our pain be redeemed and made meaningful. We can finally give thanks that a path from death to life has been forged for us and given to us freely. For this we join with all creation as we declare our love for Jesus as our Lord and Savior. All pray:

Father, all-powerful and ever-living God,
we do well always and everywhere to give you
   thanks through Jesus Christ our Lord.
The days of his life-giving death and glorious
   resurrection are approaching.
This is the hour when he triumphed over Satan's pride, the time when we celebrate
   the great event of our redemption.
Through Christ the angels offer their prayer of
   adoration as they rejoice in your presence
   forever.
May our voice be one with theirs in their
   triumphant hymn of praise.
Or share the solemn blessing for the feast in some way,

perhaps by inviting the participants to bless each other while the text is read:

> Solemn Blessing: Passion of the Lord
> The Father of mercies has given us an example of unselfish love in the sufferings of his only Son.
> Through your service of God and neighbor may you receive his countless blessings. Amen.
> You believe that by his dying, Christ destroyed death forever.
> May he give you everlasting life. Amen.
> He humbled himself for our sakes.
> May you follow his example and share in his resurrection. Amen.
> May almighty God bless you, the Father and the Son and the Holy Spirit. Amen.

References

Catholicism, Richard McBrien, Minneapolis: Winston Press, 1980 (see Chapter XII)

A Lenten Pilgrimage—Dying and Rising in the Lord, Richard Chilson, C.S.P., Mahwah, N.J.: Paulist Press, 1983

Liturgy with Style and Grace, Gabe Huck, Chicago: Liturgy Training Pub., 1984

Parish Path Through Lent and Eastertime (Second Edition), ed. Mary Ann Simcoe, Chicago: Liturgy Training Publications, 1985

Sadhana: A Way to God, Anthony de Mello, S.J., New York: Doubleday, Image Books, 1978

The Three Days: Parish Prayer in the Paschal Triduum, Gabe Huck, Chicago: Liturgy Training Publications, 1981

Doctrinal/Pastoral Issues: Paschal Mystery, Redemption

Ellen Bush

EASTER

The New Creation

By Eugene A. LaVerdiere

The Easter triduum is the highpoint of the liturgical year. It begins on Holy Thursday with a preparatory celebration of the whole paschal mystery, when we focus on Jesus' Last Supper, his farewell to history in word and deed and a gathering up of the Church into his death-resurrection. Its second day is Good Friday, when we dwell on John's account of the passion and focus on Jesus' glorious return to the Father. It climaxes with the Easter vigil, a celebration of the resurrection, an event which touched creation itself to the core and transformed all of history.

The Easter triduum is a transitional period. It can be viewed as the conclusion of Lent, but it is also the introduction to the Easter season, with its seven Sundays of Easter, the Feast of the Ascension and Pentecost Sunday. Most of the readings are taken from John's Gospel for this season, and fittingly so, since the resurrection of Jesus permeates that entire Gospel.

The Last Supper

On Holy Thursday, the Gospel reading for the Mass of the Lord's Supper is John 13:1–15. Passover was approaching, and the decisive hour had come, when Jesus would demonstrate the total gift of his love and return to the Father. The forces of treachery had not really triumphed (vv. 1–2). The body of the reading includes the washing of the feet (vv. 3–12a) and part of a brief discourse by Jesus (vv. 12b–15).

To appreciate the force of Jesus' action, we need to realize who participated—the disciples, an extremely varied gathering which still included Judas, and Jesus, the Lord. Kneeling before each disciple in turn and washing their feet, the Lord not only showed humility but destroyed any claims to human status and social prestige among the disciples. When the Lord himself kneels before the powerful and the humble of the world, they have to recognize their equality as persons before God. Peter's resistance when Jesus approaches him is an expression of pride, not of humility.

In the discourse, Jesus asked his disciples to do for one another and for others what he had just done for them. He thus showed the Church how to pursue its mission to the ends of the earth and gather all nations and peoples into one family of God.

The Glorification of Jesus

On Good Friday, we read John's account of the passion, death and burial of Jesus (Jn 18:1—19:42), an account quite different from that of Matthew, which we heard on Passion Sunday. Matthew's telling of the events would have been incomplete without the resurrection account. Not so with John's, whose passion is the story of Jesus' glorious return to the Father. Unlike Matthew, John does not speak of the resurrection event. Like Mark and Luke, he presupposes it and focuses on the disciples' experience of the risen Lord.

Throughout the passion and to the very moment of his death, Jesus is in full command of the events. John gives no hint of Jesus' anguished prayer at Gethsemane. The arrest takes place in the garden, and Judas is there with the others, but there is no need for a betrayal sign. Jesus steps forward and presents himself (18:4–5). Before Pilate, Jesus makes a solemn statement on the nature of the kingdom and the purpose of his life (18:36–37). Before dying, he shows how his death and passage to God transforms our relationship to one another: "Woman, there is your son . . . there is your mother" (19:26–27). Finally, when Jesus sees that everything has been fulfilled, he declares it so and gives us his spirit. He has drunk the cup the Father has given him to drink (see 18:11).

The Resurrection

At the Easter vigil, the Gospel reading is Mark 16:1–8, our earliest account of the women's visit to the tomb of Jesus. The women come to the tomb wondering who will roll away the huge stone which had been rolled across the entrance. The stone is the barrier which blocks their entry and cuts them off from joining Christ in his burial. We too must ask about the things which prevent us from dying with Christ and being buried with him, and with the women we must learn that only God can roll away this stone, for it is indeed a huge one. Once inside, we hear a young evangelist proclaim the good news of the resurrection of Jesus, the one who had been crucified. We also receive the mission to proclaim this same good news. Shall we do so, or shall we remain silent like the women who were overcome with fright at what had happened?

The Visits to the Tomb

On Easter Sunday, the Gospel is either John 20:1–9, which tells of two visits to the tomb, or Mark's account of the women's experience at the tomb (16:1–8) which we have already heard at the Easter vigil (see above).

Mary Magdalene went to the tomb on the first day of the week, literally on day one of the week, an expression which recalls Genesis and its account of day one of creation. Like the other evangelists at this point in their Gospel, John is announcing a new creation, a new beginning for the human race in Christ the Lord. The creative word of God was about to burst into the world and destroy all darkness, but when Mary went to the tomb it was still dark (Jn 1:4–5). For her the empty tomb was a sign of death and hopelessness.

Hearing of her experience, Peter and the disciple whom Jesus loved also went to the tomb. Early in the tradition, this disciple may have been an historical figure, but by the end of the first century he represented every Christian. Together the two saw not only that Jesus' tomb was empty but that everything associated with Jesus' death, the wrappings, had been left behind. The early Church thus presented the empty tomb as a symbol of resurrection, Christian hope, and eternal life.

The Breaking of Bread

The evening Mass for Easter Sunday presents the story of two disciples leaving Jerusalem in discouragement and going to Emmaus (Lk 24:13–35). On the way they met the Lord but were unable to recognize him. They presented their view to him, a seeming stranger, of what had happened, and Jesus proceeded to expand their understanding of the Scriptures so they might see in them a reflection of what they had experienced. With this, they invited Jesus, still a stranger to them, into their home. In the sharing of bread with Jesus the stranger, their eyes were opened in recognition, and they returned to Jerusalem to share the good news with the assembled community.

This reading is vital for understanding how to interpret the Scriptures in personal and pastoral situations. Sometimes, they remain opaque because our approach to them is too limited and we fail to look at all the Scriptures. We are also taught that to recognize our risen Lord in the breaking of bread, we must be able to extend Christian hospitality to those who are strangers to us.

The Gift of the Spirit

The first day of the week, the day of the new creation and the day on which the early Christians first experienced the risen Lord is also the day on which the Lord breathed the Holy Spirit on the Christian community (Jn 20:19–23) and on which the early Christians continue to experience the risen Lord, share their faith and proclaim it in the weekly assembly (Jn 20:24–29). On the Second Sunday of Easter we thus learn much about the origins of Sunday as well as about the first Easter. We also learn that John's Gospel did not try to present all of Jesus' signs, but only as many as would enable us to have faith and life in his name (Jn 20:30–31).

We should note that Jesus came with the witness of his wounds to bring peace to disciples who were afraid of being wounded, and he sent them on their mission as he had been sent on his. As Lord, he could now breathe into them a Spirit of new life, his own, as God had breathed his life into Adam. Like him they were to be reconcilers, and this brought with it a serious responsibility. If they withheld Christ's peace, many would never be reconciled.

The appearance to Thomas and the disciples on the following first day of the week develops some of the same elements for Christians who were far removed from the first experiences of the risen Lord. With Thomas we are called to hear the voice of the risen Lord in the life and message of the Christians who preceded us in the Church and to experience his presence in our Christian assembly.

The Mission to All Nations

On the Third Sunday of Easter, the Gospel begins by recalling the story of Emmaus (Lk 24:35). The two disciples have returned to Jerusalem and the entire community is assembled. Jesus who already had appeared to Simon (Lk 24:34) and to the Emmaus disciples (Lk 24:13–35) appears once again, this time to the whole community, that is to the eleven and all the others, including the group of women who earlier had gone to the tomb (see Lk 24:9–11).

It is very important to note who is present for this appearance. Jesus' teaching concerning the nature of his risen presence and his commission to go forth in his name to preach to all nations is addressed to the entire Church, not just to a few designated members. The Church as such is apostolic and in one way or another all of its members share in its mission. The passage's insistence that Jesus' presence is not merely spiritual is a call to respond to the physical hungers of all those in whom he is present.

The Good Shepherd

The Fourth Sunday of Easter is popularly called

Good Shepherd Sunday. As we continue to celebrate Jesus in his resurrection, we turn to John's Gospel and Jesus' discourse on the good shepherd (10:11–18). On the Fourth Sunday in Cycle A, we read the first part of this discourse (10:1–10). On the same Sunday in Cycle C, we read part of another short discourse on the shepherd and the sheep which follows this one (10:27–30).

The passage speaks to us of Jesus the good shepherd who knows his sheep. He is also aware of other sheep who are not of his fold. They too in a sense are his and one day they will hear his voice, as do those who already belong to his flock. The Gospel thus invites us to reflect on the relationship of non-Christians to Jesus the risen Lord and of the Christian need to reach out to them with the voice of his Gospel.

The good shepherd is also very different from a hired shepherd who runs away when the sheep are threatened. The good shepherd freely lays down his life for his sheep.

The True Vine

On the Fourth Sunday of Easter, the Gospel presented our relationship to Jesus with the image of the shepherd and the flock. On the Fifth Sunday, it does so with that of the vine and branches (Jn 15:1–8). Both of these are extremely important. They show us that we must be able to reflect on the person of Jesus and the life of the Church with images which are close to creation, nature and everyday experiences such as are used in Old Testament wisdom literature. These images are quite universal and easily communicated, whereas it takes historical background to approach Jesus through titles such as the new Moses, the new David, and even the Messiah.

The image of the vine and branches is very clear. Only when the branches are attached to the vine does life flow through them. Jesus himself is the vine. This does not mean that barren branches should not be pruned away. Jesus' Father is the vinedresser.

The Great Commandment

On this Sixth Sunday of Easter, we explore the relationship between the life we have in Christ our Lord and the way we live. Faith and ethics are inseparable. The core of Christian life is love, the love the Father has for Jesus and which he has for us. Our life is in that love, which we might compare to the air we breathe. Without it we die as Christians. The life which we live in Christ's love is expressed in the observance of his commandments. This should be obvious, since the greatest of these commandments and the one which gives meaning to all the others is the commandment that we love one another as Jesus has loved us. Just as he gave his life for us, so must we be able to give ours for others. In a sense every other commandment is but an expression of this most basic one (Jn 15:9–17).

Ascension

For the Feast of the Ascension in Cycle B we turn to the ending which was appended to Mark's Gospel sometime in the second century (16:9–20). The first part of that ending summarizes accounts of appearances of Jesus which are found in other Gospels (16:9–14). The reading for today refers to the ascension and Jesus' instructions on that occasion. It includes one of the most basic and revolutionary aspects of the Gospel message, its universality. As Jesus returns to his Father, everything which was limiting about his humanity is left behind, and all who related to him in faith must reach out to all human beings with the life and message he has given them (16:15–20).

Prayer for Protection

On the Seventh Sunday of Easter, we read from the prayer of Jesus in John 17. In Cycle A, we read the first part of that prayer (17:1–11a). In Cycle B, we read the second part (17:11b–19). In Cycle C, we shall read the third and last part of that prayer (17:20–26). If the Fourth Sunday of Easter is Good Shepherd Sunday, the Seventh Sunday is Prayer of Jesus Sunday.

In this second part of the prayer, Jesus asks his Father to protect all those he had given to him. Jesus' prayer should be a source of great confidence for all of us. Jesus says that none of those given to him to that point had been lost except him who had been destined to be lost according to the Scriptures. As Jesus prays, he is confident that God will guard all the others from ultimate harm. There is no indication in Jesus' message or in the Scriptures that anyone else was destined to be lost.

Pentecost

We are accustomed to viewing Pentecost through the eyes of St. Luke and the episode he presented in the Acts of the Apostles (Acts 2:1–13). In the vigil celebration for Pentecost we learn to see it through John 7:37–39. The Spirit flows from Jesus, the one who has been glorified, as living water from which all who believe in Jesus can drink. The waters of Pentecost, which recall the water from the well at Samaria, are the waters of baptism. There is no Christian baptism apart from the gift of the Spirit, and the gift of the Spirit is inseparable from the presence of the risen Lord. Jesus, through the Holy Spirit and the baptismal waters, reaches out beyond his historical life, in order that none of those he had taught and none of those who would draw near to him later would ever be lost.

On Pentecost itself, the Gospel is John 20:19–23. The first day of the week, the day of the new creation and the day on which the early Christians first experienced the risen Lord, is also the day on which the Lord breathed the Holy Spirit on the Christian community. Jesus came with the witness of his wounds to bring peace to disciples who were afraid of being wounded, and he sent them on their mission as he had been sent on his. As Lord, he could now breathe into them a Spirit of new life, his own, as God had breathed his life into Adam. For John, there is no separating Pentecost from Easter. It is there that we see most clearly why it must be the last Sunday of Easter.

Holy Thursday

Mass of the Lord's Supper

Exodus 12:1–8, 11–14
1 Corinthians 11:23–26
John 13:11–15

GATHERING PRAYER

Choose either another musical setting of the text from the liturgy "Where charity and love are found" or repeat the chant used at the liturgy

i.e., "Ubi Caritas," Taize (GIA)

"Where Charity and Love Prevail," Benoit (World Library Publications)

"Where Love Is, There Is God," Eugene Lindusky

Then pray together:

> This is the pasch:
> holy the feast we celebrate today.
> New and holy is the pasch,
> mystic,
> all-venerable,
> and Christ, who redeemed us,
> is the paschal victim.
> The pasch breathes balm,
> is great,
> was made for the faithful;
> the pasch opens to us
> the gates of paradise.
> O pasch, sanctify all believers.
> (Early Greek Hymn)

If singing is not possible, pray together:

> Where charity and love are found, there is
>   God.
> The love of Christ has gathered us together
>   into one.
> Let us rejoice and be glad in him.
> Let us fear and love the living God,
> and love each other from the depths of our
>   hearts.
> Therefore when we are together,
> let us take heed not to be divided in mind.
> Let there be an end to bitterness and quar-
>   rels,
> an end to strife,
> and, in company with the blessed,

> may we see your face, in glory, Christ our
>   God,
> pure and unbounded joy
> forever and ever. (Roman Ritual for Holy
>   Thursday)

REFLECTIONS/RESPONSE

1. The Gospel reading and foot washing gesture bring together many meanings in this first celebration of the triduum. It is not accidental that our memorial of the Last Supper focuses this way. Table fellowship and foot washing place before us through Jesus a way of life as well as a way of worship. In the action of foot washing we experience the meaning of the meal.

    What is the meaning of and the call to table fellowship and foot washing?

    How do these meanings relate to my life this year?

    Since table fellowship and foot washing are communal tasks, where am I called to be receptive, open to the gifts of others?

2. The Gospel of John expresses at least two levels of meaning in the foot washing. The most basic meaning pertains to the cross, the ultimate sign of Jesus' love. It follows immediately after Jesus' assertion that he was about to return to his Father. The action of washing his disciples' feet was an anticipation of what he would do on the cross. Peter does not grasp this connection. What Jesus knows, Peter will only realize later on, that his submission to Jesus' washing of his feet is the symbolic acceptance of Jesus' death as an act of love.

    Secondly, the foot washing is intended to serve as an example of how the disciples should humbly serve one another. The depth of his love is revealed.

    In one of the acclamations during the eucharistic prayer, we pray: "When we eat this bread and drink this cup, we proclaim your death, Lord Jesus, until you come in glory."

    How do we proclaim the death of the Lord when we share in the Eucharist?

    In what situation are we like Peter, protesting that Jesus cannot wash our feet?

3. Discuss the following statement in light of the previous reflections: "Do this in memory of me, break bread, share the cup, serve one another—this is the way the Lord taught us. It is our way of life and our way of worship."

4. In the Mass of the Lord's Supper on Holy Thursday, we begin the Easter triduum. From the beginning the Church has seen this celebration as the one feast of the Pasch (Passover). The General Norms for the Liturgical Year describe it:

> The Easter triduum of the passion and resurrection of Christ is thus the culmination of the entire liturgical year. What Sunday is to the week, the solemnity of Easter is to the liturgical year. The Easter triduum begins with the evening Mass of the Lord's Supper, reaches its high point in the Easter vigil, and closes with evening prayer on Easter Sunday.

> The Easter act of salvation or paschal mystery embraces the entire three days of the crucified, buried and risen Lord.

   Discuss ways in which you will celebrate the unity of the triduum in the liturgies.

5. Israel remembered the saving deed of the exodus in the annual celebration of Passover. More than a recalling of God's action in the past, the celebration rejoices in God's saving deeds in the present and promises for future fullness of life. It is this sense of memory that we celebrate in the liturgy.

   In the eucharistic prayer we pray: "In memory of his (Christ's) death and resurrection we offer you, Father, this life-giving bread, this saving cup." "We celebrate this memorial of our redemption." The prayer goes on to pray in unity with all our brothers and sisters, wherever they may be, those throughout the world and those who have left this world in God's friendship.

   Discuss how we experience as a Church the fullness and power of the paschal mystery when we celebrate the Eucharist.

6. At the end of the liturgy this evening there is a procession to transfer the remaining Eucharist to a chapel for use on Good Friday. This is simply a functional gesture. Often, a time for prayer is provided in the place of reposition.

   If you participate, use the time of quiet to remember the passion, death and resurrection of Christ and its saving power for you. The real presence of the Eucharist is in its celebration of our commitment to table fellowship and foot washing in daily life.

CLOSING PRAYER

Pray together Psalm 116:

> Our blessing cup is a communion with the
> blood of Christ.
> How can I repay the Lord for his goodness to
> me?
> The cup of salvation I will raise;
> I will call on the Lord's name.
> O precious in the eyes of the Lord
> is the death of his faithful.
> Your servant, Lord, your servant am I.
> You have loosened my bonds.
> My vows to the Lord I will fulfill
> before all his people,
> in the courts of the house of the Lord,
> in your midst, O Jerusalem.

References

Doors to the Sacred, Joseph Martos, New York: Doubleday and Co., Inc., 1981

The Eucharist and Human Liberation, Tissa Balasuriya, Maryknoll, N.Y.: Orbis Books, 1979

A New Look At the Sacraments, William J. Bausch, Mystic, Conn.: Twenty-Third Publications, 1983

Of Fast and Festival, Barbara O'Dea, D.W., Mahwah, N.J.: Paulist Press, 1982

The Passover Celebration, ed. Rabbi Leon Klenicki, Chicago: Liturgy Training Program, 1980

Real Presence: Worship, Sacraments and Commitment, Regis A. Duffy, O.F.M., San Francisco: Harper and Row Publishers, Inc., 1982

Study Text 9: The Liturgical Year: Celebrating the Mystery of Christ and His Saints, Washington, D.C.: BCL, NCCB, USCC, 1985

The Three Days: Parish Prayer In the Paschal Triduum, Gabe Huck, Chicago: Liturgy Training Publications, 1981

A Triduum Sourcebook, ed. Gabe Huck, Mary Ann Simcoe, Chicago: Liturgy Training Publications, 1983

Doctrinal/Pastoral Issues: Eucharist, Service, Triduum, Memorial (Anamnesis)

Ellen Bush

Good Friday

The Passion of the Lord

Isaiah 52:13—53:12
Hebrews 4:14–16; 5:7–9
John 18:1—19:42

GATHERING PRAYER

Sing: "I Will Sing of the Lord," John Foley, S.J. (NALR) (option: play the record or tape)

or "Father, Mercy," Bob Dufford (NALR)

Pray: The cross, O God, is a sign of our covenant of love.

Help us to see the hope and the glory it raises before us.

Strengthen us, O God, in all our sufferings and lead us to the new life the cross promises.

All praise and glory be to you, now and forever and ever.

REFLECTIONS/RESPONSES

(The session is based on the dismissal taking place after the veneration of the cross)

1. Today's liturgy is different in that there is not a celebration of Eucharist. The liturgy of the word is followed by the veneration of the cross, the symbolic action for the day. As a prayer for part-way in the triduum, the service has no gathering rite or dismissal rite. The Communion service was a later addition.

   Discuss your experience of the liturgy in light of the following: Christians have instinctively used the paradox "good" for this day. The term is not really misplaced as the liturgy is not morose. The image of resurrection begins to show faintly. After all, it is part of the Easter feast (triduum).

   How did you experience the paradox of "Good" Friday?

2. Reflect on the veneration of the cross. We glory in the cross of our Lord Jesus Christ. It is a symbol of Christ's victory over death and all the powers of evil. Here we celebrate the paradox of Good Friday; a large cross, not a crucifix, is used for the rite. We

are challenged to live the paradox of life in the midst of death today, not to cling to the memory of Jesus' death. We must live the mystery in present day suffering, pain, and death.

   How can we glory in the cross?

   Discuss the following statement:

   Jesus' passion goes on in the passion of our suffering people. Everywhere we find a thrust for justice, a hunger for equality and a yearning for brotherhood. . . . The condemnation of Jesus is perpetuated in these people who fight for justice. Jesus will continue to be condemned to death so long as we do not establish the human and historical conditions that will allow justice to flower and right to flourish, and without justice and right the Kingdom of God will not be established (Leonardo Boff, *Way of the Cross—Way of Justice*, pp. 7–9).

3. Discuss attitudes toward death that you have and have experienced.

   Is death something morbid?

   Is death something we try to hide?

   Do our funeral customs celebrate death or shield us from death?

   Jesus confronts the fear of death head-on, and he invites us to do the same. He also invites us to let go of any other fears we may have.

   If we cannot live without letting go of the fear of death, is it possible to be married without letting go of the fear of the failure of the marriage?

   Is it possible to be American without letting go of America?

   What other fears do I carry?

   Of what am I most afraid to let go?

   How can the example of Jesus who confronts the fear of death enable me to do the same?

4. In the passion account, John sees in the cross the "hour" of Jesus, that for which he was born, the moment of his glorification. In this Gospel Jesus is not a passive victim or a reluctant captive. With full awareness of all the events and their meaning for himself and for others, he controlled what was happening to him and freely brought them to the fulfillment expected of him.

In the garden and before Pilate, Jesus speaks on his own behalf indicating his awareness of what is happening. Then Jesus carries his own cross to the place of execution. Even his death is described as his own action: "Then he bowed his head and delivered over his spirit."

Does Jesus' coolness or calmness affect your understanding of his humanity or take away from his experience of passion?

The people cried, "Crucify him!" Does that mean that Christians ought to blame the Jews for the death of Jesus?

5. How is signing with the cross
    an act of faith?
    an act of remembering?
    an act of hope?
    an act of love?

CLOSING PRAYER

Father, I put my life in your hands.
In you, O Lord, I take refuge.
Let me never be put to shame.
In your justice, set me free.
Into your hands I commend my spirit.
It is you who will redeem me, Lord.
In the face of all my foes
I am a reproach,
an object of scorn to my neighbors
and of fear to my friends.
Those who see me in the street
run far away from me.
I am like a dead man, forgotten,
like a thing thrown away.
But as for me, I trust in you, Lord.
I say, "You are my God.
My life is in your hands;
deliver me from the hands of those who hate
        me.
Let your face shine on your servant.
Save me in your love.
Be strong, let your heart take courage,
All who hope in the Lord (Ps 31).

References

A Commentary on the Gospel of John, Robert E. Obach and Albert Kirk, Mahwah, N.J.: Paulist Press, 1981

The Gospel of John, John O'Grady, New York: Pueblo Publishing Co., Inc. 1982

A Lenten Pilgrimage—Dying and Rising in the Lord, Richard W. Chilson, C.S.P., Mahwah, N.J.: Paulist Press, 1983

Of Fast and Festival, Barbara O'Dea, D.W., Mahwah, N.J.: Paulist Press, 1982

Original Blessing, Matthew Fox, Santa Fe: Bear and Co., Inc., 1983

The Three Days, Gabe Huck, Chicago: Liturgy Training Publications, 1981

A Triduum Sourcebook, ed. Gabe Huck, Mary Ann Simcoe, Chicago: Liturgy Training Publications, 1983

Way of the Cross—Way of Justice, Leonardo Boff, Maryknoll, N.Y.: Orbis Books, 1980

Doctrinal/Pastoral Issues: Glory in the Cross, Cross, Death, Letting Go

Ellen Bush

Introduction to the Easter Season

Each session for the Easter season follows these steps:

> Opening Prayer
> Reflections
> Response
> Closing Prayer

In each session the catechist is invited to choose one or three suggestions for focusing on the Scriptures. In some sessions it is recommended that two of the suggestions be used to deepen the integration of the word with the participants' lives.

It is suggested that the catechist share with the participants their responses to the word broken open so as to assist in the development of the questions and discussion. As the catechist prepares the session he or she may want to adapt the questions to the particular group and their specific needs.

The session ends with an activity that invites the participants to respond to the sharing that has taken place during the breaking open of the word. The response invites the participants to focus on the specific way they will live the Gospel or the reading the coming week, furthering the integration of the word in their lives.

The suggested closing prayer is a time to bring to prayer the issues, concerns and hopes that have emerged from the session.

Doctrinal and pastoral issues are also indicated for each session.

Easter Sunday

Acts 10:34, 37–43
Psalm 118:1–2, 16–17, 22–23
Colossians 3:1–4 or 1 Corinthians 5:6–8
John 20:1–9

OPENING PRAYER

Leader: Let us pray on this Easter morning to be renewed in our commitment to the risen Lord.
(silence)
God of life and new creation, today we celebrate the joy of Easter. This is the morning that the Lord appeared to women and men who had begun to lose hope. Through the resurrection, their eyes were opened to the new life and the new hope offered by the life, death and resurrection of Jesus. May the Holy Spirit breathe on our minds and open our eyes that we may come to know and to follow the risen Lord in our lives. Grant this through Christ our Lord. Amen.
(Adapted from the alternative prayer for early morning liturgy.)

REFLECTIONS

A. Reading of the Gospel
   1. Invite the participants to close their eyes, to relax and to imagine themselves involved in the events of Easter morning as told in the Gospel of John.
   2. Read the Gospel slowly.
   3. One minute of silence
   4. Invite the participants to reflect on the following questions, suggesting that they respond in their journals.
      a. How did you feel being involved in the experience of finding the empty tomb, of telling the disciples, of returning and entering the empty tomb with the disciple and with Peter?
      b. What touched you most about the Easter story?
      c. What does the Easter story say to you about who God is in your life, in the Church, in the world?
   5. Invite the participants to share in small groups (5–6 persons) their responses to the questions. (15–20 minutes)

B. After the reflection on the Gospel using A, choose one of the following (C or D) for further faith reflection.

C. Reading of the Gospel
   1. The Gospel tells us that when the disciple looked in the tomb, he saw the folded linen cloths and believed. For the beloved disciple the linen cloths were a sign which led him to believe. In our own lives there have been signs that have led us to belief. Signs can be events, persons or things which point or lead us to the risen Lord in our lives. Invite the participants to reflect on the following questions.
      a. Name one specific event or relationship in your life that pointed to or was a sign that led you to believe in the risen Lord.
      b. In your experience what are the signs for you in the Church today that have led you to believe in the risen Lord?
      c. How do you see your life as a sign that points to the risen Lord? Be specific and concrete.
   2. In small groups share the responses to the above questions. (20–25 minutes)

D. Reading of the Gospel
   1. The disciples' experience of Jesus' death was an experience of the absence of Jesus in their life. Although physically absent, Jesus was present to the disciples in a new way through the Holy Spirit. As well, our lives are experiences of the absence and presence of the Lord. Invite the participants to respond to the following questions in silence or through journaling.
      a. Name a specific event or time in your life when you have experienced the absence of God.
      b. What were the feelings you had before, during and after that event or time in your life?
      c. Were there significant people involved in

your life during this event and if so how were they part of this experience?

    d. Who or what was your experience of Church at that time in your life when you experienced the absence of God?

    e. What questions did this event raise for you about who God is in your life?

    f. In small groups share the reflections on these questions. (10 minutes)

2. Name a specific event or time in your life when you experienced the presence of God in your life.

    a. What were the feelings you had before, during and after that event or time in your life?

    b. Were there significant people involved in your life during this event and if so how were they part of the experience?

    c. Who or what was your experience of Church at that time in your life when you experienced the presence of God?

    d. In small groups share the responses to the above questions.

3. In looking at both the experience of the absence and of the presence of God in your life what is similar and what is different between the two?

    a. What do the experiences say to you about who God is for you in your life today?

    b. What questions do these events raise for you about who God is in your life, in the Church and in the world?

    c. In small groups (of 5 or 6) share the responses to the above questions. (20–25 minutes)

RESPONSE

From the word that was shared in this session, invite the participants to respond to the following:

1. From the breaking open of the word today, how are you challenged to live the Gospel this coming week. Name one specific and concrete way.

    a. What will it cost you to live this Gospel this coming week?

2. Invite the candidates/catechumens to share their responses with their sponsors. (10–15 minutes)

3. As a large group, invite the participants to respond to the following questions:

    a. What do you need, specifically, from your sponsor, from your spouse or from the other partici-

pants gathered here so that you can live the Gospel this coming week?

    b. What do you need from the Church in order to live the Gospel this coming week?

CLOSING PRAYER

From the sharing in the large group invite the participants to join their own prayers of petition:

Leader: Let us pray. God of new life and creation, we come before you, expressing our needs, our hopes to live the Gospel this coming Easter week. We desire to be a sign and to be the presence of the risen Lord to one another. Hear our prayers that we ask in confidence to you:

Response: Open our eyes, O Lord.

Doctrinal and Pastoral Issues: Revelation, Church, Incarnation, Theological Virtues, Immanent and Transcendent God, Absence and Presence of God, Faith Experience

Kathleen Brown

Second Sunday of Easter

Acts 4:32–35
Psalm 118:2–4, 13–15, 22–24
1 John 5:1–6
John 20:19–31

OPENING PRAYER

Leader: Let us pray. Almighty and powerful God, through your Son's resurrection you revealed to us your love and mercy for all people. We thank you for the on-going revelation of your love. Send your Holy Spirit to deepen our faith in you so that we can become a people of peace, mercy and love to all our brothers and sisters. We ask this through Christ our Lord. Amen.

REFLECTIONS

A. Reading of the Gospel
   1. Before reading the gospel invite the participants to listen for the word or phrase that touches them today in their lives.
   2. Reading of the Gospel.
   3. One minute of silence.
   4. Invite the participants to speak the word or phrase that touched them from the Gospel reading. Break them into small groups (5–6) and request that the word or phrase be spoken without comment or explanation. (2 minutes)

B. After the response to the Gospel using A, choose one of the following (C or D) for further faith reflection.

C. Reading of the Gospel, verses 19–23 only.
   1. As the frightened disciples were gathered Jesus appeared to them, greeting them with peace. He then breathed the Holy Spirit on them, empowering them and sending them, as he was sent by his Father, to forgive or not to forgive others. Invite the participants to respond silently or in writing to the following questions.
      a. Name a recent and specific experience in your life when you forgave someone. How

did you feel before, during and after you forgave someone?
      b. Name a recent and specific experience in your life of being forgiven. How did you feel before, during and after the experience of being forgiven?
      c. Name an event or time in your life when you found it difficult to forgive someone. Why was it difficult for you to forgive?
      d. In your experiences of forgiving and being forgiven, who was/is God for you?
      e. Name a specific experience of knowing you were forgiven by God or an experience of forgiving God.
   2. In small groups share the responses to the above questions. (15–20 minutes)

RESPONSE

Invite the participants to respond to the above faith sharing by answering the following:

1. From the reading and the sharing of the Gospel today, how are you enlightened, or challenged about forgiveness in your life?

2. Name one concrete, specific way you feel called to live the Gospel this week.

3. What will be the obstacles to living the Gospel this coming week?

4. From the community gathered here, what help do you need from them?

REFLECTION

D. Reading of the Gospel, verses 24–31 only
   1. In the Gospel, the disciples told Thomas they had seen the risen Lord. Thomas refused to believe upon the strength of their testimony and instead would only believe when he saw the Lord himself. Invite the participants to reflect and/or write their responses to the following questions.
      a. Name a concrete event or time in your life when you experienced doubt in a relationship, in your faith or in God.

b. What questions did your experience of doubt raise for you about relationships, about your faith or about God?

c. Name a concrete event or time in your life when you experienced strong faith in a relationship, in your faith, or in God.

d. What are the similarities and differences between your experience of doubt and of faith?

e. How did you move from doubt to faith?

2. In small groups share the responses to the above questions. (20–25 minutes)

RESPONSE

Invite the participants to respond to the above reflection on the Gospel by answering the following questions individually and then by sharing them with your sponsor or in a small group for 10–15 minutes.

1. Name a concrete and specific way you feel enlightened or challenged about doubt and faith in your life.

2. Name a specific and concrete way you feel called to live the Gospel this coming week. What will it cost you?

3. From the community gathered here today, what help do you need to live the Gospel this coming week?

CLOSING PRAYER

From the breaking open of the word in this session, invite the participants to include their prayers with that of the leader.

Leader: Let us pray. Loving and merciful God, we thank you for revealing yourself to us through this community. We welcome your word of enlightenment and challenge in our lives and now come to you asking for your strength and courage to live the word enfleshed within us today. Hear the prayers of this community and be with us this coming week.

Response: Lord, hear our prayer.

Doctrinal and Pastoral Issues: Forgiveness, Reconciliation, Peace, Faith, Holy Spirit, Doubt

Kathleen Brown

Third Sunday of Easter

Acts 3:13–15, 17–19
Psalm 4:2, 4, 7–8, 9
1 John 2:1–5
Luke 24:35–48

OPENING PRAYER

Song: "We Remember" by Marty Haugen, GIA Publications.

Pray together Psalm 67.

REFLECTIONS

A. Reading of the Gospel
   1. The Gospel tells us that when the risen Lord stood in the midst of the disciples, they experienced "panic and fright." Invite the participants to respond silently or in writing to the following exercise.
      a. Remember an event or time in your life when you experienced panic, fear or excessive worry.
      b. Recall the feelings before, during and after the event.
      c. To whom did you turn during this event or time in your life when you experienced panic, fear or excessive worry?
      d. Who was God for you at that time in your life?
   2. Reading of the Gospel
      a. What does the Gospel say to you about how you deal with fear, panic or excessive worry in your life?
      b. What does the Gospel say to you about your understanding of what it means to trust God in all things?
   3. Share in small groups (5–6 persons) the responses to the above questions. (20–25 minutes)

B. Reading of the Gospel

   1. One minute of silence.
   2. In the Gospel Jesus reminds the disciples that it was foretold in the Scriptures that he was to die and rise from the dead. The disciples are witnesses of this and therefore are charged to preach the remission of sins in Jesus' name to all the nations. Invite the participants to respond silently or in writing to the following questions.
      a. Name a concrete event or a person that has witnessed the presence of Christ for you in your life.
      b. What does it mean for you to be a witness of Christ? Give specific examples of how you have witnessed the presence of Christ in your family, in your work, in your neighborhood.
      c. Name an experience where someone who is going through or has gone through suffering has been a witness of Christ to you.
   3. Share in small groups the responses to the above questions. (25–30 minutes)

RESPONSE

Invite the participants to respond to the above reflection on the Gospel by answering the following questions and then sharing them with the sponsor or in their small group. (10–15 minutes)

1. Name one concrete and specific way you feel challenged or called to live the Gospel this coming week as a result of the word shared here today?

2. What will it cost you?

3. What do you need from your sponsor or from the community gathered here in order to live the Gospel this coming week?

CLOSING PRAYER

Leader: Loving God, through your Son you have shown us that we have nothing to fear, that you are with us in all things. Increase within us our faith in you and give us courage to be witnesses of your saving love to the world. We ask this in Christ's name. Amen.

Doctrinal and Pastoral Issues: Death and Resurrection, Sin, Mission and Witness, Trust and Hope

Kathleen Brown

Fourth Sunday of Easter

Acts 4:8–12
Psalm 118:1, 8–9, 21–23, 26, 21, 29
1 John 3:1–2
John 10:11–18

OPENING PRAYER

Leader: Let us pray. God and Father of our Lord Jesus Christ, though we may struggle in our lives with fear or worry, we are reminded that you have not left us alone. For we follow in faith the call of the shepherd whom you have sent for our hope and our strength. Attune our minds to the sound of the shepherd's voice, lead our steps in the path shown to us by the shepherd, that we may know the strength of your outstretched arm and enjoy the light of your presence forever. We ask this through Christ our Lord. Amen.
(Adapted from the alternative opening prayer for the Fourth Sunday of Easter.)

REFLECTIONS

A. Reading of the Gospel

1. The Gospel speaks about the wolf who comes to "snatch and scatter" the sheep away from the fold. In our own lives we can be drawn away from following Christ. Invite the participants to respond to the following questions either silently or in writing.
   a. What are the "wolves" or those areas in your life that would draw you away from following the Lord? Be specific and concrete.
   b. Name a concrete example from your life during the past week or month when you have experienced being drawn away from the Lord.
   c. From your experience, where, when and how do you hear and recognize the voice of the Lord in your life, especially when you are being pulled or drawn away from following the Lord? Give an example that is concrete and specific.

2. Reading of the Gospel
   a. One minute of silence
   b. What does the Gospel have to say to you about remaining close to the Lord, about hearing and recognizing the Lord in your life?

3. Share in small groups the responses to the above reflections. (25–30 minutes)

B. Reading of the Gospel

1. In the Gospel today we are presented with the image of Jesus as the Good Shepherd. In the Old and New Testament there are many images and names given to God. In our own lifetime very often the names and images we have for God change as we go through various events or experiences in our life.

2. The catechist is invited to develop a lifeline for the participants to use that traces the unfolding images and names of God for them. Include the following:
   a. Divide the lifeline so that it includes the ages of the participants in ten year segments, that it includes a space for them to indicate what was taking place in their life at certain times, that indicates the significant people in their life at that time, and finally that includes a space for them to write the name and/or image of God for them at that time in their life.

3. Invite the participants to respond to the following questions once the lifeline is completed:
   a. Has the image/name of God changed during your life? Has God moved away from you or come closer to you?
   b. Do you see any relationship between what was going on in your life and your relationship or understanding of God?
   c. What have you learned or discovered about your images or names for God in your own life?

4. Share in small groups the responses to the above reflection. (20–25 minutes)

RESPONSES

Invite the participants to respond to the above reflections by answering the questions below and then share with the sponsor or in small groups. (10–15 minutes)

1. What does the image of the Good Shepherd mean for you right now in your life?

2. How have you been enlightened or challenged by the word that was shared today in this gathering?

3. Name a specific and concrete way you feel called to live the Gospel this coming week. What will it cost you?

CLOSING PRAYER

Song: "Like a Shepherd" by Bob Dufford, S.J., N.A.L.R.

Doctrinal and Pastoral Issues: Images of God in the Old and New Testament, Leadership, Universality of Christ, Ecumenism

Fifth Sunday of Easter

Acts 9:26–31
Psalm 22:26–27, 28, 30, 31–32
1 John 3:18–24
John 15:1–8

OPENING PRAYER

Song: "All the Ends of the Earth" by Bob Dufford, N.A.L.R.

Read Psalm 22 together.

REFLECTIONS

A. Reading of the Gospel
   1. Invite the participants to listen to the imagery of the vine and the branches as presented in the Gospel and then to respond either in silence or in writing to the following questions.
      a. How does a plant receive life? Think about all the necessary ingredients in order for a plant, a vine to survive. List these ingredients.
      b. How does a branch receive life from the plant or the vine?
   2. Reading of the Gospel
      a. One minute of silence
      b. From the reading of the Gospel about the vine and the branches what new insight or challenge do you hear about your relationship to others, to God, to the Church?
   3. In small groups (5–6 persons) share the responses to the above reflection. (10–15 minutes)

B. After the reflection on the Gospel using A, choose one of the following (C or D) for further faith reflection.

C. Reading of the Gospel
   1. In the Gospel Jesus uses the analogy of the vine and branches to describe our relationship with him. As a branch connected to a vine receives the necessary ingredients for it to survive, so do we receive the necessary ingredients or nourishment for us to survive if we remain attached to Christ. Invite the par-

ticipants to respond to the following questions either in silence or in writing.
      a. Name a specific and concrete event or time in your life when you needed to be cared for, supported or nourished in your personal life, in your family, in your faith, in your relationships with others.
      b. How did you seek the care, the support or the nourishment that you needed? Where did you go and to whom did you turn?
      c. During this event or time in your life when you needed care, support or nourishment, who or what was the Church for you?
      d. During this event or time in your life who was God for you?
      e. How has your understanding of how you seek and receive care, support and nourishment changed for you in the past week, month or year? Be specific.
   2. Reading of the Gospel
      a. One minute of silence.
      b. What does the Gospel say to you about how and where you seek care, support and nourishment?
      c. What does the Gospel say to you about what the Church is?
      d. What questions does the Gospel raise for you about your relationships, about God, about the Church?
   3. In small groups share the responses to the above reflections. (25–30 minutes)

D. Reading of the Gospel
   1. In the Gospel Jesus says that the Father is glorified in our bearing much fruit and becoming his disciples. To be a disciple is to be a follower of Christ, and when we follow Christ our lives reflect that reality in all we do; therefore, our lives bear the fruit of what it means to be a Christ-follower, a Christian. Invite the participants to respond to the following questions either in silence or by writing.
      a. Name a specific and concrete example of what it has come to mean to you to be a follower of Jesus Christ.
      b. In your life, in your work, in your family, in your neighborhood, in your relationships, how are you called to be a Christian?
      c. What are the obstacles that you encounter

to becoming/being a follower of Christ?

    d. What are the gifts or the fruits that you witness in your life to others about what it means to be a Christian?

2. Reading of the Gospel

    a. One minute of silence.

    b. How does the Gospel speak to you about your life as a Christian?

3. In small groups respond to the above questions. (20–25 minutes)

RESPONSES

Invite the participants to respond to the above reflections by answering the following questions and then sharing them as a large group:

1. As a result of the sharing of the word today in this gathering, how are you enlightened or challenged by the Gospel?

2. How do you understand yourself called to live the Gospel this coming week and what will it cost you to live it?

3. What care, support and/or nourishment do you need from this gathering or from your sponsor this coming week so that you can live the Gospel?

CLOSING PRAYER

Leader: (Invite the participants to include their prayers of petition)

Let us pray. God of life and nourishment, through your word today you have invited us to cling to you, to turn to you, to live in you. We desire to be one with you, nourished by your word and by this community. You say to us that if we live in you and your words stay part of us, then we may ask what we will and it will be done for us. We come now with thankfulness for hearing our prayers. Receive these petitions which come from our needs in our lives.

Response: Lord, hear our prayer.

Doctrinal and Pastoral Issues: Church, Leadership, Body of Christ, Mission, Ministry, Discipleship, Gifts, Sin, Petition, Prayer

Kathleen Brown

Sixth Sunday of Easter

Acts 10:25–26, 34–35, 44–48
Psalm 98:1, 2–3, 3–4
1 John 4:7–10
John 15:9–17

OPENING PRAYER

Leader: Let us pray that we may practice in our lives the faith we profess. Ever-living God, help us celebrate our joy in the resurrection of the Lord and to express in our lives the love we celebrate. Grant this through our Lord Jesus Christ. Amen.

Read Psalm 103 together.

REFLECTIONS

A. Reading of the Gospel
  1. Invite the participants before the reading of the Gospel to listen to the word or phrase that speaks to them today.
  2. Invite the participants in small groups (5–6 persons) to share the word or phrase from the Gospel that touches them today.
    a. Ask them to share the word without comment or discussion.
    b. Two minutes.

B. After the reflection on the Gospel using A, choose one of the following (C or D) for further faith reflection.

C. Reading of the Gospel
  1. Name and describe a concrete time you have experienced loving someone.
    a. What were the feelings that you had before, during and after the experience of loving another person?
    b. As a result of your experience of loving someone what did you receive in your life?
    c. How were you affirmed as a person as a result of loving another person?
  2. Name and describe a time in your life when you have been loved by another person.
    a. What were the feelings you had before, during and after that event?

    b. How were you affirmed as a person as a result of being loved by another person?
  3. In small groups share the responses to the above questions. (10–15 minutes)
  4. Reading of the Gospel
    a. One minute of silence.
    b. Name a concrete event or time in your life when you have known you are loved by God.
    c. Describe the feelings you had before, during and after this event of knowing you were loved by God.
    d. How were you affirmed as a person as a result of being loved by God?
  5. Reading of the Gospel
    a. What does the Gospel say to you about your understanding of love, about your love for others and others' love for you and God's love for you and others?
    b. What questions does the Gospel raise for you about God's love for you and others?
  6. In small groups share the responses to the above questions. (25–30 minutes)

RESPONSE

Invite the participants to respond to the above reflections by answering the questions below and then sharing them as a large group.

1. As a result of the sharing of the word in your groups today how are you enlightened or challenged in your life of loving?

2. How do you hear yourself called to live the Gospel this coming week? What will it cost you?

3. What do you need from your sponsor, from your family, from this gathering to help you live the Gospel this coming week?

REFLECTION

D. Reading of the Gospel
  1. Silence.
  2. In the Gospel Jesus continues to speak about being disciples of his by going forth and bearing fruit which must endure. In fact Jesus says

that we were chosen to go forth and bear fruit. Invite the participants to respond to the following questions either in silence or in writing.

   a. Recall a time in your life when you were chosen to do something, to join a group, to be included in some plans.

   b. Name the feelings you had when you were chosen.

   c. Recall a time when you were not chosen for something you really wanted to do or be part of.

   d. Name the feelings you had when you were not chosen or when you felt rejected.

3. Reading of the Gospel

   a. Before the Gospel is read, invite the participants to listen to the Gospel as though it was being written for only them.

   b. Read the Gospel slowly.

   c. From your hearing of the Gospel, what did you learn or relearn about what it means to be chosen, to be called, to be loved by God?

   d. What questions does the Gospel raise for you about who God is in your life?

4. In small groups share the responses to the above questions. (25–30 minutes)

Doctrinal and Pastoral Issues: Theological Virtues, Commandments, Death and Resurrection of Christ, Martyrs and Saints, Revelation, Mission and Ministry, Call

Kathleen Brown

RESPONSE

Invite the participants to respond to the above reflection by answering the following questions and then sharing the responses as a large group.

1. As a result of the breaking open of the word, what have you come to understand by being chosen and being called forth to bear fruit in your life, in your work, in your neighborhood, in the world?

2. What questions has it raised for you about your being chosen by God to bear fruit?

3. How are you challenged to live the Gospel this coming week and what will be the obstacles to living the Gospel this week?

4. What do you need from your sponsor or from the community gathered here in order to help you live the Gospel this coming week?

CLOSING PRAYER

Song: "Anthem" by Tom Conry from N.A.L.R.

Ascension

Acts 1:1–11
Psalm 47:2–3, 6–7, 8–9
Ephesians 1:17–23
Mark 16:15–20

OPENING PRAYER

Song: "Let All the Earth" by Marty Haugen, GIA Publications.

Read Psalm 47 together.

REFLECTIONS

A. Reading of the Acts of the Apostles

1. One minute of silence.
2. In the reading the apostles are told by Jesus that they will receive the power of the Holy Spirit and then they are to be his witnesses to the ends of the earth. But the apostles continue to stand there, looking up into heaven as Jesus ascends. Two men ask them why they continue to stand there and tell them to believe that Jesus will return someday.
3. At times we stand around waiting or we move too quickly in our decisions. As witnesses of Christ we are empowered by the Spirit. The question is in recognizing that now is the time to move, to act, to go forth, to be sent. Invite the participants to respond to the following questions either in silence or in writing.
   a. Name an event or time in your life when you have felt prompted, moved or believe you were called by God to do something or not to do something.
   b. How do you recognize the activity or the promptings of the Holy Spirit in your life? Give a concrete example.
   c. Name a specific time or event in your life when you have felt that God had empowered you to do or not to do something?
   d. What were the feelings you had before, during and after the event?
4. In small groups share the responses to the above reflection. (20–25 minutes)

B. Reading of the Gospel

1. One minute of silence.
2. In the Gospel, the risen Lord commissions or sends forth the apostles to all the world where they are to proclaim the good news of Jesus Christ. After listing the many signs that will accompany their ministry, Jesus was taken up into heaven. However, the story continues to speak about how the Lord continued to work with them and confirm their message. Our words and deeds proclaim who Jesus is to other people. Invite the participants to reflect on the following questions either in silence or in writing.
   a. Name an event, a person or a relationship that led you to believe that knowing Jesus Christ was good news for you in your life. Be specific.
   b. What does it mean for you in your life that Jesus is good news? Give a concrete example of how Jesus has been good news for you in your life.
   c. By your words and deeds, how does your life speak about Jesus being good news for others?
3. Share in small groups the responses to the above questions. (20–25 minutes)

RESPONSE

Invite the participants to respond to the above reflections by answering the following questions and sharing the answers with at least one other person or as a large group.

1. Through the sharing of the word today, how have you been enlightened or renewed or how did you receive new insight?

2. How are you challenged to live the Gospel this coming week? Give a concrete example.

3. What will it cost you to live the Gospel this coming week?

4. What do you need from your sponsor or from the group gathered here to help you live out the Gospel?

CLOSING PRAYER

Leader: Let us pray. God of all creation, through your Son you have revealed to us the good news of salvation. You have entered our world, continuing to reveal your love for us and for all creation. We thank you for the gift of life through the good news of your Son and our Lord, Jesus Christ. We ask you to send your Spirit upon us, blessing us that we may become good news for one another. Send us forth, enlightening our minds and guiding our lives toward you. Remember as well those whom we present to you as needing our prayers and your support.

Response: Lord, have mercy.

Doctrinal and Pastoral Issues: Salvation, Evangelization, Holy Spirit, Gifts, Ascension, Afterlife

Kathleen Brown

Seventh Sunday of Easter

Acts 1:15–17, 20–26
Psalm 103:1–2, 11–12, 19–20
1 John 4:11–16
John 17:11–19

OPENING PRAYER

Leader: God of truth and life, you have shown us the way to life and to true joy through the life, death and resurrection of your Son. We have come to know your love for us, and we desire to follow you in all of our lives. Guide us, protect us and bring us to your eternal life. We ask this in Christ's name. Amen.

REFLECTIONS

A. Reading of the Gospel
   1. One minute of silence.
   2. Jesus' prayer for us is that we live in the world but not be of the world, that we not belong to the world. Invite the participants to respond to the following questions either in silence or in writing.
      a. In your life, in your work or in your relationships, how are you challenged most often as a follower of Jesus? Give a concrete, specific example.
      b. What are the events, the people or the happenings in our world today that challenge your belief in Jesus Christ or in a loving God?
      c. What are the events, the happenings, or the people in the world in your life that affirm your belief in Jesus Christ or in a loving God?
   3. In small groups share the responses to the above questions. (15–20 minutes)

4. Reading of the Gospel
   a. One minute of silence.
   b. Jesus understood himself as sent into the world. After listening to the word shared in the small groups and after hearing the Gospel proclaimed, how do you understand yourself as being sent into the world?
   c. Give concrete examples of how you understand yourself being sent as Jesus was sent.
5. Share in large groups the responses to the above questions. (10–15 minutes)

RESPONSE

Invite the participants to respond to the following questions as a response to the faith sharing. These responses may be shared with the sponsor or small group.

1. As a result of the faith sharing, how are you challenged and/or enlightened to live in the world today?

2. Name one specific, concrete way you are challenged to live the Gospel this coming week. What will it cost?

3. What do you need from your sponsor or the gathering here to help you live the Gospel this coming week?

CLOSING PRAYER

Song: "Here I Am, Lord" by Dan Schutte, S.J., N.A.L.R.

Doctrinal and Pastoral Issues: World and Church Relationship, Mission and Ministry, Morality, Social Justice, Truth and Wisdom

Kathleen Brown

Pentecost

Acts 2:1–11
Psalm 104:1, 24, 29–30, 31, 34
1 Corinthians 12:3–7, 12–13
John 20:19–23

OPENING PRAYER

Song: "Lord, Send Out Your Spirit" by Mike Balhoff, Gary Daigle and Darryl Ducote, N.A.L.R.

Read together the prose text of the sequence.

REFLECTIONS

A. Read 1 Corinthians.
   1. Before reading the epistle invite the participants to list on a piece of paper or in their journals what talents or gifts they believe they have.
   2. Read the epistle.
      a. One minute of silence.
   3. In the letter Paul speaks about how each of us has a different gift, a different ministry, and that as different as they are they are for the common good. Each of us has been the benefactor of the talents and gifts of others in our lives, and these other people have affirmed us in who we are.
      a. Name three people in your life who have been very important in influencing who you are today.
      b. What are the qualities, the gifts, the talents that these people had and how did they share them with you?
      c. How did you change as a result of knowing these people?
   4. In small groups share the responses to the above reflection. (15–20 minutes)
   5. Reading of the epistle
      a. After hearing the epistle again and after your discussion, relook at your list of your gifts and/or talents.
      b. Add to or delete from your list of gifts and talents.

6. Ask the participants to get into pairs. Invite each person to read the list of gifts/talents of the other person and to add to the list or to delete.
7. As a large group invite the pairs to present each other to the group, sharing the gifts of the other. (15–20 minutes)

B. Reading of the Gospel
   1. In the Gospel Jesus says to the disciples that they are sent as he was sent by the Father. In the previous exercise we explored the gifts each of us has to give to another and for the common good.
   2. Invite the participants to reflect upon their gifts and the gifts of each one present and how they are a gift for the common good.
      a. Small groups.
   3. Invite them to reflect on the following:
      a. Understanding that our gifts are from God, name one concrete way you see your gift being used for the common good of your family, at work, in your neighborhood, in the Church, in the world.
   4. Share in small groups the responses of the participants.

RESPONSE

Invite the participants to respond to the above reflections by answering the following questions. Share the responses with the sponsor or small group.

1. From the listing and sharing of your gifts with another, how were you enlightened in your life as a follower of Christ?

2. What questions did these reflections raise for you about yourself, your gifts and the gifts of others?

3. What questions does it raise for you about the use of your gifts in your life, in your work, in your neighborhood, in the Church?

4. How are you challenged to live the epistle and the Gospel this coming week? What will it cost you?

5. What do you need from your sponsor or from those gathered here to help you to live the word this coming week?

CLOSING PRAYER

Leader: Let us pray. God of power, God of new
life, God of re-creation, we thank you
for the many gifts of your people.
Send your Holy Spirit upon us to renew us, to recreate us, to enable us to
share our gifts with all your people.
Enlighten us so that we grow in your
life. We thank you for the many people who have touched us in our lives
with their gifts, and we come before
you in confidence with our prayers:

Response: Lord, send forth your Spirit and renew the
face of the earth.

*Doctrinal and Pastoral Issues: Holy Spirit, Church,
Mission, Ministry, Community, Pentecost*

Kathleen Brown

Trinity Sunday

Sunday after Pentecost

Deuteronomy 4:32–34, 39–40
Romans 8:14–17
Matthew 28:16–20

OPENING SONG

"Everyone Moved by the Spirit," Carey Landry, N.A.L.R.

Or: Prayer: Gloria from Mass or solemn prayerful sign of the cross.

THEMATIC FRAMEWORK

One of the earliest learned and most familiar prayers is the sign of the cross—a proclamation of the Trinity. The life and faith of a Christian are marked from their outset "in the name of the Father, and of the Son, and of the Holy Spirit." Prayers and Scripture readings often speak of the Father (Creator, God) sending his Son (Word, Jesus) for our salvation and communicating the Spirit (Power, Voice, Breath, Presence) related to our rebirth and strengthening in faith.

Description of the Trinity—unity of Father–Son–Spirit—defies our own human language. We can understand somewhat who God is for us, in a unique relationship. It is more important to develop that relationship with God—Father–Son–Spirit—than it is to find definitions for the mystery of three persons in one God. To be in relationship with God who is Father and Creator is quite different than coming to know and follow the Son of God become man in the historical and yet living Jesus the Christ. Our relationship with the Spirit is a sense of presence, wisdom, gift, grace and strength. What faith seeks is knowledge of the God in relationship.

Even the prayers of the Mass focus on the Trinity in relationship rather than definition.

The reading from Deuteronomy indicates that the Hebrews experienced and believed in God as *one*, as Lord of all creation, and as their protector. They claimed a special relationship and covenant with him; they perceived God as immanent as well as transcendent, as someone who revealed himself and who drew forth a response from his people.

Paul's Letter to the Romans here expresses the facets of Trinity which were yet not clearly defined. His experience is of the triune God–Spirit which cries out and gives witness that we are children of God (Father) and thereby heirs with Christ.

It is the Gospel that most clearly speaks the Trinity, as Jesus commissions his disciples to baptize "in the name of the Father and of the Son and of the Holy Spirit." As disciples, his chosen followers did not merely learn from Jesus; they established a strong personal relationship with him, believing in him. Others who become disciples and believers are to be baptized, initiated into the family of believers, intimately related to the Father through Jesus with whom he is one and to the Spirit, who proceeds from both.

REFLECTING ON LIFE

In most of our relationships, we do not spend a lot of time trying to define and describe the relationship itself. We are more concerned with the person and our ways of being and doing together, about caring, listening, responding.

It is also a part of our faith to not have all the answers in neat little packages. We stand before the mystery of the Trinity, simply accepting that there is a reality and expression beyond our words. Our personal experiences that parallel or hint at this mystery may be our relationship with someone we admire deeply, as we begin to realize we do not fully know or understand everything about that person. Each of us has a core, an internal, spiritual or motivational facet that is unique and too complex to put into words. Only those to whom we choose to reveal these deeply personal inner workings have a clearer understanding of who we are and why we do what we do.

Individually, participants could take several minutes to think about a person or two with whom they feel very close. Think about how that relationship first started. When did it take a turn and become more special and deeper?

1. How did I feel when I first shared a deep part of myself with another? What risk, trust, care, love did I feel?

2. How did I respond when someone revealed a deeply

personal part of himself or herself to me? Did I feel honored, welcomed and trusted, or were there other feelings?

3. Have there been any changes in me or in other relationships because of what I have learned about myself and others?

KNOWING OUR FAITH

The mystery of the Trinity was not revealed in the Old Testament. It was only when Jesus Christ came on earth proclaiming his bond of Sonship to God as the strength of the disciples that the teaching was revealed. The specific mention of Father, Son and Spirit in this episode from Matthew's Gospel has given us both the foundation for the doctrine and the Christian formula for Trinitarian prayer.

God has revealed himself in numerous ways throughout the scriptural accounts. At times he reveals himself as immanent (present on earth and in our hearts), as transcendent (in the heavens, above or beyond our human experiences). He reveals himself in and through human or tangible form—in the fire, wind, "angel" messengers and ultimately in Jesus the Christ. He also evokes a response in the hearts of those who hear; he graces the faithful with a sense of presence of relationship, of strength that are indicated by the term "spirit."

Most likely, it was only gradually that the early Christian community understood better what they did not doubt in Jesus' teaching—the existence and meaning (nature) of the Trinity. It is a doctrine that the Church itself has grappled with in its explanation over the centuries. Richard McBrien, in *Catholicism*, devotes a chapter to "The Trinity" which may be helpful for the catechist as resource information. A simple way to reflect on what we proclaim is by study of our credal statements. The importance of our belief in the Trinity is evident in the frequent use of the Trinitarian formula in the daily prayers and sacramental liturgies of the Church.

INTEGRATION

The revelation of God as Father, Son and Spirit tells us what God is for us, as we "break open" the meanings of those relational words. But the mystery of God himself is our call to be in wonder, to grow in relationship with that God whom we experience. We realize that more important than knowing about God is knowing God. In personal reflection, small group sharing and especially in journaling, each of us needs to spend time with the questions:

1. How do I experience God in my daily life?

2. What is my response to that discovery of God's presence and care?

3. Do I sometimes feel that God is distant? Why? What can I do about that feeling?

4. How am I most comfortable with God at this point in my life, as Creator/Nurturer, as Son/Brother/Friend, as Spirit/Presence/Peace/Strength?

5. How has my relationship with God changed in the recent past? How do I see that relationship developing in the future?

Discussion about the Creed—Apostolic or Nicene—may also help participants become more aware of the significance of the simple statements we often pray. Again, some media may be helpful—your parish or diocesan media center could help with obtaining that kind of resource.

CLOSING PRAYER

Leader: Let us pray
to the one God, Father, Son and Spirit,
that our lives may bear witness to our
    faith.
God, Creator, Nourisher,
you send your Word to bring us truth
and your Spirit to make us holy.
Through them we come to know
the mystery of your life.
Help us to worship you
by proclaiming and living our faith in you.
Grant this through our Lord Jesus Christ,
    your Son,
who lives and reigns with you and the
    Holy Spirit,
one God forever.

All: Glory be to the Father,
and to the Son,
and to the Holy Spirit,
as it was in the beginning,
is now and ever shall be
world without end.
Amen.

Doctrinal and Pastoral Issues: Trinity, Prayer of the Church as Proclamation of Its Teaching, Creed

Clare M. Colella

(Note: An explanation of the methodology employed in this session can be found with the introduction to the Tenth through Twelfth Sundays of Ordinary Time.)

Feast of Corpus Christi

Second Sunday After Pentecost

Exodus 24:3–8
Hebrews 9:11–15
Mark 14:12–16, 22–26

makes two references to Corpus Christi—Canons 944 and 1246.

BASIC MESSAGE: JESUS' REAL PRESENCE IN EUCHARIST

The catechist calls the catechumens (and sponsors) together and invites them to sit in a circle. He or she greets them and begins the session.

GATHERING PRAYER

Let us pray. O Lord our God, your great love for us transcends beyond all our imagination. You have given yourself to us in many ways. In these last days, your Son Jesus has given himself to us in the Eucharist. In that way he may be with us in all our days and wherever humans gather. Help us to firmly believe in you, so that, eating the Bread of Life, we may have eternal life in you. We make our prayer in the name of Jesus our Lord and Savior. Amen.

HISTORICAL CONTEXT

Corpus Christi, a doctrinal feast, was established in honor of Christ present in the Eucharist. In the mid-eleventh century there was the Berengian controversy over the real presence of Christ in the Eucharist. By the thirteenth century reception of Communion was not emphasized. The emphasis was on seeing the consecrated Host. In 1209 Juliana of Liège had a vision which demanded a feast for the Eucharist. After much persuasion the feast was celebrated for the first time in 1247.

In 1264, Pope Urban IV extended the feast to the universal Church. Its purpose was to instruct the people in the mystery, faith, and devotion surrounding the Eucharist. From the late fourteenth century, the most conspicuous feature of the feast was the procession. Today in many parts of the world, including Canada and the United States, it is not customary to hold public eucharistic processions. The new Code of Canon Law

LOOKING AT LIFE

- Recall from your experience a banquet that you were part of in which a very important person was honored. This person was moving away, celebrating an anniversary, or maybe retiring.

- Who authorized the celebration of this banquet?

- What kinds of preparation were made for this banquet?

- Who made these preparations?

- Who was present at this banquet?

- What ceremonies were used at this banquet?

- Was there anyone present who might be moved to betray the honored guest?

SHARING YOUR LIFE

Read the following questions, reflect, then discuss:

- Why was this person honored with a banquet?

- Why are banquets a good way to honor a person?

- Why are good preparations necessary before you can have a good celebration?

- Why were ceremonies and speeches included?

- Why were the disciples concerned about where to celebrate the Passover?

KNOWING OUR FAITH

Read, reflect, and dialogue about Mark 14:12–16, 22–26. Point out and discuss:

- Verses 12–16 have to do with the Passover preparation. Verses 22–26 concern the actual Passover celebration.

- The disciples were concerned about adequate Passover preparations.

- It is in verses 12–16 that Mark identifies the Last Supper with the Passover meal.

- The man carrying a pitcher of water was easy to identify, because this work was done by women.

- Parts of the preparations the disciples did consisted of the lamb, the unleavened bread, a bowl of salt water, some bitter herbs, charosheth and four cups of wine.

- There were various parts of the Passover meal as normally celebrated at that time.

- Jesus said: "Take it, this is my body." "This is my blood, the blood of the covenant, which is to be poured out for many."

- The institution narrative is not a description of the Passover meal but is restricted to those aspects of the supper that were liturgically important to the early communities.

- They departed for the Mount of Olives after the supper.

MAKING THE FAITH OUR OWN

Read the following questions, reflect, then discuss:

- Do you believe that the Last Supper is the *new* continuation of the Passover meal?

- Do you believe that the eucharistic liturgies celebrated in Catholic churches throughout the world today are a continuation of the Last Supper?

- Do you believe that Jesus is really present in the Eucharist, that the Eucharist is Jesus?

- Do you believe that it is necessary to participate weekly in the Sunday eucharistic celebration?

LIVING OUR FAITH

Read the following questions, reflect, then discuss and make a decision:

- How will you make every effort to learn to appreciate the presence of Christ in the Eucharist?

- How will you participate regularly at the Sunday eucharistic celebration?

- How will you try your best to prepare for the reception of Communion?

PRAYER

Responsorial Psalm: Psalm 116

℞.   The cup of salvation I will raise;
        I will call on the Lord's name.

Or: Alleluia.

How can I repay the Lord
for his goodness to me?
The cup of salvation I will raise;
I will call on the Lord's name. ℞.
Oh precious in the eyes of the Lord
is the death of his faithful.
Your servant, Lord, your servant am I;
you have loosened my bonds. ℞.
A thanksgiving sacrifice I make:
I will call on the Lord's name.
My vows to the Lord I will fulfil
before all his people. ℞.

You may wish to close by singing a eucharistic hymn. It could be: "I Am the Bread of Life," #569, Catholic Book of Worship II.

Spend some time in socializing and informal discussion.

Pastoral and Doctrinal Issues: Eucharist, Passover, Passover Meal, Real Presence and Eucharistic Preparation, Corpus Christi (Body of Christ)

Fr. Michael Koch

(Note: An explanation of the methodology employed in this session may be found with the introduction to the Thirteenth through Twenty-Third Sundays in Ordinary Time.)

ORDINARY TIME

Jesus and His Mission

Part I: Proclaiming the Good News

By Eugene A. LaVerdiere

In this first series of Sundays in Ordinary Time, all but one of the Gospel readings are taken from Mark 1:14—3:6, the first major unit in the body of the Gospel. Its focus is on Jesus' work of evangelization and the way he called others to join him in that mission. The readings include a summary of Jesus' ministry and his call of the first disciples (1:14–20), and several passages in which Jesus' teaching puts him in conflict with demonic forces (1:21–28), the scribes (2:1–12), a number of people (2:18–22), and the Pharisees (2:23—3:6). In all this, Jesus proclaimed the Gospel in deed as well as in word, healing many (1:29–39), including a leper (1:40–45). At every point, we must ask why such goodness and generosity led to so much conflict.

For the First Sunday, see the final Sunday of Christmastime, the Baptism of the Lord (Mk 1:7–11), with which it coincides. The second Sunday, with its reading from John's Gospel, gives John's testimony to Jesus as the Lamb of God. The event led to the call of Andrew and Simon Peter (Jn 1:35–42).

Jesus and John the Baptizer

In some ways, John the Baptizer, who lived under the old covenant, stands at the end of an era. In other ways, he marks the beginning of a new era. As the last great prophetic figure preparing the way for Jesus, his role was transitional. We see this in the way he witnessed to Jesus as the Lamb of God, the one who came from God and whose whole life was a sacrificial offering to God. But there is more. Jesus himself emerged into his ministry from the circle of John the Baptizer and so did the first disciples of Jesus. This is what we learn from John 1:35–42 on the Second Sunday in Ordinary Time.

Andrew was one of John's disciples who went to Jesus in response to John's witness. According to John's Gospel, it is Andrew who then sought out his brother and brought him to Jesus declaring that he had found the Messiah. Messiah is the Aramaic form of the Greek title Christ, and as the Gospel indicates, it means the Anointed.

Jesus and His First Disciples

It is not easy to provide a two-line summary of anyone's life message, let alone Jesus'. That is what Mark gives us at the very beginning of Jesus' mission, as described on the Third Sunday in Ordinary Time. What Jesus did was proclaim the good news of God. He did this, as the Gospel shows, in deed and word. Spelling out Jesus' message a bit, Mark then tells how Jesus announced the imminence of the reign of God, a world situation in which all would respond to God's rule fulfilling the order of creation and the promise of salvation history. For this, Jesus asked that all repent and believe in the good news he announced (Mk 1:14–15).

Jesus did not exercise his mission by himself. He called others to join him. They were fishermen, two pairs of brothers, Simon and Andrew, James and John, all called to be with him and to learn from him by actually participating in his mission. Their previous occupation as fishermen would be transformed into a concern for human beings (1:16–20).

Confrontation with Evil

Jesus taught with authority, and this meant that his teaching was acceptable to some but repudiated by those who were threatened by the power of his teaching. The Gospel reading for the Fourth Sunday in Ordinary Time (Mk 1:21–28) shows us why. The source of the authority and power of Jesus' teaching was the Holy Spirit, which had come down upon him and which he had interiorized. Wherever he went, he confronted not only the sinful and the unjust, but evil itself. Beneath every surface conflict, the life of Jesus was a confrontation between the Holy Spirit which resided in him and worked through him and the evil spirit at work in the world's disorder, crippling illnesses and death. The unclean spirit understands the nature of Jesus' mission very well when it asks: "Have you come to destroy us?" Jesus silences the demons because the Gospel of the presence of the Holy One of God among us cannot be proclaimed with authority by unclean spirits.

Proclamation in Word and Deed

Jesus' proclamation was not in word alone. His very presence was a proclamation of good news for all who came to know him. The reading for the Fifth Sunday in Ordinary Time (Mk 1:29–39) draws attention to the way Jesus announced the good news of the kingdom through his actions. The cure of Simon's mother-in-law was a Gospel message. So were his other healings and his expulsion of demons. By performing these wonders and signs in the company of his disciples, Jesus taught them and prepared them one day to join him in his mission and even to continue it after his death.

Those who witnessed what Jesus did tried to restrict Jesus' work to themselves, but Jesus pressed on to other places. The kingdom of God is as big as creation and includes all human beings. Had Jesus limited the scope of his work to a few towns and villages, he would have betrayed his mission of announcing the coming of God's kingdom. Like Jesus, we have no choice but to be missionary. Such is the nature of the Church.

The Healing of Leprosy

Lepers were expected to stay far away from other human beings. Leprosy was thought to be highly contagious, and lepers themselves were considered unclean. It is most extraordinary then that a leper should have approached Jesus and that Jesus would have touched him. The man of course was cured, but what should impress us most is the Gospel's message that anyone, no matter what the person's condition or how much the person is rejected by other human beings, can approach Jesus and receive his healing or forgiveness. On this Sixth Sunday in Ordinary Time (Mk 1:40–45) we should also take note of the leper's reaction. Healed, he goes out to proclaim the good news of his healing. Earlier, Simon's mother-in-law had done something similar. Healed, she had set about serving Jesus and the others (Mk 1:31).

The Forgiveness of Sins

On the Seventh Sunday in Ordinary Time we read the story of the paralytic who was lowered into Jesus' presence through an opening in the roof (Mk 2:1–12). Jesus cures the man, but that is not the main point. Mark draws our attention away from the extraordinary act of healing to the even more extraordinary act of the forgiveness of sins. Only God can forgive sins. Human beings can forgive others for the harm done to them, but that is not the same as restoring the bond that unites us to God and to his people. But the Spirit of God is upon Jesus (Mk 1:9–11), and he is the Holy One of God (Mk 1:24). Accordingly, Jesus is able to forgive sins. Such is his authority as the Son of Man, the ultimate human being and God's beloved Son. He demon-

strates his authority by curing the man of his paralysis, leaving everyone in wonderment at the event.

New Wine in New Wineskins

Jesus was not the only one to have disciples. John the Baptizer had disciples, and so did the Pharisees. Each of these groups differed from the others in several respects. One of the things that set Jesus' disciples apart from the others was the fact that unlike the others they did not fast. Such is the problem brought to Jesus in Mark 2:18–22 which we read on the Eighth Sunday in Ordinary Time.

In his response, Jesus justifies his disciples' behavior by distinguishing the days of his ministry, which were like a long wedding feast, from the future days of turmoil, when they would fast. He also gives two short parables which show how new his teaching and his disciples' way of life really are. There is no repairing an old cloak with a new piece of cloth. Besides, new wine calls for new wineskins.

The Lord of the Sabbath

The reading for the Ninth Sunday in Ordinary Time contains two distinct episodes. In the first, the Pharisees protest because Jesus' disciples pick a few grains of wheat on the sabbath (Mk 2:23–28). As on the previous Sunday, the Gospel shows how Jesus and his disciples differed from others. In his response, Jesus emphasizes the purpose of the sabbath, which was made for human beings, not vice versa, and he affirms that the Son of Man is consequently lord of the sabbath.

The setting for the second episode is a synagogue on the sabbath day when Jesus angers many of those present by healing a man whose hand was shriveled up (Mk 3:1–6). Again Jesus emphasizes the purpose of the sabbath which was made for our well-being. Refusing to heal because it was sabbath would have been a distortion of the sabbath's very nature.

Introduction to Sundays of Ordinary Time
Baptism of Jesus through Ninth Sunday of Ordinary Time

Liturgically this season lies between Epiphany and Ash Wednesday. The last several Sundays of this period are often not used because of actual calendar arrangement.

Each session is structured with segments:

      Opening Song or Prayer
      Thematic Framework
      Reflecting on Life
      Knowing Our Faith
      Integration
      Closing Song or Prayer

Specific mentions of songs or prayers are meant to be guides. Always feel free to adapt or substitute according to the needs and choice of your group. Sometimes songs can be sung, or played for meditation, or played and sung. Songs can easily be preceded or followed by oral or silent prayer. Often in using a missal or missalette, the catechist will find the prayers of the Sunday an appropriate springboard for prayer. Segments of the readings may also be used with a song. Many options are available.

Spontaneous prayer from the group could be encouraged, especially at the close of a session. A variety of formats and experiences of prayer would be beneficial to the group, and an aesthetic setting is highly recommended. Hospitality for the group should always include a reverent and wholesome attitude toward prayer experiences.

The method of this section presents to the catechist a framework for development of the theme for the gathering. It is the work of preparation to become familiar and comfortable with the material provided, to add to it or adapt according to the needs of the group and the insight of the catechist. Each catechist will need to personalize the presentation and develop a style of dialogue and interaction with the group.

The section titled "Reflecting on Life" attempts to focus on our experience in relation to the theme: Usually questions or statements are given for discussion. With this section as with "KNOWING OUR FAITH" and "INTEGRATION," actual methodology is developed by the catechist, whether presentations or discussions in large or small groups are used. At times media are suggested which may be helpful. Again adaptation is always possible. Appropriate time should be given for reflection before discussion is initiated. We simply trust the best judgment of a competent, prayerful catechist in the adaptation and use of the materials offered here.

Baptism of the Lord

Sunday after Epiphany

Isaiah 42:1–4, 6–7
Acts 10:34–38
Mark 1:7–11

OPENING SONG

"Come to the Water," John Foley, S.J., © 1978 John B. Foley, S.J. and N.A.L.R.

THEMATIC FRAMEWORK

With the Gospel account of the baptism of Jesus, we have another "Epiphany"—a manifestation of Jesus as the chosen one of God. John is the one who has gone before, who has prepared the way, the hearts of people. Jesus' decision to seek baptism by John gave an opportunity to focus and reflect on his mission.

Previously we have listened to the Scripture accounts of his birth, the visit by the magi, Jesus' presentation in the temple. This time we see an adult Jesus, responding to an inner call, approach John the Baptizer seeking baptism; he is making a public statement about his life, his beliefs, his choice. The affirmation of the Father is depicted through the voice and the dove.

The reading from Isaiah depicting the servant of Yahweh, the Chosen One, is here reapplied by the evangelist and the Church to identify Jesus as the beloved servant. The mission of the servant is the mission of Jesus, who is proclaimed as the "beloved Son." God's special gifts—"spirit" strength, protection—are with the chosen servant.

In the reading from Acts, Peter proclaims Jesus as the anointed one, anointed by God with the Holy Spirit, fulfilling his calling to do good works and to heal those in the grip of the devil. That healing is spiritual as well as, at times, a physical healing.

Weaving together the readings, psalms and other prayers of the Sunday, we look at John whose whole life of prayer, teaching, and simplicity called people to conversion, to a way of holiness, openness to God. We hear the call of Jesus to live as the chosen servant of Yahweh. Then we reflect on our own lives. Each of us has a calling in life. We must respond to the voice according to our personal circumstances of life and according to our gifts, the best of our abilities. That response is visible in both our vocation and our lifestyle, our way of living.

In our Church community, our individual response to the call to holiness is celebrated and affirmed in our participation in the sacraments. In the next several weeks, we will reflect on the sacraments linking themes from the Sundays with our own lives. As part of their preparation for entrance into the Church, catechumens and candidates will need to hear from catechists and sponsors a living witness to the meaning of the sacraments in our lives.

REFLECTING ON LIFE

Our lives are filled with decisions. Most of them are simply about ways to develop and continue major choices and directions or tasks we are already committed to. We have grown to a turning point—faced a choice—made a decision.

In today's Gospel reading, Jesus made a public statement of his life to God—he sought baptism from John, the holy prophet, preacher, baptizer.

John was one who by his life preceded and foreshadowed Jesus—one who taught, called people to a life of holiness. John helped them make their lives and hearts ready for God—for Jesus—to make a choice for fidelity to the covenant.

In the Gospels, the baptism of Jesus was the beginning to his public life of healing, doing good works and teaching. But the roots of that decision went far back.

Discussion

Time to reflect, then discuss—use and adapt reflections and questions as they apply to the participants.

1. Think of one central, pivotal decision you have made in your life? Name it.

   • Who or what helped prepare you for that decision and brought you to a point of wanting to make a choice?

   • What changes are a result of it?

2. How did other key people in your life respond to your decision?

   • Was it a surprise to them?

   • Did they give affirmation or disapproval? How?

   • What difference did their response mean to you?

3. How do you continue to live out that pivotal decision?

   • Does it impact your daily life?

   • How does that focused choice make life easier? Harder?

KNOWING OUR FAITH

There is an obvious connection between the feast of the baptism of Jesus and a discussion of the sacraments of initiation. Several of this Sunday's other readings and prayers include references to the Spirit, to being anointed, and to being children of God, faithful to our calling.

In our framework for sacramental theology, the sacraments are times of our encountering Christ Jesus in the living Church. We come to and celebrate the sacraments not as magical moments, but as an affirmation of what is already happening in our lives. Jesus came to John, seeking baptism, not because he sought conversion and a new way of life, but because he already had turned his heart and mind to the work of God.

In the cluster of sacraments of initiation are baptism, confirmation and the Eucharist. (If desired, a film or filmstrip may be used to give some brief background on these.)

Baptism celebrates a person's entrance into the Christian community; for us, it focuses on the Catholic Christian community. This sacrament correlates to that pivotal decision.

Confirmation is a unique affirmation by the Christian and by the Church of the person's commitment to live out his or her baptismal decision. The special attributes of preparing for and celebrating confirmation have to do with recognizing our giftedness in the community, the Spirit as our strength and guide in living out our faith, and our restatement of our baptismal decision.

For those candidates already baptized Christian but not confirmed in the Catholic Church, this will be a particularly significant sacrament of entrance into the Church.

The Eucharist is that sacrament of initiation which is, in effect, our daily decision to "keep the faith." As often as possible we say by our participation with the community at prayer and celebration that we reaffirm that earlier choice.

Each time we celebrate the Eucharist, like each time we say "I love you" to someone, we both affirm what is already and nourish deeper growth.

INTEGRATION

Attentiveness to what we say and do is a valuable way to discover ourselves more deeply and to gain insight into what we really live out in our lives.

Reflect on the pivotal decision discussed earlier. Spend some time journaling your fidelity and growth—or changes and new directions—from that decision.

Spend some time in asking yourself about a choice for God, for Jesus Christ, in your life.

Describe, in your journal, God's actions in your life and your response—the conversion process. How will you keep your conversion as an on-going experience in your life?

It may well be beneficial to have catechumen or candidate and sponsor dedicate some time in sharing their journal or reflections.

CLOSING PRAYER

"Seek Ye First" (Karen Lafferty, © 1972, Karen Lafferty, pub. Maranatha Music, *We Celebrate Hymnal*, Paluch Co. Publishing, 1982)

Doctrinal and Pastoral Issues: Call to Holiness, Pivotal Decision in Life and Faith, Sacraments of Initiation

Clare M. Colella

Second Sunday in Ordinary Time

1 Samuel 3:3–10, 19
1 Corinthians 6:13–15, 17–20
John 1:35–42

OPENING SONG

"Speak, Lord, I'm Listening," © 1978, Gary Ault and Damean Music.

THEMATIC FRAMEWORK

A choice for God, for Jesus Christ, becomes a pivotal time in our lives. The call to discipleship comes to each of us who hears the voice of the Lord. In the first and third Scripture readings today we hear stories of "vocation"—of Samuel called by the Lord and of the first disciples called by Jesus.

In the case of Samuel, once he understood who it was that called him and listened to his wise and holy teacher, Eli, he responded, "Speak, Lord, your servant is listening!" In very brief terms, the Scripture tells of his life—"Samuel grew up and the Lord was with him, not permitting any word of his to be without effect." Because of his obedience to the Lord, because he listened, Samuel's own words became effective, too. He would be listened to by others, as he had listened to his teachers, particularly Eli. The word of the Lord is passed on through his chosen ones.

Another example of call and response is given in the Gospel reading. Two disciples of John the Baptizer saw Jesus and recognized him, calling him by the very term John had used. Because of their willingness, their openness, they responded immediately to Jesus' invitation to follow him. One of those two went to call his own brother to come to meet Jesus. Jesus gave Simon a new name, an indication of a new life beginning.

The reading next week retells, from Mark's Gospel, a different version of this first call of the disciples. These two Sundays pair off in their consideration of discipleship and vocation.

What does it mean to be called and to respond? When we have heard the call of God, however it comes to us, to learn about the Lord and to follow his way, we become sharers of the word, as Samuel and Andrew were.

We find ourselves, our lives, dedicated to holiness. We recognize what Paul proclaims today—we are members of Christ, one in spirit with him, a temple of the Spirit. We belong to God. Then through our lives, the Lord can continue to reach out into the lives of others. By being open to our vocation to holiness, discipleship, we become instruments of God, bearers of his truth.

Springing from today's readings could be a discussion of the ordained and religious commitment of married and single life and lifestyle as sacraments of vocation. The vocation is a call from God to a life of fidelity to his word; how that vocation is lived out, the lifestyle, is the sacramental choice. As persons called to fidelity, we need the continuing support, strength, nourishment of the community of faith; we need to celebrate the Eucharist together.

REFLECTING ON LIFE

Today's readings relate a call to live with and for the Lord. It seems so clear and easy in the stories as they are told. In daily life it is not so simple to find or hear the call from God. It is less easy to work out in our lives what it means to follow Jesus.

Now as catechumens and candidates prepare for entrance into the community, it may be helpful and inspiring for them to hear from members of the parish who are willing to share their faith, their vocation, the meaning of the Eucharist in their lives.

Reflection and Discussion

What qualities and characteristics do you see in a close friend you admire and want others to see?

How is your own life influenced by someone you admire?

What sort of relationship would you hope to have with this person you admire?

KNOWING OUR FAITH

The Catholic Church acknowledges and celebrates two sacraments of vocational lifestyle, of "vocation." Today's readings can give rise to discussion of the sacraments of holy orders and of matrimony. There are other vocational lifestyles that are important in the life of the Church which also need explanation and discussion: religious vowed life for men and women; single life in the world. Permanent diaconate is another vocational lifestyle that uniquely blends married life with ordained ministry, not priesthood.

In dealing with the variety of vocational lifestyles, it seems the most fundamental and central point is that we are each chosen by God, called to develop and use our unique gifts for the good of the Church and the broader community. In whatever context we live out our faith, ours is an experience of servant leadership, valuing the gifts and ministries of others, knowing that all members of the body of Christ are necessary for its full development.

Media materials on ordination and matrimony are available readily; some materials on vowed religious life are also available.

An alternative or supplement to media would be a sharing by someone, preferably known to the group, of the story of his or her vocational choice. It may be valuable to have someone who is a married permanent deacon or who has chosen to live a single lifestyle share his or her story with the group, to give a broader vision of vocational lifestyle and commitment within the Church.

Remember that next Sunday's Gospel also deals with Jesus' call to the disciples. Both weeks could be used for development of the vocational theme and discipleship.

INTEGRATION

Reflection and Discussion

1. How do you see the variety of vocation lifestyles complementing one another?

2. Does there seem to be a common thread or theme in the stories of different people?

3. What are your experiences of being ministered to by those in different vocational lifestyles?

4. How do you feel you can enrich others through your life?

For Journaling and Meditation

What is required of me to respond faithfully, to the best of my abilities, to the call of Jesus to "Come, follow me?"

How can I keep a joyous, peace-filled response alive in my life?

CLOSING PRAYER

"Here I Am, Lord," Dan Schutte, S.J., © 1981, Daniel Schutte and N.A.L.R.

Doctrinal and Moral Issues: Vocation Sacraments, Universal Call to Holiness, Vocation

Clare M. Colella

Third Sunday in Ordinary Time

Jonah 3:1–5, 10
1 Corinthians 7:29–31
Mark 1:14–20

OPENING SONG

"Come Back to Me—HOSEA," Gregory Norbert,
O.S.B., © 1972 The Benedictine Foundation.

THEMATIC FRAMEWORK

The call to holiness, to discipleship, even to leadership,
is received differently. We may go through times of reluctance when it seems difficult to live up to our already made commitment. We may want to ease back,
say no or change our minds. That reluctance is a part of
human nature.

The Bible reading deals with two quite different responses to God's word. Jonah was called to preach to
the people of the city of Nineveh the need for conversion from their evil ways. The first part of the story of
Jonah tells us how he was reluctant to preach, tried to
run away, and was eventually put on the shores of the
city, through no choice of his own. Jonah, it seems,
then agreed to do what God asked—to preach conversion to the people. The people of the city responded to
the word of God, proclaimed a fast, did penance and
changed their evil ways. Jonah was, in fact, an effective
vehicle for God's word. The immediacy of the response
of the Ninevites is echoed in the second reading, from
Paul's First Letter to the Corinthians—now is the time
for conversion, now for repentance.

The responsorial psalm bridges the Scripture readings
and the Gospel: "Teach me your ways, O Lord." The
Gospel reading opens with Jesus continuing the proclamation of John: "This is the time of fulfillment. Reform
your lives and believe in the good news." In this version of Jesus' call to the disciples, he invites them to
follow him. The response of each of the four is immediate and complete. The disciples seek to learn his ways,
and to follow.

Once we make a choice for God, we are changed—our
attitudes and values may be radically changed. Are we
willing to do that? Some are called to leave all they
have and, in a singular way, be dedicated to the work of
proclaiming, of servant leadership in the Church,
among the faithful. Some of us are called to a deep,
centered holiness and fidelity to the Lord in the midst
of family, work, marketplace. We are called to come
aside to learn and pray, then to go back into our daily
settings, our families, as bearers of the message.

KNOWING OUR FAITH

Though the readings may not point directly to discussion on the sacrament of marriage, it may serve well to
develop it from last week's consideration of vocation
sacraments. While the call to discipleship is depicted as
a beckoning away from all human ties, the unspoken
side is that Jesus and each of the disciples did have a
family, a human community that nourished them,
helped form them and gave them the ability to hear and
respond to God's word. The call to discipleship happens
also within the context of a married lifestyle. To understand the sacramentality of Christian marriage is also to
celebrate the imagery used in Scripture to describe
God's intimate covenant of care for his people, and our
participation in that covenant by our faithfulness and
love of him. The central energy in marriage is loving
commitment. By it, the couple shares in the love Christ
has for the Church, and their love is a symbol of God's
love. One purpose of marriage is to help each other
grow in holiness. Here again we touch back on the call
of Jesus to his disciples—to seek him, to know him, to
become holy.

REFLECTING ON LIFE

The family is the basis of all society, its vitality and con-
tinuity. In celebrating the sacrament of marriage, the
Church affirms the choice of two people to live out
their call to holiness in the context of sharing human
love and life.

We find joy and hope in the commitment and love of
persons who promise their fidelity to one another. It is
a deeper commitment, wise from experience, gentle
and compassionate from growing together through the
years that we celebrate in anniversaries of twenty-five
or thirty or fifty years of married love. It may not have

been easy, but it has been worthwhile, my friends said, on the occasion of their twenty-fifth anniversary.

Reflection and Discussion

1. What have married people communicated to you about married love?

2. How do their lives speak to you about love?

3. How did they balance out the not-so-easy times?

4. Is love blind? Or is it more deep-seeing and trusting?

INTEGRATION

1. In some prophetic books and poetic literature of the Scriptures, images of a marriage covenant and of the fidelity of spouses are used to depict God's relationship to his chosen people. Infidelity is the graphic telling of a broken covenant.

2. In the play "Fiddler on the Roof," after hearing his daughter proclaim her love for her beloved, Tevye goes home to his wife of twenty-five years and says: "Do you love me?" The dialogue of the song reveals a love that has been lived out in unquestioning service and commitment for those many years, and now gives Tevye and Golda the chance to say what has been taken for granted—"That I love you too!"

Reflection and Discussion

1. How do you feel about the response of the disciples who got up and left everything immediately to follow Jesus? What is the heart of the story as it is told—what is the truth we are called to recognize?

2. What do you think is unique in the call to holiness for a married person?

3. How would you describe marriage as an appropriate image for fidelity to God's word?

4. How might the way the Church views marriage and holiness reflect your hopes and experiences about marriage? About holiness?

Journaling

How could you bring together your insights about Christian marriage and your response to the call to holiness?

CLOSING PRAYER

Tobit 8:4–9

Romans 8:31–35, 37–39

Matthew 19:3–6

Doctrinal and Pastoral Issues: Sacrament of Marriage, Universal Call to Holiness

Clare M. Colella

Fourth Sunday in Ordinary Time

Deuteronomy 18:15–20
1 Corinthians 7:32–35
Mark 1:21–28

OPENING SONG

"Remember Your Love," Darryl Ducote and Gary Daigle, © 1978, Damean Music.

THEMATIC FRAMEWORK

The readings today and in the Sundays ahead center on the question: Who is Jesus? Each week new facets of Jesus will surface, foreshadowed in Hebrew Scripture, recounted and reflected upon in the Christian Scriptures. Even the psalms and prayers of the Mass add insights. Throughout the discussions of these weeks we also keep in mind that we are walking through the life of Jesus as we approach Lent. Aspects of the readings evoke our personal reflection on belief in Jesus Christ. We need to be more deeply aware of who it is that we have faith in and follow, in Jesus, so that we will be strengthened to live out the Gospel and turn our hearts to God—the challenge of the weeks and months ahead.

For this week and next the sessions outlined here will focus on the sacraments of healing—reconciliation and anointing of the sick. As the Gospels depict Jesus as one who forgives sin and heals both spiritually and physically, we look into our own lives for our capacity to forgive and to heal. It is our love of God, of one another, our acceptance of others and compassion that make this presence of Jesus alive in our surroundings.

Parenthetically, most years that keep cycle B readings do not celebrate the Seventh, Eighth or Ninth Sundays of Ordinary Time. Chronologically, those Sundays simply do not fit in.

This is a great loss, though unavoidable, because the readings of those Sundays center on penance, forgiveness, miracles, faith and love. A parallel to this week's focus on healing and forgiveness may be found in the Seventh Sunday.

The readings from Deuteronomy, the responsorial psalm and Paul's First Letter to the Corinthians point to a prophet, a person chosen by God to be a spokes-person for himself, someone dedicated to the Lord. That someone appears in the Gospel account of Jesus who spoke with authority, sure of his relationship to God, of his fidelity to the word he taught. It was this Jesus who had the faith and compassion to drive out demons, to heal and to forgive. In doing so, Jesus is fulfilling his mission, but he is also challenging those around him, who are amazed at his power and authority.

The casting out of demons was in itself an amazing event. What is unspoken here, but told elsewhere, is Jesus' word of forgiveness and call to conversion to those he heals. It is the external miracle of healing that points to the interior grace of forgiveness and reconciliation. It is faith and love that heal—on the part of the penitent as well as on the part of the person assuring forgiveness and healing.

REFLECTING ON LIFE

When we do something wrong in our lives, we know there is a sense of having done less than our best, an awareness that somehow we have "missed the mark." Brokenness and selfishness have surfaced in us. We can, in response to that awareness (consciousness–conscience), choose to acknowledge our limitations, weakness, sinfulness, or we can ignore the insight into ourselves. When we acknowledge our weakness, we can again choose—to mask the reality and escape, or place blame elsewhere—or we can forthrightly seek forgiveness—within ourselves, from another who has been involved, and from God.

Reflection and Discussion

1. Remember a situation when you were forgiven by another person. What were your feelings?

2. Remember a situation when you were asked to forgive another person. What was your attitude about forgiving another? How did you feel?

3. Recall a circumstance when you had to accept and forgive yourself. Was it easy or difficult? Why?

Journal your responses and share with your sponsor some of these reflections.

KNOWING OUR FAITH

Reconciliation is personal, interpersonal and sacramental. It is a movement of the heart and the whole person. It is multilateral and pivotal in our spiritual growth if we are attentive to what is really called for. Reconciliation, the sacrament of penance, has had quite a history of development and change. A good filmstrip or brief history might help the group appreciate the Church's present teaching on reconciliation.

Suggestions: "Sinner Sam" (Teleketics) is excellent for historical background. Many other materials from PAULIST, Teleketics, ROA, Winston Press or Our Sunday Visitor are available. Again, as with other media suggestions, your parish or diocesan media center should have a wide variety of resources for you to preview and choose from.

In Scripture, forgiveness of sin is often linked with physical healing, with miracles. Perhaps harder to define, forgiveness of sin is linked, then and now, with inner healing, with that new freedom to accept, to let go of, to move beyond our limitations and weakness. Our current sacramental practice highlights reconciliation as a time of spiritual direction, intentional spiritual growth. It connects the interpersonal aspects of reconciliation with the deeply personal. It is an integral part of growth in holiness.

INTEGRATION

There is an essential place for spiritual guidance in the catechumenate process, for all those involved, not just for candidates and catechumens but for sponsors and team members as well. Attentiveness to spiritual growth is central to the conversion process we are participating in. Consideration of daily experiences of reconciliation and the graces of sacramental celebration are a valuable portion of that growth.

It may be helpful to have members of the parish community or team share an experience of reconciliation and reflect on how the Church's sacramental celebration of reconciliation affected that experience.

Reflection and Discussion

In journaling, share with sponsor or spiritual guide:

Do you remember a situation where, after asking forgiveness, you wanted to change your attitudes or behavior? How well did you follow through on your "conversion"?

Where do you gain strength and patience to persevere in your conversion process?

CLOSING PRAYER

Use the traditional act of contrition, or a similar prayer composed for this session. It may be useful to have the prayer typed on cards for each participant. Use a quiet, candlelit setting for meditation with the prayer.

Doctrinal and Pastoral Issues: Sacrament of Reconciliation, Spiritual Direction, Conversion as an On-Going Call

Clare M. Colella

Fifth Sunday in Ordinary Time

Job 7:1–4, 6–7
1 Corinthians 9:1–19, 22–23
Mark 1:29–39

OPENING SONG

"You Are My God," John Foley, S.J., © 1970, John B. Foley, S.J. and N.A.L.R.

THEMATIC FRAMEWORK

Continuing the development of the sacraments of healing, today's session focuses on the anointing of the sick. The Gospel account includes Jesus' healing of Simon's mother-in-law and many others. This Jesus who heals—who is he? What are we to learn from him? What is his response to suffering?

The story of Job in the first reading points out the pain in human existence. Suffering is not the only reality, but it is present and we must consider it. We are to make a personal response to the suffering of others. But our efforts are not isolated or in vain. The responsorial psalm assures us that it is the Lord who heals the brokenhearted. We may serve as instruments of his healing through our efforts and compassion.

From Paul's First Letter to the Corinthians we hear of his urgency to proclaim the good news. The joy and fullness of the Gospel give him no rest, give him strength to go out to others. He becomes a servant to them, growing in compassion and empathy in order to identify with those he preaches to. His understanding of the Gospel is also his hope to share in its blessings.

Proclaiming the good news and healing went hand-in-hand for Jesus. In reading about his healing ministry, we remember that freedom from evil—forgiveness—was part of the messianic mission. Healing the sick and brokenhearted is integral to the work Jesus undertook. We see that suffering and pain are part of our passage to eternal life, part of our journey of faith, an important element in working out our salvation. Our attitude and response in the presence of pain and suffering—our own and others'—may reflect the measure of our faith and trust in God. Our readiness to be compassionate may indicate our awareness of unity with all God's people. And our efforts to go beyond physical pain to spir-

itual healing and peace may be our growth in faith.

As Jesus took quiet time to pray, so too do we need time to focus, to center on the spiritual realities that can get crowded out by busy, day-to-day concerns and by pain and grief. Fortified by inner peace, by prayer, we can be better companions on the way. We might share our strength with others or be more receptive to their sharing. Those who suffer, or who are close to a loved one suffering, have a need both to give and to receive: their burden and grief may make them both vulnerable and strong. We need to learn how to walk the painful journey with them—when to console and when to learn from their experiences.

The sacrament of anointing is celebrated in our pastoral practice as a part of the community's care and concern for the sick. In this, we live out Jesus Christ's compassion for the suffering.

REFLECTING ON LIFE

Suffering and pain, growing old and facing death are all around us. We may not have had the experience ourselves, or in a loved one, but we cannot pass through one day, it seems, without an awareness of suffering in the lives of others. It may be helpful to have participants in your group reflect on how their lives have been touched, shaped by suffering.

1. What were your feelings when you have been with a loved one who was seriously ill or facing death? Has that kind of illness been an experience in your own life? What were/are your thoughts and feelings about it?

2. How has the illness of loved ones influenced your life?

3. Have you gained any insights through your encounters with suffering or pain? What are they? Can you share some of your own life?

4. Where do you find any hope or strength in the presence of suffering?

KNOWING OUR FAITH

From the Gospel, we learn that Jesus' response to sickness was to heal, to cure, to come to the heart of the illness. Through the cures he brought about, Jesus gave a sign that God's kingdom had come—that forgiveness and healing were an important response to suffering. But not all suffering has been taken away, not all illness is cured. Jesus himself took on suffering, pain and death as a part of what it meant for him to "be like us in all things"—a part of his own humanity.

Through the disciples and on through the development of the Church, prayer for the sick and healing have been handed on to our present community. Always there have been elements of prayer, faith, anointing of the sick, healing, forgiveness and the power of the Lord made manifest. The Church continues Jesus' healing ministry through this sacrament among those who suffer and who face death. Pastoral care of the sick is a growing ministry, including parish visitation, bringing the Eucharist to the homebound and those in bed, celebration of the sacrament of anointing in the parish community as well as at the request of individuals.

Facing illness and death is a "threshold experience" for persons, and the community of faith is present as companions and supporters, offering prayer, friendship, strength and peace as an individual deals with the radically intimate and personal encounter with his or her own limitations, hope and faith.

The sacrament can bring us into the powerful presence of the Lord who heals our broken spirits, strengthens us in the face of fears, gives us peace to endure suffering on our life's journey. We can, through celebration of this sacrament, understand better the meaning of dying and rising, can grow in our hope of resurrection beyond death, can deepen our trust in God's great, gentle care and compassionate love for each of us.

INTEGRATION

Depending on the group's response to this topic, it may be helpful to use a film or filmstrip that deals with anointing of the sick. It would be excellent to have a parish celebration of the sacrament of anointing and have the group participate, and perhaps invite to the group as speakers some from the parish who have experienced the sacrament or who are actively ministering to the sick and elderly in the parish.

Reflection and Discussion

1. What is the Christian belief about death and about life after death? When you think about illness and death, how do you feel about Christian hope and belief in resurrection?

2. How would you like the faith community to minister to you when you are faced with illness or death?

3. What can you do to be present with and to help the sick and elderly in your community?

CLOSING PRAYER

From the sacramentary, Prayers from the Rite of Anointing of the Sick, or Song, "All That We Have," Gary Ault, © 1969, 1979, Damean Music, or Song, "Lay Your Hands," Carey Landry, © 1977, N.A.L.R.

Doctrinal and Pastoral Issues: Sacrament of Anointing of the Sick, Healing, Forgiveness, Suffering

Clare M. Colella

Sixth Sunday in Ordinary Time

Leviticus 13:1–2, 44–46
I Corinthians 10:31–11:1
Mark 1:40–45

OPENING SONG

"A Creed," Joe Wise, © Joe Wise, album "A New Day," or "I Believe in the Sun," Carey Landry, © 1973, Carey Landry and N.A.L.R.

THEMATIC FRAMEWORK

Most often, this Sunday is just a few days before Ash Wednesday, the opening of the Lenten season. In this setting, the readings take on added significance. The outcast lepers of Leviticus are healed in the Gospel account. The balancing of sinfulness and forgiveness are words of hope for us as we approach the penitential season. The Gospel continues to probe the question: Who is this Jesus? What are we to learn from him? How are we to follow him? What does he ask of us?

The responsorial psalm invites us to turn to the Lord in time of trouble, for he will fill us with the joy of salvation. We are forgiven, made glad. That, too, seems to be the message of St. Paul, to find our fulfillment and peace in the Lord. For Paul it is in imitating Jesus Christ, doing what he does for the glory of God, that he finds that joy of salvation.

As we conclude our consideration of the sacraments as the touchstones of our faith journey, celebrating our encounter with the living God, we move into a time of reflection on faith. The leper in the Gospel story came to Jesus with a deep faith in the possibility of being healed. We do not know if the leper believed in Jesus' proclamation of the good news, or believed in Jesus' power to forgive, but his approach to Jesus and whatever faith he had were sufficient. His healing was the result not so much of his own efforts but of God's free gift, given through Jesus. That sense of faith, however much or little, was a beginning. Since the leper, now cured, went out to proclaim what happened to him, it appears that his faith became deeper as a response to Jesus' action. We grow in faith—through experiences, reflection, insight, through grace and love. Our faith response to Jesus and to life reflects our on-going rela-tionship in which we grow in knowledge and love of God. Our faith forms the basis of our outlook and attitudes, our values and efforts. In these terms, "faith" may seem a little vague, hard to grasp, measure, nurture. In this session, we will look at some ways to consider faith in more concrete or verifiable terms, in human and spiritual contexts. Special consideration is given to the Creed as one of the traditions of our Church, and a heritage-formulation of the beliefs of the Catholic community. This time is proximate to the time when the presentations of the traditions may be celebrated with the catechumenate group.

REFLECTIONS ON LIFE

On a day-to-day basis, we live by faith—in human relationships and concerns. We believe in the sincerity of others, we shape our interactions with others according to our previous experiences or our intuitions, and we depend in numerous ways on our knowledge of and trust in human beings. Basic human faith is essential to normal living. Clarification may be gained through consideration and discussion of the following:

1. Describe the relationship you have with a person who is significant in your life at the present time.

2. What do you do to keep that relationship alive and growing?

3. How do you respond to your friend's efforts or interests or ideas?

4. What difference has that relationship made in your life?

Most often, members of the group will find that it is a personal relationship that has shaped their lives, that even if inspired by a book, a hero or ideal, it is only when that inspiration became personally "owned" that it had a lasting impact on them. That human experience is the foundation for the faith experience of "Creed."

KNOWING OUR FAITH

Growth in faith involves a process of maturing—experience, reflection, insight, response. In their document "Sharing the Light of Faith, The National Catechetical

Directory for Catholics," the bishops of the United States indicate the importance of continued development of the human person in the process of faith growth (#173, 174). Because our experiences are different, each of us possesses aspects of our faith to differing degrees. Growth is a lifelong process. There is no one way that is right for all. Our faith reflects the on-going relationship in which we grow in knowledge and love of God.

As a community, the Roman Catholic Church has, over the centuries, expressed its beliefs in formulas or Creeds, statements of doctrine. Through a Creed, the Church and its members declare their understanding of God who reveals himself in faith. There are two commonly used Creeds familiar to Catholics today: the Apostles' Creed, a very ancient statement of beliefs, and the Nicene Creed, formulated in the fourth century and proclaimed during the Sunday liturgy.

The Creed is one of the traditions which, along with the Lord's Prayer, are special heritage prayers presented to the catechumens and candidates as they prepare to enter the Catholic community. Time to reflect on the meaning of these two prayers of the Church is encouraged prior to the celebration of the presentation of the traditions. A day of prayer may be one way to focus on understanding the prayers, along with time spent with sponsors, or even at a catechumenal session. Team members will need to decide in advance how they will study, pray with and present the Creed and Lord's Prayer to the catechumens and candidates. There are several books and some media that give background history that might be helpful to the catechists.

INTEGRATION

Faith is a free personal response; it cannot be forced or expected. As the catechumenate community approaches the time of election, it may be helpful to consider some of the ways of evaluating or reflecting on a person's growth in faith. There is no one right way to be or to respond, but it is important to spend time in prayer, looking at one's present faith-style, seeking continued growth. This reflection is a responsibility shared among the team, candidate/catechumen and sponsor/godparent. John Westerhoff describes four styles of faith that may be useful (cf. "Will Our Children Have Faith?" Seabury Press, 1976).

1. *Experienced Faith:* Our earliest style, when feelings are most important. Persons must experience for themselves being loved, trusted, accepted in order to believe.

2. *Affiliative Faith:* Strong identification with a community is central in this style. A recognized community with a sense of authority provides a basis for the individual who still relies on religious feelings, especially the experience of awe, mystery and wonder.

3. *Searching Faith:* In a time of transition, a person questions the meaning and purpose of a community, seeks some form of commitment, even briefly, while looking at the way a community lives out what it proclaims it believes. This style of faith is meant to be transitional as a person progresses from the community's understanding of faith to his or her own personal understanding and integration.

4. *Owned Faith:* The fullness of faith growth is in itself a beginning. The culmination of the process of conversion calls a person to witness faith in word and action. Owned faith gives birth to a lifestyle centered on growth and commitment. One does what one believes. There is no perfect product, because our believing and doing are woven into our daily rhythmic growing.

But a personal choice has been made, and *that* makes the difference. There may be media or print materials to present this or alternative considerations in looking at the stages in human and faith development. The team will need to have spent time in choosing whether or how to deal with this whole issue. There surely does have to be some process planned for helping catechumens and candidates discern their readiness for the next steps in the catechumenate process.

Reflection and Discussion

1. What attitudes of faith do you carry into daily Christian living?
2. What consequences will these have in your relationships and actions? Are some changes being required of you by the challenge of the Gospel and the Church's beliefs and teachings?

Journaling

How comfortable am I with my present style of faith? If I want to grow, what am I to do?

CLOSING SONG

"What You Hear in the Dark," Dan Schutte, S.J., © 1975, Daniel Schutte, S.J. and N.A.L.R.

Doctrinal and Pastoral Issues: Faith Development, Stages of Growth, Creed, Presentation of the Traditions

Clare M. Colella

Seventh Sunday in Ordinary Time

Isaiah 43:18–19, 21–22, 24–25
2 Corinthians 1:18–22
Mark 2:1–12

OPENING SONG

"Turn Back, O Man," Godspell, © Bell Records.

or "Seek the Lord," © St. Louis Jesuits and N.A.L.R., album: "Earthen Vessels."

THEMATIC FRAMEWORK

This week's readings are a wonderful insight into forgiveness, repentance, healing and fidelity. The first reading from Isaiah declares the Lord's forgiveness, his power to create something new, to renew his people. The responsorial psalm might well reflect the response of his people—in return we ask for healing, acknowledging our sinfulness, which is already forgiven. Even physical healing is a part of the psalmist's prayer. Today's message of penance and forgiveness of sin shows clearly that God has promised mercy. Paul reminds the people of Corinth and of our local communities of God's absolute fidelity, his presence and strength in us through the Spirit in our hearts.

The stage is set, scripturally, for the healing of the paralytic—the faith of those who brought him to Jesus, the forgiveness of sins, and the validation through a miracle of physical healing. The miracles must be understood as faith-events—occasions for people to believe in Jesus and in the One who sent him. The miracles, integral to his proclamation and mission, are signs, making visible a deeper reality of inner healing and wholeness. They show God's power at work and lead people to faith in God.

In today's Scriptures, we are called to believe in God's mercy and readiness to forgive our sins, and to acknowledge his healing power to enable us to lead righteous lives. He does not stop simply at forgiveness—his love is everlasting, ever-present.

REFLECTING ON LIFE

An open-eyed perusal of our own lives will yield some insight into our personal need for forgiveness, for penance and conversion. We may be able to look back at a time when we have experienced a conversion that led to a change in our lives—a statement of renewed faith in God, in ourselves, and which may have led to an inner healing.

We may also discover, or become more deeply aware of, an area of our lives that is still paralyzed by sinfulness, a stumbling block to our growth in holiness. What can we do? Do we have others who will, by their faith and care for us, bring us to the Lord for healing, who will help us recognize the need for repentance and forgiveness? If we cannot bring ourselves to discuss our area of weakness with another, do we honestly deal with it in our own internal forum, or do we avoid it, making excuses, procrastinating? Do we want to be converted, healed? Do we really believe God can forgive and heal us and help us on our way?

KNOWING OUR FAITH

Events and parables of forgiveness and healing are numerous in the Christian Scriptures as well as in the Hebrew Scriptures. Since an earlier session focused on the sacrament of reconciliation, this session will center on the scriptural stories of forgiveness and our insights from them. Whether it was the woman with the hemorrhage, the man born blind, the death of the young girl, the son of the widow, or the death of Lazarus, the lepers or the paralytic, miracles and healing are woven into the fabric of faith and forgiveness. The textures of the settings may change, but the elements are there. There are miracles of Jesus' power over nature and other miracles, for the nurturing of faith, to lead his followers and us to belief—belief in the power of God to heal us, to forgive us, and to give us the strength to choose good, to stand upright before the Lord. Some time could be spent in reading these different stories, finding and discussing the common threads of what Jesus asked of those to be healed, how persons came to him with belief/doubt, and whether there is any parallel in our current Church for healing ministry. If there is a community of believers who have experienced healing, someone from that community may be invited to share his or her faith and experiences with the group. This exposure to the variety of expressions of faith and expectation in the Church today may need considerable preparation and discussion afterward. But if there is a valid healing ministry in the Catholic community, it may be a valuable time for those who seek to know more about the Church in its fullness.

INTEGRATION

Give the group time to reflect, even to look through the Scriptures at the suggested readings, to select a story of forgiveness which has special meaning for them. Some may choose to consider an event in their own lives which was an encounter with a loving, forgiving God.

Reflection and Discussion

1. What is my response to an experience or story of God's forgiveness, even expressed through miracles?

2. What signs do I see in my own life that remind me of the forgiveness of the Father?

3. What does it mean to be faithful to the Lord?

4. Why do we find it hard to forgive ourselves?

5. What helps us to feel forgiven?

CLOSING PRAYER

Psalm 15: "Preserve me, O God. I take refuge in you . . ." (Leader begin, alternating sides according to paragraphs in your Bibles.)

Doctrinal and Pastoral Issues: Forgiveness, Miracles of Healing

Clare M. Colella

Eighth Sunday in Ordinary Time

Hosea 2:16–17, 21–22
2 Corinthians 3:1–6
Mark 2:18–22

OPENING SONG

"I Have Loved You," Michael Joncas, © 1979, N.A.L.R.

THEMATIC FRAMEWORK

The covenant of love is given image in today's readings. The antiphons, prayers and responsorial psalm all develop the theme of overwhelming love, the imagery of covenant and fidelity that appear.

The Scriptures see human beings as relating to God in sacred partnership, in agreement, covenant. Hosea is the first prophet to use language of marital characteristics to describe this relationship. His own unhappy marriage and his willingness to take back his unfaithful wife provide an insight into God's willingness to do the same with his unfaithful people.

Paul's imagery of covenant is that it is written in our hearts, a covenant of spirit. He calls his people of Corinth to be faithful to the message he has given them, for they are God's ministers of the new covenant. In them the Spirit gives life.

The imagery of marriage was familiar to Jesus, so that in this Gospel segment he uses the terminology of a marriage. In speaking of a time when the bridegroom will be taken away he is referring to his death, a foreshadowing of what is to come. But while he is present, do we stand ready to be faithful to him? Two similes, or images, Jesus speaks of show that the new covenant which he is founding is not just a mending or repairing of the old. It is distinct, different from the former covenant. It goes further than the old: it establishes a new relationship of love and family membership with God.

REFLECTING ON LIFE

The strongest bond between persons and the greatest motivation for action is love. It is love that calls us to respond in fidelity; it is love that challenges us to a new way of living, or perceiving, or valuing. We can recognize in our lives certain individuals who have shaped us and given us a direction that has made a real difference in our lives. When we try to describe our relationship with that person—or persons—one of the first words we would use is that of love.

1. Describe some of the persons who have really affected your present life. How did they influence you?

2. How will you influence others?

3. How do you feel about needing or accepting direction in your life?

KNOWING OUR FAITH

From ancient times, Israel was a "chosen people" because the people of the nation acknowledged no other king but God alone. That unique relationship established between God and his people, the *covenant*, forged a union: "You will be my people. I am your God." It was a union based on fidelity, not fear, on loving service, not slavery. Israel had an important part in this relationship, but its continuation depended ultimately on Yahweh, the Lord of the kingdom. As time went on, the concept of the kingdom of God came to mean many things to the Hebrew nation—for some it meant freedom from Roman oppression; for others it meant renewed power and glory; for others it meant that God would again intervene in their affairs for their protection and safety.

But when Jesus proclaimed that the kingdom was already here—the bridegroom was among his people—he presented a problematic statement. The kingdom Jesus declared called for a change of heart, a conversion. He offered a new relationship between God and those who believed his message. Jesus was to bring about that new relationship through his own life, death and resurrection; a relationship that resulted in harmony, integrity, wholeness and freedom from fear. That new way of life called for compassion, concern, acceptance, forgiveness, fidelity and service, love of neighbor. It was almost too much to hear. In fact, for some who did hear, it could not be accepted. Some followers were hurt, angry, disappointed in the proclamation of the new covenant. It was too much to ask, and did not measure up to their expectations. So Jesus spent much of his public life continuing to teach, explain, nurture the faith of his followers.

INTEGRATION

Our Christian living is a response to God's gift of the kingdom, a response made possible in and through Jesus Christ. It is because we have both the Scriptures and our encounter with the living Christ in the Church today that we can know what we are called to do as participants of the new covenant.

Reflection and Discussion

1. Do you see yourself as related to God in a partnership of love? How do you grow in that relationship?

2. How do you live that relationship out in daily life?

CLOSING SONG

"Beginning Today," Mike Balhoff, Darryl Ducote, sung by the Dameans © 1973, Damean Music and N.A.L.R.

Doctrinal and Pastoral Issues: Seeing Ourselves as Members of the New Covenant, Living Gospel Values, Love

Clare M. Colella

Ninth Sunday in Ordinary Time

Deuteronomy 5:12–15
2 Corinthians 4:6–11
Mark 2:23—3:6 (long form) or 2:23–28 (short form)

OPENING SONG

"Pause Awhile," The Dameans, album: "Tell the World," © 1969, F.E.L.

THEMATIC FRAMEWORK

After an opening prayer which speaks of God's care and protection, the first reading proclaims the observance of the sabbath. The importance of the sabbath for the Hebrews and for us is a time of abstinence from work in order to remember and renew our covenant with God. The sabbath was seen as a grateful response to the safe exodus from Egyptian bondage. The early Christians from Jewish background continued to observe the sabbath and celebrated the Eucharist on the Lord's day (day of his resurrection). Later, as more Gentiles joined the Church, the Lord's day, Sunday, became the Christian day of worship.

The responsorial psalm depicts a joyous celebration, a clear connection to sabbath/Sunday worship.

The Gospel reading focuses on Jesus' experience of and teaching about the sabbath. "The sabbath was made for man, not man for the sabbath." The Pharisees had gone far beyond the intention of sabbath rest and worship, creating myriad detailed laws about what could or could not be done. Jesus clearly opposes the yoke of such legalism. Jesus also proclaims that the Son of Man is Lord even of the sabbath. If there is an act of mercy, or healing, that is opportune or necessary, Jesus declares, by doing it, that good deeds are appropriate, regardless of the legalistic limitations imposed.

This week's reading from Paul's Second Letter to the Corinthians does not seem to fit the theme but carries its own message of Paul's affirmation of God's revelation to him. The glory of God was shown to him so that he, weak and human as he is, could proclaim it to others. It is for the Corinthians to look to Christ, not himself as the revelation of God's treasure.

REFLECTING ON LIFE

Observing the spirit of the sabbath may be one of the great challenges offered to us. Our lives are so often crowded and clouded that we forget to really set aside time for the Lord. It is at times a grudging participation in weekly Sunday worship; an excuse to minimize time with the Lord can pretty easily be found. Sometimes even the time of fellowship is something we want to escape.

Let's look at what is happening—or could be. At this time you and the catechumenate community are spending extra time together, on Sunday, perhaps also during the week. This time together, in reflection, study, prayer, sharing, is one way of keeping Sunday holy. Do you manage to find some extra few moments to pause, in solitude, to look at the Lord and listen to his word to you this day? Is part of your preparation and follow up to speak with the Lord about these concerns, these people, about your own spiritual growth?

KNOWING OUR FAITH

To keep holy the Lord's day is one of the ten commandments, part of the covenant between Yahweh and his people through Moses, sealed solemnly and upheld as sacred by succeeding generations. If there is a need to study briefly the Hebrew covenant, the ten commandments, this may be an opportunity to do so. However there are so few times that Cycle B includes the Ninth Sunday of the Year that this session, as with the Seventh and Eighth Sundays, is often omitted.

INTEGRATION

When this session is utilized and the topic of the Hebrew covenant commandments is not vital, it may be beneficial to reflect on how we keep the Lord's Day holy, whether our participation in Sunday Mass is an adequate sum total of time set aside, or whether some members of the group may have some valuable insights or customs to share. This is one area where we may learn from other faiths the value they attach to keeping holy the sabbath or Sunday. Many religious denominations expect that several hours be given to worship, study and fellowship. At home too there are ways of not crowding in tasks—plan to save some time for family events or for simple quiet time. There should be something different about the time we want to dedicate to God.

CLOSING PRAYER

The Lord's Prayer.

Doctrinal and Pastoral Issues: Keeping the Sabbath, Time for Prayer, Commandments

Clare M. Colella

Jesus and His Mission

Part II: The New Israel

By Eugene A. LaVerdiere

In this second series of Sundays in Ordinary Time, most of the readings are again taken from Mark, but from the Seventeenth to the Twenty-First Sundays and on the Thirty-Fourth and Last Sunday, they come from John 6 and 18. The readings from Mark focus first on the implications of Jesus' life for the universality of the Church and the scope of the Christian mission. From the Tenth to the Sixteenth and again on the Twenty-Second and Twenty-Third Sundays, the readings are drawn from Mark 3:7—8:21. As the new Israel, the Church transcends every people, race and ethnic group. It is universal in principle. Through its mission it must become so in fact. The readings also focus on the kind of commitment that is required to fulfill the Christian mission. From the Twenty-Fourth to the Thirty-Third Sundays, the readings are taken from Mark 8:27—13:37. The universal mission requires total selflessness. Christians must be able to be baptized with the baptism of the passion and to drink deep of the cup of the new covenant in Christ's blood.

Jesus' True Relatives

At first reading, it may appear from the Gospel for the Tenth Sunday in Ordinary Time (Mk 3:20–35) that Jesus is quite harsh and uncaring with regard to his family. Not so when we read the passage in context and recognize that its purpose is to elevate all who do the will of God, not to lower his immediate family. As they receive the word of God from Christ, all find a new relationship in him. The mission of the Church reaches beyond blood ties, beyond any particular people, and invites everyone to become a relative of Jesus. As relatives of Jesus, we also become relatives of one another.

Parables of the Kingdom

Two short parables, in which the reign of God is compared to the planting, the growing and the harvesting, which anyone could observe in Galilee, as well as to the very tiny mustard seed which becomes a large shrub, form the substance of the Gospel for the Elev-enth Sunday in Ordinary Time (Mk 4:26–32). To appreciate such parables, we must be attentive to the images used and allow them to express the mystery of God's reign for us. It is important not to reduce them to abstract summary statements. In addition, Mark adds that the purpose of Jesus' parables was to help his hearers to understand his message (Mk 4:33).

A Stormy Crossing

After the discourse on parables (Mk 4:1–34), which Jesus had presented from a little boat in the lake, the scene shifts to the lake which becomes stormy and threatening as Jesus crosses it accompanied by his disciples. The crossing, which is the Gospel for the Twelfth Sunday in Ordinary Time (4:35–41), is an important transitional moment in the Gospel of Mark. Until now Jesus has been teaching and preaching on the Jewish side of the Sea of Galilee. He now moves toward the Gentile side and the Gerasene territory. The stormy crossing mirrors the history of the early Church in its passage from a Jewish Christian community to a comprehensive community which included both Jew and Gentile. This too was a stormy crossing, and it appeared to many in the little Church that they would founder.

Raising the Dead to Life

On the Twelfth Sunday in Ordinary Time, the Gospel moved from a Jewish to a Gentile setting. On the Thirteenth Sunday, Jesus and his disciples have returned to Jewish territory. For the Gentiles, the Christian message expelled demons and cast them into the abyss (Mk 5:1–20). Now for the Jews it meant healing and even their being raised from the dead. No doubt the story of the daughter of Jairus and of the woman with the hemorrhage once had a point independently of their present context. However, at this point in Mark's Gospel, they speak to us of what is needed to become part of the new Israel which embraces all of humanity (Mk 5:21–43).

The Identity of Jesus

The question of Jesus' identity is at the heart of the mystery of the new Israel. We saw this already on the Tenth Sunday in Ordinary Time (Mk 3:20–35). It is taken up again on the Fourteenth Sunday. The setting is Jesus' home country, and Jesus is in the synagogue on the sabbath. Those present, all of whom had known Jesus and his family, were amazed at what he said and did. However, they were not able to see beyond appearances and accept that there was more to Jesus than a carpenter, the son of Mary. For this they would have needed faith (Mk 6:1–6). Without faith, they could not see that Jesus' identity and mission transcended the boundaries of their village and even of their people. The Gospel was meant for all.

Instructions for the Mission

On the Fifteenth Sunday in Ordinary Time, we leave Mark's section on the scope and nature of the new Israel (3:7—6:6a) and move on to the mission of the disciples (6:6b—8:21). Like the new Israel, the mission was to be universal. In today's reading (Mk 6:7–13), the Church focuses on the instructions Jesus gave for the mission. These include a series of do's and don'ts, both of which are important. The disciples are to go without money, without bread and without baggage. They are to accept the hospitality offered them. However, they are to carry a staff, wear sandals and a tunic (only one). These items evoke the exodus in the Old Testament and especially the night of Passover. The Christian mission is to be like a new exodus.

With Jesus in the Desert

The introduction for the long section on the multiplication of loaves is our reading for the Sixteenth Sunday in Ordinary Time (Mk 6:30–34). Having returned from their missionary journey, the disciples are exhausted and Jesus invites them to come apart from the crowd and rest, but the crowd preceded them to their retreat. Jesus' reaction becomes a challenge for the disciples. It also summarizes their ministry. Looking at the crowd, his heart was deeply moved. He reached out to them because they were like sheep without a shepherd. Like Jesus, the disciples must reach out lovingly toward the flock and nourish them with the word of God.

The Miraculous Sharing

The introduction for what we call the multiplication of loaves (Sixteenth Sunday) is taken from Mark's Gospel, but the story of the multiplication itself (Seventeenth Sunday) is taken from John (6:1–15). Every Gospel has a distinctive way of presenting this event. In John it is one of the great signs which manifested the identity of Jesus and the nature of the work the Father accomplished through him. As part of the background, we should recall 2 Kings 4:42–44 which helped to set the pattern for this story at a very early moment in Christian tradition. The story was also influenced by the early Christian Eucharist.

The Bread of Life

On this Eighteenth Sunday in Ordinary Time and for the next three Sundays, the Gospel reading is taken from the discourse which follows John's story of the multiplication of loaves. We begin with the introduction to the discourse (6:24–25) and a number of verses from the first part (6:26–35). The crowds had experienced the multiplication of loaves. They had seen and marveled at the sign Jesus had performed among them, but they had not appreciated its meaning. For them Jesus was but a miracle worker who provided perishable food. Jesus wants them to seek food that remains for eternal life. When they actually ask for this bread, Jesus tells them that he himself is the bread of life. Jesus, the Word of God made flesh, the light and the life, is also our nourishment.

Bread from Heaven

As on the previous Sunday, the crowd is unable to penetrate beneath appearances and see with the eyes of faith. On this Nineteenth Sunday, it is a matter of the very identity of Jesus (6:41–51). The question "If he is the son of Joseph, how can he claim to have come down from heaven?" is still with us today. In this part of the discourse, Jesus explains how everyone who comes to him in faith and sees how he reveals the Father has eternal life and will be raised up on the last day.

Flesh for the Life of the World

Jesus now speaks in very concrete and physical terms. His person, which is offered to them as heavenly nourishment, is among them in a very human and mortal way. The nourishment he gives is his very flesh and blood (Twentieth Sunday in Ordinary Time). As background for this, we should recall John's prologue and its statement about the incarnation: "The Word was made flesh." Jesus' discourse responds to any and every tendency to spiritualize Christianity to the exclusion of simple fleshly realities. This includes the Eucharist, where Christ is present, not in a vague spiritual way, but in very physical and visible signs. Among these signs are all the Christians present. We must be concerned for earthly human needs and not merely for other-worldly needs (6:51–58).

The Life-Giving Spirit

After emphasizing the incarnational nature of Christian life and worship (6:51–58), Jesus shows how those incarnational realities, including his flesh and blood, his mortal person among us, receive their life-giving value from the spirit (6:60–69). The spirit, that is, Jesus' message which is spirit and life, enables us to penetrate the signs of the Father's presence and to see that there is more than meets the eye in the flesh and blood of Jesus. The discourse concludes on this Twenty-First Sunday in Ordinary Time as some of those present leave Jesus. His message is too demanding. Others remain with him. His presence is the only place to be. The Gospel invites us to make our own decision.

God's Commandment and Human Tradition

On the Twenty-Second Sunday in Ordinary Time, we return to our reading of Mark's Gospel. We start with an issue that is as important today as it was in the first century, the relationship of human religious traditions to the commandment of God. Among the Pharisees, religious traditions often neutralized divine commands or had nothing to do with them. For Jesus, religious traditions were of value precisely because they gave concrete expression to the divine commandments. It was obvious that they could not be tolerated if they prevented the commandment from being observed. Such traditions no longer had religious value (Mk 7:1–8, 14–15, 21–23).

Hearing and Speaking the Word of God

In today's Gospel, Jesus meets a man who was both deaf and dumb (Mk 7:31–37). This is the only such incident in the Synoptic Gospels, and it forms part of the transition from the mission of the disciples to the Jewish people (the first multiplication of loaves) to the mission to the Gentiles (second multiplication). The event occurs in the land of the ten Greek cities (the Decapolis). As on other Sundays, the Gospel for this Twenty-Third Sunday in Ordinary Time deals with more than a physical healing. Jesus opens the man's ears to hear words as the word of God and to speak human words which are also God's good news.

The Passion of the Son of Man

The Gospel reading begins by raising the question of Jesus' identity. Jesus is more than Elijah, John the Baptizer and the other prophets. He is the Messiah, the Christ. Such is Peter's profession of faith. However, when Jesus goes on to identify himself as the Son of Man, the epitome of all humanity, and as one who will suffer and die, Peter protests. He does so, not so much because of what will happen to Jesus, but because of what will happen to him as a follower of Jesus. In reply Jesus tells him to get back into his following. Peter was also tempting the others, and so Jesus addresses him as Satan. The last part of the reading for the Twenty-Fourth Sunday in Ordinary Time begins to spell out the implications of the passion for all those who follow Christ (Mk 8:27–35).

Rank and Importance Among Disciples

On the Twenty-Fifth Sunday in Ordinary Time, we continue the themes introduced last Sunday with a reading of the second prophetic statement concerning the passion-resurrection of the Son of Man and the disciples' reaction to it (Mk 9:30–37). Like Simon Peter, the other disciples are unable to accept Jesus' message, but instead of confronting it directly as Peter had done, they spoke of something else. Jesus had announced his passion and resurrection. They discussed who was the most important among them. In response, Jesus called their attention to a little child—a truly important person. By welcoming the child, the disciples would be welcoming him. Their discussion about personal importance was thus made to appear quite foolish.

Those Not of Our Company

With Mark 9:38–43, 45, 47–48, the Gospel for the Twenty-Sixth Sunday in Ordinary Time examines a number of important issues affecting those who follow Christ to the passion and resurrection. We begin by considering those who are not of our company and who invoke Jesus' name. If they are not against us, they are for us. Even a complete outsider will be rewarded for doing good to us because of our relationship to Christ. We then turn to the question of leading others astray. No hyperbole could be too exaggerated for showing the seriousness of this matter.

Divorce and Remarriage

The subject for the Twenty-Seventh Sunday in Ordinary Time is quite delicate: divorce and remarriage (Mk 10:2–16). It includes two important points. The first is in a discussion with Pharisees who allowed for divorce and remarriage and based their position on the law of Moses. For his position, which excluded divorce and remarriage, Jesus appealed to the story of creation, which is even more fundamental than the law of Moses. Jesus saw marriage as a lifetime commitment. The second point is given later in a discussion with the disciples who wanted Jesus to explain further. Jesus had not been speaking of divorce as such but of divorce and remarriage. His position presupposes the disciples' commitment to take up the cross and follow Jesus. Without this radical commitment, it would not have made any sense.

Wealth and the Kingdom of God

What must one do to share in everlasting life? A rich man brought this question to Jesus. In response, Jesus first recalls the commandments, but he then goes a step further. To enter the kingdom of God, one must give one's goods to the poor and follow Christ. On hearing this, the man went away sad. Jesus then refines his position for the disciples, and it is here that he challenges them with the famous hyperbole about the camel and the eye of the needle, forcing them to recognize the seriousness of the matter (Mk 10:17–30). On this Twenty-Eighth Sunday, as on the previous Sunday, Jesus and Mark's Gospel presuppose the radical commitment to take up the cross of Christ.

Drinking the Cup of Christ

On the Twenty-Ninth Sunday in Ordinary Time we join Jesus and his disciples on the road to Jerusalem, which for Mark was the place of his passion-resurrection. Jesus has just spoken of his passion for the third time (10:32–34) and, as on the two previous occasions, his disciples try to evade its implications. This time the sons of Zebedee, James and John, immediately ask Jesus if they can sit one at his right and one at his left when he comes into his glory. Jesus answers with a question: "Can you drink the cup that I will drink?" The disciples are being told that they should be concerned about their commitment to follow Christ all the way instead of focusing on the journey's glorious end (10:35–45).

Opening of the Eyes

The story of the blind beggar, Bartimaeus, is our reading for this Thirtieth Sunday in Ordinary Time (Mk 10:46–52). The story's message is a summary of this whole section of the Gospel on the following of Christ. At the beginning of the passage, Bartimaeus is seated beside the road. He is not a disciple with Jesus and the others on the road. When Jesus hears him calling and invites him onto the road, he shows himself ready to follow Christ. At the story's conclusion, we find Bartimaeus, his eyes now open, following Jesus on the way to Jerusalem, the passion and the resurrection.

The First Commandment

In Mark 11:27—12:44, Jesus meets up with all the various groups already encountered in the course of the Gospel and addresses each of them on the issue which more than all the others blocks their participation in the life of the kingdom. On the Thirty-First Sunday in Ordinary Time, a scribe comes to him inquiring about the greatest commandment (12:28–34). Jesus responds with the double commandment to love both God and neighbor. The unity of these commandments stems from their common source in God. One does not love God without loving the neighbor, and one does not love the neighbor without loving God.

Scribes, Widows and Jesus' Disciples

In Mark 12:38–44, Jesus addresses his disciples. His message on this Thirty-Second Sunday is that they are to avoid behaving like the scribes who are taken up with their own importance, prestige, and power over others. They even despoil widows of their savings. The passage ends with an extreme example of a widow who has been brought to abject poverty by the scribes. Jesus warns the disciples against religious exploitation of the poor, as the scribes had done before them.

The Return of the Son of Man

As we approach the end of the liturgical year (Thirty-Third Sunday in Ordinary Time), the Gospel turns to the return of Christ as Son of Man and the extraordinary cosmic events which will accompany his return (Mk 13:24–32). The purpose of this passage is not to frighten us but to try to express just how significant the return of Christ will be. The event has historic and cosmic implications. The power and glory of the sun, the moon and the stars fade before that of the Son of Man. The discourse also means to warn us against trying to guess the day or hour when this will happen. Only the Father knows—no one else.

A Kingdom Not of This World

On the Last Sunday in Ordinary Time, the Thirty-Fourth, we turn once again to John's Gospel for the reading (18:33–37). The theme is the nature of Jesus' kingdom. The setting is the passion and the trial before Pilate at the praetorium. Jesus is a king, but his kingdom is not of this world. He refuses to answer Pilate directly, because Pilate hears Jesus' message in purely this-worldly terms. Jesus had no political ambition. His kingdom is the reign of God, a reign exercised over the hearts and minds of human beings everywhere. By so transcending history, the kingdom of Jesus relativizes every human and earthly kingdom, calling them to the heavenly kingdom of the King of kings.

Introduction to Trinity Sunday, Tenth through Twelfth Sundays in Ordinary Time

Trinity Sunday, Corpus Christi (Feast of the Body and Blood of Christ), and the following Sundays are an unfolding of the story of salvation. With the Scriptures, we continue to hear Jesus' proclamation of the kingdom and we see evidence of his love, power, and his compassion as the Son of God. In our own lives, we reflect on our growth in faith, the teachings of the Church, and the importance of Scripture in our faith.

Each session is designed to include:

Opening Song or Prayer
Thematic Framework
Reflecting on Life
Knowing our Faith
Integration
Closing Song or Prayer

As before, specific songs or prayers mentioned follow the theme, but are offered only as suggestions. It may be preferable to use songs your group knows, or different music for meditation. As team members and catechists, feel free to adapt or substitute according to the needs and choice of your group. Prayers from the Mass or readings from Scripture can be used by the entire group if they have missalettes or Bibles available. Spontaneous prayer from the group is encouraged, especially at the close of a session.

We recommend a variety of prayer formats and experiences, trusting in the prayerful insights and skills of the leaders to develop these. Always the qualities of aesthetic setting and comfortableness with prayer are an integral part of the essential hospitality of the catechumenate ministry.

The method of this section presents to the catechist a framework suggesting a theme for the gathering. During preparation time, the catechist will need to become familiar with the materials provided, adding and adapting according to the needs of the group. The segment titled "Reflecting on Life" attempts to focus on our own experiences in relation to the theme. Questions or statements for discussion are offered and could surely be adapted for small or large groups, for journaling or for private reflection.

"Knowing Our Faith" highlights the doctrinal or catechetical theme, often suggesting media and additional resources to enhance the catechist's own background for preparation and presentation. The segment under "Integration" weaves the catechetical and pastoral elements into real-life application or conclusion. Questions or statements offered could be used for discussion and/or journaling. It would be helpful to assure some quiet time for reflection or journaling within the weekly gathering itself. The sponsor or godparent, team members or spiritual director may want to plan to spend some time with the individual candidate/catechumen other than the session times to keep pace with questions, growth and development of the individuals in the group.

We trust the best judgment of the competent and prayerful team members and catechists in the use and adaptation of the materials offered here. We also recommend that the team begin to maintain a notebook of themes, materials and resources that are available or have proven useful for future reference. An on-going reference shelf for the members of the catechumenate ministry would be helpful as well.

Tenth Sunday in Ordinary Time

Genesis 3:9–15
2 Corinthians 4:13—5:1
Mark 3:20–35

OPENING SONG

"Only In God," John Foley, S.J., © 1976 by John R. Foley, S.J. and N.A.L.R.

THEMATIC FRAMEWORK

As persons undertaking a deliberate journey of faith who are seeking to know the Lord better in our lives, we might turn to the last segment of today's Gospel reading for direction and encouragement: Jesus is not so much dismissing his relatives as he is declaring a deeper bond between people of faith. The common acceptance of the Father's creating and saving will is central in our lives.

The first two readings set up the polarizations we know in our own lives; the experience of weakness, of human sinfulness over against the promise of redemption. That promise is lived out, as explained by Paul in the Second Letter to the Corinthians: we do not lose heart because we are renewed each day; we have been given Jesus and abundant grace.

The Gospel story spells out the polarization; Satan cannot fight against himself. It is because a person has chosen to follow the way of holiness that Satan has taken up battle. There is here a suggestion of the basic option each person has—to choose God or to choose Satan. The two are not compatible in one person's life. The choice for God, however, does not take away all weakness or solve, once for all, the questions, doubts and tensions we feel in trying to be faithful. So the words of Paul and the assurance by Jesus of the profound strength of the bond between God and the faithful are our strength in our day-to-day life.

This season of Ordinary Time seems to parallel our life. There are not too many liturgical high points (or life high points). Most of the time we need to look deeply to find meaning; we remind ourselves of the choices and dedications we have made in our lives as we reflect on the promises and teachings of Jesus and the vitality of the presence of the Spirit of Pentecost. These serve as the center to which we return time and again when in the doldrums.

The question may be: Having made a choice, how do we live it out? What difference does it make in our lives that we have made a choice for God?

REFLECTING ON LIFE

"No one ever said it would be easy." How many times have we said—or heard—that line? Sometimes it is an effort of consolation in a difficult time, sometimes an encouragement or goad in facing hurdles on our way to a goal. As ordinary and trite as it may seem, that saying holds a deep truth. A choice or decision once made is only the beginning of something, not the end or solution all wrapped up.

To have said yes to a proposal, to have celebrated "I do" in a marriage, is only a beginning. To have said yes to a job or a job change, to have given physical life to a child, to have said "Here I am" to a friend—these are all only the first step. Not everyone or everything around us will be a help in living out our choices. We decide again and again to affirm our decision. Or we may find ourselves questioning a choice and perhaps changing our minds (or hearts).

As a springboard for discussion of spiritual choices, participants may find it helpful to spend some time reflecting on the following questions, then discussing them in small groups. Some reporting back to the large group or whole group feedback may be helpful.

1. In my own life, what is one pivotal choice I have made? How have I prepared for that choice? How have I lived it out?

2. What is it that brings me to—or keeps me in—patterns or actions that are different from that basic choice?

3. Am I aware of the diminishment or demise of something in my life because of neglect?

4. Is there something in my life that I want to help grow stronger? How can I do that?

KNOWING OUR FAITH

Being a part of the pilgrim people, the chosen, the family of the Lord, is both a challenge and a comfort. From the early years in our lives we are aware of the tension between good and evil, fidelity and sinfulness, self-gift and selfishness.

Since the promise of redemption first made in the covenant between Adam and Yahweh, there has indeed been a "people of God."

Paul proclaimed that the promise of redemption has been fulfilled in Jesus Christ who is with us, renews us, and calls us to a heavenly goal. But what does it mean for us to be chosen? If we are members of the family of Jesus, what are we called to?

Acknowledging our human and spiritual weakness, nourishing our strengths, trying to become and remain faithful—these are some characteristics of God's people. Overcoming evil and sinfulness is a personal and a communal task. Conversion, "turning to the Lord," is interior and exterior. Conversion is a communal experience because each person's life impacts other persons, and because the broader Christian community is also growing in faith and fidelity.

We gather as a community in search of faith; we do not hold all the answers to everyone's questions, nor can we resolve everyone's tensions and difficulties. We are the family on the Way, sharing what we have and offering our support to one another in living the Gospel values.

If Catholic Christianity seems to be the family and the path we have chosen, have we decided to let go of all else that hinders us or binds us elsewhere?

What and who has brought us to this point of faith, of growth, of search? How are we tracking our journey?

INTEGRATION

To recognize where we are going, it is most helpful to reflect on what in our past has brought us to the present moment.

Journal keeping in some regular form is an increasingly popular and valuable way to "track" our lives and thoughts. If it has not been done yet, this may be an opportune time to introduce or broaden the practice of journaling to the group. For beginners, it often helps to use a notebook journal to reflect on/respond to questions posed during the sessions or given as points to ponder between sessions.

A few guidelines may be offered:

1. Set aside a regular time to write in your journal.

2. Be brief and thoughtful. Put yourself in a quiet setting.

3. Focus on the point at hand, but keep track of other insights or questions that arise.

4. Let your journal be a place for "telling your story," in whatever form is most comfortable. Experiment with various formats until you find the most effective one(s) for you.

5. Mark down milestones along the way—events, insights, memories.

6. Express prayer in your own words. Again, various experiments with methods or formats may be useful. Also remember that God may be speaking to you at these times.

7. Set up some time to speak with your spiritual director, spiritual guide or a trusted friend about the growth, questions or insights you discern through journaling.

The catechumenate team may well spend time studying some of the journal/prayer books available for ideas that could be adapted and included in sessions to stimulate journaling exercises. The questions of today's session may be journaled as well.

CLOSING PRAYER

Setting: Lighted candle; dimmed lights if possible.

Leader: Let us pray for the guidance of the Holy Spirit.
God of wisdom and love,
source of all good,
send your Spirit to teach us your truth
and guide our actions in your way of peace.

All: Psalm 27 (or read meditatively by members of the group)

Doctrinal and Pastoral Issues: Promise of Redemption, Basic Option in Our Lives, Intentional Spiritual Growth, Journal Keeping

Clare M. Colella

Eleventh Sunday in Ordinary Time

Ezekiel 17:22–24
2 Corinthians 5:6–10
Mark 4:26–34

OPENING SONG

"Anthem," Tom Conry, © 1978, N.A.L.R.

THEMATIC FRAMEWORK

Images of the kingdom—or the reign of God—form the backdrop of this week's Gospel reading. Last Sunday we heard the kingdom likened to a family of one mind, one purpose. This Sunday we hear two parables depicting the kingdom, one of planting and harvesting, the other of the mustard seed. In Matthew 13 we read a fuller development of the image of the mustard seed. But here, it is simply a brief sketch, to remind hearers of the whole story, but also to show that indeed Jesus taught through parables. The mystery of growth that underlies these two parables today is the sort of mystery that permeates the proclamation/acceptance/growth of the kingdom—that the sowing of the seed and the planting of the word will bear fruit.

In the first reading from Ezekiel, the prophet uses a gentle image of God as planter and protector to give hope to his listeners. God is able to do all things—make a healthy tree wither (the fate of the enemy) or make a withered tree bloom (protection of the chosen people).

The message of hope continues through the responsorial psalm on to the reading from Paul's Second Letter to the Corinthians. We walk by faith, full of confidence, he says. Why? Because we are one with the Lord, because his kingdom is within, for we are a part of the kingdom.

But the key to the images of the kingdom as plant is the purpose of the plant—the shelter, the fruit, the harvest. Paul's parallel is the confidence we are to have as our lives are revealed—the recompense appropriate for us, the fruits of our labors, so to speak.

REFLECTING ON LIFE

It seems that this season of being and becoming, of seed unfolding into plant into bloom into harvest, speaks to so many facets of our life. Our faith is always developing—that means changing, unfolding. We see much in the world around us that challenges our faith, perhaps even our trust. We need a strong theology of hope today, perhaps more than ever before.

Injustice, poverty, bigotry, nuclear weapons, materialism, selfishness seem overwhelming. Discouragements and despair, individualism and aggressive competition diminish our sense of social and personal well-being. Somewhere deeper than all these, somehow beyond these forces, there is something positive and affirming that gives us grounds for hope; we need to strengthen our belief in a God of the future, a God who is present now in compassionate wisdom, our God whose reign of peace, justice and harmony will be established.

Many of us have planted seeds, taking for granted the simple expectation of growth, the mystery of what really happens between planting and harvesting.

Invite participants to recall their experiences of planting, waiting, watching, watering, harvesting. What feelings surface? Being co-creators, gardeners with faith, planning and appreciation? Discouragement or sense of loss when plants have died?

What have been experiences of nurturing relationships? What have we hoped for? How do we show our belief in another person?

KNOWING OUR FAITH

Christian hope requires patience, understanding and belief in the power of the Spirit. God's word is like a seed in us, hopeful, patient for growth, yet believing in the nourishment God will provide. There is a principle of tension in the New Testament writings between what God has already done in Christ Jesus and what still remains to be done among all people. It is the tension the Hebrew people felt between being the chosen people of the covenant and yet having to work out their salvation and livelihood as a people in the midst of hardship and unfriendly surroundings. It is the tension we feel between being planted in faith and yet not fully ready for harvest, the tensions between ideals and weakness, between hope and despair. It is hope that will carry us—individually and communally—through to the har-

117

vest time. As the promise and potential of the harvest is borne within the seed, so is the kingdom in its fullness within us. We do not wait for a future heaven; heaven has, in a certain sense, already begun. The power and reality of the kingdom are now. The future element of the kingdom indicates the need for continued growth and conversion. We do not "have it made." We are chosen, redeemed, but we also know our weakness and our capacity for failure. In the risen Jesus, the victory—kingdom, harvest—has been assured, but we must continue to seek nourishment and respond to grace. That is the context for a deep sense of hope that is part of being both seed and harvest.

INTEGRATION

In dealing with a theme like hope, people may become aware of an habitual outlook of hopefulness—or helplessness—issues and feelings may surface that are not directly related to our expectations for these sessions, but those feelings may indicate the person's questions, faith, hope. We are called not to passivity or quiet desperation, but to hope-filled energy and commitment to life. If our approach to life is one of hope, then our stance in faith will be one of hope—realistic, balanced and persevering.

Reflection and Discussion

Is our basic attitude or outlook on life one of hope? How do we give evidence of our belief? Is our outlook harmonious with belief in a loving, forgiving, ever-present God?

What do we want our outlook to be? How can we go about nurturing that belief?

CLOSING PRAYER

Psalm 92

Doctrinal and Pastoral Issues: Christian Hope

Clare M. Colella

Twelfth Sunday in Ordinary Time

Job 38:1, 8–11
2 Corinthians 5:14–17
Mark 4:35–41

OPENING SONG

"Be Not Afraid," Bob Dufford, S.J., © 1975, Robert J. Dufford, S.J. and N.A.L.R.

THEMATIC FRAMEWORK

Through pairing of images and ideas, we hear today assurances of the presence and power of God in the midst of life's storms. Many of us have experienced the awesome power of storms or certainly read in papers or seen on television their force and fury. The first reading places God in the storm as he speaks to Job; the responsorial psalm and Gospel reading tell of God's power over the storm, especially in compassionate response to the fear of the people. Prayer in faith in the midst of fear or anxiety gives us strength, because it helps us to recognize who we are—God's people—and where our strength truly is. Paul emphasizes the fact that the faithful are, indeed, one in Christ, redeemed and a new creation. As Jesus spoke to the winds and the sea to calm them, so he speaks to us to create and build a new creation.

Again, the readings from the New Testament grapple with the question: Who is this man Jesus? What are we to learn of him? As we continue to explore our questions of faith, of religious insight, how are we coming to know Jesus better? Is it readily a part of us to turn to Jesus, to God, in prayer? It seems that we too easily focus on the storms and the dangers present in our lives, and too frequently we neglect to look to Jesus for the guidance, comfort, and security he offers to us. In the climax of the Gospel story there are two facets: the calming of the storm and Jesus' question "Why are you so terrified? Why are you lacking in faith?" Is our personal response similar to the disciples' query: "Who can this be that the wind and sea obey him?" Who is this man that we do not really know well enough yet?

Our reflection may well focus on how we have come to recognize God's presence and action in our lives, and acknowledge the power of Jesus as Redeemer and Savior, Protector, Friend, Companion with us.

REFLECTING ON LIFE

In the heat of struggle, in the midst of difficulties, we often rely on our own resources, individually, and feel abandoned, weak or hopeless; sometimes we have experienced the panic of seeing things get out of control. We grasp at whatever may be at hand for help. And often we find all else inadequate that does not lead us to and anchor our trust in God.

Spend some time in individual reflection; then invite participants to move into small groups to share their insights from the following questions:

1. Recall a time when you encountered a "storm" in your life—a time of tension, doubt or difficulty. What was the core problem? How did you first respond? As time went on, did you handle the problem differently?

2. Was there an element of faith or prayer in your response to the situation?

3. Was there an insight or wisdom that you gained through grappling with the problem?

KNOWING OUR FAITH

The event recounted in today's Gospel reading is one that is included in the three Synoptic Gospels. It may be opportune to use a Gospel parallel resource to see the different emphases of the various versions of the story. It would be good to develop a broader understanding of the different Gospels, their historical development, and the authors/communities from which they arose.

The Scriptures form such a central part of our belief, heritage and liturgy that it is advisable to use various opportunities to give participants a better education on the Scriptures. Some simple booklets, for example those published by Channing Bete or Catholic Update, could be selected for use. There are a variety of filmstrips on the formation of Scriptures and of the Gospels in particular that would be a valuable resource. If there is someone in the area who has a strong background in scriptural studies, a presentation might be very helpful, especially for a basic introduction to the Scriptures.

The totality of today's readings and prayers also form a

network, so that connections can be easily made between Hebrew Scriptures and Christian Scriptures. The theme of God's power over the sea threads from Genesis through Job through Psalm 107 (today's responsorial) into the New Testament books. There are numerous other references throughout the Bible to this theme. Participants may begin to see the connections in each Sunday's readings between the Hebrew and Christian Scriptures, and the various changing prayers and psalms incorporated into the liturgies. The sequencing of readings and themes from Sunday to Sunday is also a valuable insight and aid in appreciating the importance of Scripture in our faith development.

Again, if needed, consult your parish or diocesan resource personnel for media, books or other recommendations in developing the "input" for this session.

Doctrinal and Pastoral Issues: Formation of Scriptures, History of the Gospels, Scripture in the Liturgy, Trust in God in Our Lives

Clare M. Colella

INTEGRATION

Throughout his Gospel, Mark emphasizes the message and person of Jesus—"Who is this man?"—as the Son of God, the Anointed One, the Christ. In the Gospel, specifically in today's reading, we sense the mystery that surrounds Jesus, the wonder and the questions that must have been felt by the followers of Jesus. Who is Jesus and how do we come to know him? He is Christ, the Son of God, with power over nature, with compassion for his disciples. We encounter him when we are open to his presence and action in our lives, when we acknowledge that Jesus is our Lord. The logical response to this Gospel story is the segment not written: often asking "Who is this man?" and experiencing the calming of the storm, our response would be: This is surely a man of God. Our statement of faith springs not only from the Gospel but also from our own life's experiences. There are the times when things flow smoothly and we are comfortable with ourselves, our God, our faith. But as a storm arises, we are unsettled. Where is our security, our help? To whom do we turn? God is present, and the storm will calm. Have we been strengthened by the experience? Have we grown in faith and prayer? Do we experience God—or Jesus Christ—as present and close in our lives?

CLOSING PRAYER

Psalm 107 (group reading) or "You Are Near," Dan Schutte, S.J., © 1971 Daniel L. Schutte, S.J. and N.A.L.R.

Introduction to Sundays 13–23 in Ordinary Time

Each catechetical session in this section contains the following parts:

> Looking at Life
> Sharing Your Life
> Knowing Our Faith
> Making the Faith Our Own
> Living Our Faith
> Prayer

Additionally, the *basic message* of the Sunday readings is summarized in a few words. This focuses the session and assists the catechist in planning.

As an aid to prayer, the responsorial psalm of the day is noted at the end of each session. The catechist may wish to expand the prayer time by inviting the catechumens to pray spontaneously, and by summarizing the session with a prayer drawn from additional sources. After the prayer concludes, allow some time for informal discussion and socializing.

The method followed in these sessions moves from experience to tradition to application. In Looking at Life and Sharing Your Life the catechumens are invited to reflect and share on an aspect of their lives that relates to the basic message. In Knowing Our Faith, the group listens again to a reading of the Gospel. Discussion starters are offered to lead the group into a deeper understanding of the Gospel and to appropriate it in Making the Faith Our Own. Living Our Faith suggests directions and possibilities for putting this dimension of faith into practice. Finally, the Doctrinal and Pastoral Issues most relevant to the readings are highlighted.

Thirteenth Sunday in Ordinary Time

Wisdom 1:13–15; 2:23–24
2 Corinthians 8:7–9, 13–15
Mark 5:21–43

BASIC MESSAGE: JESUS' HEALING LIFE-GIVING TOUCH.

The catechist calls the catechumens (and sponsors) together and invites them to sit in a circle. He or she greets them and begins the session.

GATHERING PRAYER

Let us pray. (silence)

Blessed are you, Lord God, for your profound magnanimity. Many times we ignore you and go our own merry way. We forget to thank you. When we run into crises, we faithlessly turn to you as a last resort, when no one else delivers. In your greatness, you do not despise our neglect of you but come to our rescue. Help us, Lord, to recognize you not only in bad times but in good times as well. We make our prayer in the name of Jesus our Lord. Amen.

LOOKING AT LIFE

- Recall a situation in your life experience when you decided that you would never stoop to a certain person for help. Examples might be a doctor, a priest, a business man, a politician not from your party, a neighbor or relative.
- How did you feel toward this person?
- What brought on this negative feeling? this rift?
- Some time after your decision, you had a crisis in your life. The only person who could help you was the person you decided you would never let help you.
- Did you finally ask the person for help?
- How much does it take to swallow pride?
- Were you later grateful and reconciled with that person?

SHARING YOUR LIFE

Read the following statements, reflect, then discuss:

- Why did you initially feel negatively toward this person?
- Why did you think you would never need this person's help?
- Why do people sometimes refuse to let certain other people into their lives—e.g., prejudice, another race, another religion, economic status etc.?
- Why is it important to be open to all people?
- Why do we turn to God when no one else delivers?

KNOWING OUR FAITH

Read, reflect, and dialogue about Mark 5:21–43.

Point out and discuss:

- Jairus, the synogogue official, was a man of great importance and status. He would have looked down upon Jesus as an outsider with dangerous teachings.
- The anguish of Jairus when his child was sick and at the point of death. The girl was twelve years old, the threshold of womanhood. It would have been especially sad to see her die at this age.
- Jairus finds himself in a crisis. The only person left to turn to is Jesus, the man he had avoided with disgust.
- Jairus did not send a messenger to summon Jesus but went himself. Jairus, in his last resort, falls at the feet of Jesus and pleads with him in earnest.

  (a) Jairus forgets his prejudice. No doubt, Jairus saw Jesus as an outsider, a dangerous heretic, a person an orthodox Jew should avoid. Jairus was big enough to abandon his prejudice in an hour of need.
  (b) Jairus forgets his dignity. He, the ruler of the synagogue, falls at the feet of Jesus, the wandering teacher.
  (c) Jairus forgets his pride. It was hard to be indebted to a man he disliked.

- The objection of Jairus' friends to allow Jesus to come.
- The love and humility of Jesus who did not snub Jairus but quickly went with him to see the sick girl.

- With Jesus' life-giving touch and healing words, "Tal-
  itha, kum," he restores the girl to good health.
- The astonishment of those present.
- The human touch of Jesus: "Give her something to
  eat."

MAKING THE FAITH OUR OWN

Read the following statements, reflect, then discuss:

- A person totally ignores you, but when in need of
  help, he or she comes to you demandingly. How will
  you respond?
- You totally ignore a particular person. One day you
  need his or her help. How will you respond?
- Do you believe in the healing word and life-giving
  touch of Jesus?
- Do you believe in the efficacy of the sacrament of the
  anointing of the sick?

LIVING OUR FAITH

Read the following statements, reflect, then discuss and
make a decision:

- What effort will you make to forget your prejudice,
  dignity and pride in the face of human need?
- Will you extend a healing life-giving touch when the
  occasion calls for such an action?
- Will you learn as much as you can about the sacrament of the anointing of the sick?
- When will you start doing these things?

PRAYER

Responsorial Psalm

Psalm 30

℞.   I will praise you, Lord, you have rescued
            me.

I will praise you, Lord, you have rescued me
and have not let my enemies rejoice over me.
O Lord, you have raised my soul from the
      dead,
restored me to life from those who sink into
      the grave. ℞.
Sing psalms to the Lord, you who love him,
give thanks to his holy name.
His anger lasts but a moment; his favor
      through life.

At night there are tears, but joy comes with
      dawn. ℞.
The Lord listened and had pity.
The Lord came to my help.
For me you have changed my mourning into
      dancing.
O Lord my God, I will thank you for ever. ℞.

Spend some time in socializing and informal discussion.

*Doctrinal and Pastoral Issues: Healing, Prejudice and
Pride, The Power of Jesus, The Anointing of the Sick,
Miracles, Reconciliation*

Fr. Michael Koch

Fourteenth Sunday in Ordinary Time

Ezekiel 2:2–5
2 Corinthians 12:7–10
Mark 6:1–6

BASIC MESSAGE: PAIN OF REJECTION

The catechist calls the catechumens (and sponsors) together and invites them to sit in a circle. He or she greets them and begins the session.

GATHERING PRAYER

Let us pray. (silence)

Blessed are you, Lord God, revealer of the universe. You reveal yourself in many ways, but most profoundly in your Son Jesus. When Jesus speaks and we listen, we are led into the mystery of life. Help us, Lord, to be open and receiving. Do not let our fears and pride close our minds and petrify our wills. For unless we accept you at all cost, we cannot enter into eternal life. We make our prayer in the name of Jesus, our Lord. Amen.

LOOKING AT LIFE

– Recall a situation in your life when you had good news and truth to share with enthusiasm, but when you shared it, you were belittled and ignored. Examples might be your insight into social justice, some depth in spirituality, ecumenical development, the virtue of tithing, or inclusion of women.
– Who were these people who rejected you?
– Were they threatened by your good news?
– How did you feel when you started your conversation?
– How did you feel after being ignored?
– What do you think of these people now?
– What did you do after being ignored?

SHARING YOUR LIFE

Read the following statements, reflect, then discuss:

– Why did these people reject you?

– Why did they think you were too insignificant, too ordinary to have anything worthwhile to say?
– Why did the good news and truth threaten them?
– Why could they not see the extraordinary in the ordinary?
– Why was Jesus not accepted in his home town?

KNOWING OUR FAITH

Read, reflect, and dialogue about Mark 6:1–6.

Point out and discuss:

– When Jesus came to Nazareth, he did not come as a private visitor to see old friends and familiar sights, but as a rabbi with his disciples.
– Jesus' profound teachings in the synagogue were not received with wonder, but with a kind of contempt. They could not believe that this workingman had become a big shot.
– The people of Nazareth did not accept him because:

 (a) "This is the carpenter." They could not see how an ordinary workingman like themselves could become so sophisticated.
 (b) "Is not this Mary's son?" Jesus lived in Nazareth for some thirty years. People would have known him well. His being referred to as "Mary's son" shows that Joseph probably had died some time ago. It could also be a term of contempt.

– Jesus' amazement at their lack of faith.
– The early Christian community would have treasured this pericope. After they were converted to Christianity, they would have gone back to their Jewish or pagan friends. They would have been rejected and regarded as "holier than thou." Reflecting back on Jesus' rejection would have brought them some comfort.

– Read and enjoy Ezekiel 2:2–5.

MAKING THE FAITH OUR OWN

Read the following statements, reflect, then discuss:

– Do you believe you can be a sign of belief in an environment of disbelief?
– When you are rejected can you identify with Jesus'

rejection in his home town?
- Do you believe that you, with the grace of God, can continue to be a witness for Christ even if it hurts?

LIVING OUR FAITH

Read the following statements, reflect, then discuss and make a decision:

- Will you continue to live a Christian life even in the midst of rejection?
- Will you be able to relate positively with those who belittle you?
- How will you deal with your old non-believing friends?
- To whom will you turn for support?

PRAYER

Responsorial Psalm

Psalm 123

℞.   Our eyes are on the Lord till he show us
        his mercy.

To you have I lifted up my eyes,
you who dwell in the heavens:
my eyes, like the eyes of slaves
on the hand of their lords. ℞.
Like the eyes of a servant
on the hand of her mistress,
so our eyes are on the Lord our God
till he show us his mercy. ℞.
Have mercy on us, Lord, have mercy.
We are filled with contempt.
Indeed all too full is our soul
with the scorn of the rich,
with the proud man's disdain. ℞.

Spend time in socializing and informal discussion.

Doctrinal and Pastoral Issues: Divinity and Humanity of Christ, Discipleship, Pain of Rejection, Witness, Truth

Fr. Michael Koch

Fifteenth Sunday in Ordinary Time

Amos 7:12–15
Ephesians 1:3–14
Mark 6:7–13

BASIC MESSAGE: CALL TO MINISTRY

The catechist calls the catechumens (and sponsors) together and invites them to sit in a circle. He or she greets them and begins the session.

GATHERING PRAYER

Let us pray. (silence)

O Lord our God, how wonderful are your works. You always bring good news into our lives. Often we are fearful of what you offer us. Blindly we reject what is good for us. You have invited us to bring good news to others, to be your messengers. Help us to be faithful like the Twelve; help us to bring your good news to others, even at the point of rejection. We make our prayer in the name of Jesus our Lord. Amen.

LOOKING AT LIFE

– Recall a time in your life when you were called to participate in some money-raising enterprise. It may have been for your parish, a service club, or some tragedy. Its purpose was to enhance the lives of a certain group of people.
– What was your first response to the call?
– Did you agree to participate?
– Did you go from door to door in pairs?
– Did you find asking for money a hard thing to do?
– What was it that kept you motivated?
– What was the authority of those who called you?
– How did people respond to your request?
– What would have been the consequences had you not participated?

SHARING YOUR LIFE

Read the following statements, reflect, then discuss:

– Why did you agree or not agree to participate in this project?
– Why was it better to go in pairs?
– Why is asking for money such a hard thing to do for most people?
– Why did you continue even when you were rebuffed?
– Why did Jesus send out the Twelve?
– Why did Jesus instruct the Twelve to travel light?

KNOWING OUR FAITH

Read, reflect, and dialogue about Mark 6:7–13. Point out and discuss:

– Jesus has been teaching and forming the Twelve. Now he sends them out on mission. The Twelve are sent out in pairs. This is for two very good reasons: one is for mutual support; the second is that the two can "sacramentalize" before the non-believer the love which they are preaching. This provides the non-believer with a greater opportunity to believe.
– The Twelve are to travel light. Too many material possessions become an obstacle to effective ministry. They are to take only staff and sandals, nothing else, nothing extra. They take with them the authority and power which Jesus gives them. The Twelve are to trust that all other needs will be met by the people to whom they preach the good news.
– The Twelve are to accept the hospitality which was offered.
– In the East, hospitality was a sacred duty. When a stranger came to a village it was not his duty to search for hospitality; it was the duty of the village to provide it.
– The Twelve are to preach repentance. They did not ask the people for money for a good cause, but they told them they must change their lives. The good news they brought was clearly disturbing news, news which challenged the hearer's life style. They were called to repent, to change their heart and change their actions. The good news was painful. Changing from vice to virtue, from sin to grace is always painful. Usually in order to alleviate this pain, the messenger is belittled and rejected.
– The Twelve, despite many rejections, had a high degree of success. Many people unhappy with their lives were open to conversion, to repentance.

MAKING THE FAITH OUR OWN

Read the following statements, reflect, then discuss:

- Which is the harder task, to ask people for money, or to ask them to change their way of life?
- How did you respond when you were asked to inquire into the Catholic Church?
- How did this person approach you?
- Why were you willing to accept this invitation?
- Have "devils" been cast out of your life, have you experienced healing, because you have accepted the good news into your life?

LIVING OUR FAITH

Read the following statements, reflect, then discuss and make a decision:

- Do you feel called to bring this good news to others?
- How enthusiastic would you be if you were sent to bring this good news to others?
- Do you think you are adequately prepared at this point?
- How hard will you work to prepare yourself to participate in the mission of Jesus?
- Will you try to learn as much as you can about how leadership in the Church has been developed and exercised?
- Will you study about the sacrament of holy orders?
- Will you study the variety of ministries found in the Church today?

PRAYER

Responsorial Psalm

Psalm 84

℞.   Let us see, O Lord, your mercy
        and give us your saving help.

I will hear what the Lord God has to say,
a voice that speaks of peace,
peace for his people.
His help is near for those who fear him
and his glory will dwell in our land. ℞.
Mercy and faithfulness have met;
justice and peace have embraced.
Faithfulness shall spring from the earth
and justice look down from heaven. ℞.
The Lord will make us prosper
and our earth shall yield its fruit.
Justice shall march before him
and peace shall follow his steps. ℞.

You may wish to sing an appropriate hymn.

Spend some time in socializing and informal discussion.

Pastoral and Doctrinal Issues: Christian Call to Mission, Discipleship, Holy Orders, Ministry in the Church, Stewardship

Fr. Michael Koch

Sixteenth Sunday in Ordinary Time

Jeremiah 23:1–6
Ephesians 2:13–18
Mark 6:30–34

BASIC MESSAGE: THE COMPASSION OF JESUS

The catechist calls the catechumens (and sponsors) together and invites them to sit in a circle. He or she greets them and begins the session.

GATHERING PRAYER

Let us pray. (silence)

Blessed are you, Lord God, immortal King. You gave us David, shepherd become king. You sent us Jesus, eternal king become shepherd. In his compassion he teaches us compassion. Help us, Lord, to learn compassion by putting us with suffering people, with elderly people, with lonely people. For it is in exercising compassion that we learn compassion. We make our prayer in the name of Jesus our Lord and God. Amen.

LOOKING AT LIFE

– Recall a time when you had done a long day's work and you were very tired. The telephone rang. Someone at the other end of the line (a relative, friend, parishioner or client) needed help—for example, someone in a family may have died, a marriage has broken-up, someone has economic problems, a person discovers a close friend is taking drugs.
– In your tiredness, how did you feel about this request for help?
– In your tiredness, what did you do:

  • Did you say you were too sick to help?
  • Did you send someone else—e.g., your spouse who was equally tired?
  • Did you go yourself?

– How did you feel after you hung up the phone?

SHARING YOUR LIFE

Read the following statements, reflect, then discuss:

– Why did you respond in the way you did?
– Why would you describe yourself as a compassionate person?
– Why would you describe yourself as lacking compassion?
– Why would you show compassion:

  • to yourself first?
  • to other needy persons first?

– Why did Jesus show compassion:

  • to the tired apostles?
  • to the needy crowd?

KNOWING OUR FAITH

Read, reflect, and dialogue about Mark 6:30–34.

Point out and discuss:

– The excitement of the apostles to share with Jesus and each other what "they had done and taught."
– What might these stories have sounded like?
– The cost of serving in the mission ("the apostles had no time even to eat").
– The compassion of Jesus when he saw the tired apostles. He tells them: "You must come away to some lonely place all by yourselves and rest for a while."
– The deep need of the many who were coming and going.
– The compassion of Jesus toward the crowd, who "were like sheep without a shepherd."
– The love of the tired Jesus, who set about the task "to teach them at some length."
– The reprimand of the shepherds in Jeremiah 23:1–6.

MAKING THE FAITH OUR OWN

Read the following statements, reflect, then discuss:

– Jesus is the model of compassion. How well developed is your compassion?
– When you exercise compassion, do you have a healthy balance between compassion for yourself and compassion for others?
– When do you believe you come first? others come first?
– How does an employer balance compassion toward employees with compassion toward the customers?

LIVING OUR FAITH

Read the following statements, reflect, then discuss and make a decision:

– What effort will you make to develop the virtue of compassion in your life?
– When will you start making this effort?
– To whom will you turn to help you develop this virtue of compassion?
– Will your love and admiration for Jesus increase because of his compassion?
– Will you be pleasantly compassionate toward others even if you are tired?
– Will you visit a suffering person this week?

PRAYER

Responsorial Psalm

Psalm 23

℞.   The Lord is my shepherd;
          there is nothing I shall want.

The Lord is my shepherd;
there is nothing I shall want.
Fresh and green are the pastures
where he gives me repose.
Near restful waters he leads me,
to revive my drooping spirit. ℞.
He guides me along the right path;
he is true to his name.
If I should walk in the valley of darkness
no evil would I fear.
You are there with your crook and your staff;
with these you give me comfort. ℞.
You have prepared a banquet for me
in the sight of my foes.
My head you have anointed with oil;
my cup is overflowing. ℞.
Surely goodness and kindness shall follow me
all the days of my life.
In the Lord's own house shall I dwell
for ever and ever. ℞.

You may prefer to sing "The Lord's My Shepherd," Catholic Book of Worship II #689.

Spend some time in socializing and informal discussion.

Pastoral and Doctrinal Issues: The Compassion of God, Love for Others, Christian Justice, Suffering

Fr. Michael Koch

Seventeenth Sunday in Ordinary Time

2 Kings 4:42–44
Ephesians 4:1–6
John 6:1–15

BASIC MESSAGE: FEEDING THE HUNGRY—PHYSICAL BREAD

The catechist calls the catechumens (and sponsors) together and invites them to sit in a circle. He or she greets them and begins the session.

GATHERING PRAYER

Let us pray. (silence)

Blessed are you, O Lord our God, who cause bread to come forth from the earth. May you who once miraculously fed five thousand continue to teach us that in sharing our resources wisely and generously, you can feed all the hungry on earth. We make our prayer in the name of Jesus our Lord. Amen.

LOOKING AT LIFE

– Were you ever in a situation where there was not enough food to go around—a family situation, a social function, a disaster problem, a third world country?
– Were there pessimists who complained of the shortage?
– Were there optimists who generated alternative ideas?
– Were there those preoccupied with number one?
– What finally happened at that event?

SHARING YOUR LIFE

Read the following statements, reflect, then discuss.

– Why is there a constant anxiety about running out of resources?
– Why are some people pessimists?
– Why are some people optimists?
– Why do some people hoard rather than share?
– Why does Philip represent pessimists?
– Why does Andrew represent optimists?
– Why did Jesus work this miracle?

KNOWING OUR FAITH

Read, reflect and dialogue about John 6:1–15

Point out and discuss:

– The circumstances of the story.
– Many of the crowd were probably pilgrims on their way to Jerusalem to celebrate the Passover.
– Philip, a native of Bethsaida, was the natural person to ask where food could be found.
– Barley bread was the cheapest of all bread and was held in contempt.
– The fish were probably pickled and no larger than sardines.
– Philip's pessimism and Andrew's optimism: Who had the real faith?
– Three possible interpretations of the event:

   (a) Jesus in a miraculous way multiplied the loaves and the fish.
   (b) It may have been a sacramental meal. Each person ate only a morsel. The language of Jesus is the language of the Last Supper. The satisfaction came from recognizing God in Jesus. The morsels of bread became the symbol through which Jesus touched the people's hearts and souls.
   (c) The people, if they were pilgrims, probably had some food with them. They probably, because of fear of scarcity, did not want to share, but keep all for themselves. Jesus, because of his attitude of gratitude and sharing, moved the others to do likewise. Then there was not only enough for all, but there were twelve baskets left over.

– The desire of the selfish, narcissistic dependency of some people to only reach and take Jesus exclusively for themselves.
– The desire of Jesus to be free to give himself to everyone.
– Read and enjoy the first reading, 2 Kings 4:42–44.

MAKING THE FAITH OUR OWN

Read the following statements, reflect, then discuss:

- Are you anxious that resources like food, petroleum, timber, clean air and clean water will soon run out?
- Do you, like Philip, believe that the gap between resources and need is so big that final shut-down is imminent?
- Do you believe, like Jesus, that our God is a resourcing God who cares for his children?
- Do you believe that all the world is for all the people?
- Do you believe that if we share freely, there will be enough for all?
- Do you believe that global social justice is possible?

LIVING OUR FAITH

Read the following statements, reflect, then discuss:

- Are you prepared to surrender your "five barley loaves and two fish" to Jesus and let him multiply them to satisfy many?
- Are you willing to experience deeper conversion from hoarding to giving?
- What is the cost of this new attitude of sharing?
- When are you going to begin?
- Who will be your support in this conversion?

PRAYER

"God does not ask about our ability or inability but our availability."

Responsorial Psalm

Psalm 145

℟.   You open wide your hand, O Lord,
            and grant our desires.

All your creatures shall thank you, O Lord,
and your friends shall repeat their blessing.
They shall speak of the glory of your reign
and declare your might, O God. ℟.
The eyes of all creatures look to you
and you give them their food in due time.
You open wide your hand,
grant the desires of all who live. ℟.
The Lord is just in all his ways
and loving in all his deeds.
He is close to all who call him,
who call on him from their hearts. ℟.

Spend some time in socializing and informal discussion.

Doctrinal and Pastoral Issues: Eucharist, Social Justice, Responsibility to the Poor, World Hunger, Corporal Works of Mercy, Poverty

Fr. Michael Koch

Eighteenth Sunday in Ordinary Time

Exodus 16:2–4, 12–15
Ephesians 4:17, 20–24
John 6:24–35

BASIC MESSAGE: FEEDING THE HUNGRY— SPIRITUAL BREAD

The catechist calls the catechumens (and sponsors) together and invites them to sit in a circle. He or she greets them and begins the session.

GATHERING PRAYER

Let us pray. (silence)

O Lord our God, we come before you in mystery. Free us from the temptation to settle into the comfortable pew. Help us to transcend the various gods we are tempted to adore and lay down our lives for. Help us to realize as St. Augustine did many centuries ago that "our hearts are made for you, O Lord, and they shall not rest until they rest in you." We make our prayer in the name of Jesus, our Lord.

LOOKING AT LIFE

- Name some passing thing into which you deeply invested your whole self. Examples might be saving for a car, career, making money, sports champion, education, physical pleasure, etc.
- Were you tempted to act immorally to serve this purpose?
- Did you step on other people to serve this god?
- Did this god you served initially bring you happiness?
- Was there a time you outgrew your god?
- Were you happy?
- Where did you turn next?

SHARING YOUR LIFE

Read the following statements, reflect, then discuss:

- Why did you begin to worship (serve) this particular god?
- Why did you soften your morals to serve this god?

- Why did this god not bring you ultimate happiness?
- Why did your peers try to convince you not to give up serving this god?
- Why did you outgrow your god?
- Why did Jesus say, "Do not work for food that cannot last, but work for food that endures to eternal life"?

KNOWING OUR FAITH

Read, reflect, and dialogue about John 6:24–35. Point out and discuss:

- How Jesus got from Bethsaida to Capernaum.
- The desire of the people for Jesus to give them more physical food.
- The effort of Jesus to lead the people from preoccupation with physical bread to eternal life.
- The teaching of Jesus, "This is working for God: You must believe in the one he has sent."
- The resistance of the people to believe in Jesus.
- The effort of Jesus to bring about conversion from preoccupation with Moses and manna in the desert in the past to "It is my Father who gives you bread from heaven" now.
- When the people were open and ready to accept this new bread, Jesus said, "I am the bread of life. He who comes to me will never be hungry; He who believes in me will never thirst."

MAKING THE FAITH OUR OWN

Read the following statements, reflect, then discuss:

- How big is the gap between your "gods" and "I am the bread of life"?
- Do you believe that Jesus is the incarnation of God?
- Do you believe that the fullness of life can only be found in Jesus?
- Do you believe it is necessary to feed on Jesus?

LIVING OUR FAITH

Read the following statements, reflect, then discuss:

- Are you ready to throw in your lot with Jesus, the bread of life?

– If not, when will you be ready?
– What is the cost of conversion, the cost of discipleship?
– Who will support you in your conversion?

PRAYER

"Our hearts were made for you, O Lord, and they shall not rest until they rest in you."

Responsorial Psalm:

Psalm 78

℞.   The Lord gave them bread from heaven.

The things we have heard and understood,
the things our fathers have told us,
we will tell to the next generation:
the glories of the Lord and his might. ℞.
He commanded the clouds above
and opened the gates of heaven.
He rained down manna for their food,
and gave them bread from heaven. ℞.
Mere men ate the bread of angels.
He sent them abundance of food.
He brought them to his holy land,
to the mountain which his right hand had
      won. ℞.

Spend some time in socializing and informal discussion.

Pastoral and Doctrinal Issues: Worship, Eucharist, Incarnation and Conversion, Economic Pastoral, Greed, False Gods

Fr. Michael Koch

Nineteenth Sunday in Ordinary Time

1 Kings 9:4–8
Ephesians 4:30—5:2
John 6:41–51

BASIC MESSAGE: THE EUCHARIST—CHRIST REALLY PRESENT

The catechist calls the catechumens (and sponsors) together and invites them to sit in a circle. He or she greets them and begins the session.

GATHERING PRAYER

Let us pray. (silence)

Blessed are you, Lord God, for your marvelous love for us. You revealed your divinity through flesh and blood, our humanity. In the mysterious hypostatic union in Jesus we experience your closeness, our solidarity with our everlasting God. Help us, O Lord, to recognize your real presence in the Eucharist. We make our prayer in the name of Jesus, our Lord. Amen.

LOOKING AT LIFE

– Recall a situation where you did a kind deed for someone and later that person spread stories accusing you of false motivations.
– How did you feel when you did the kind act?
– How did you feel when you heard the misinterpretations of your kind act: toward yourself? toward the other?
– Did you try to convince the non-believer of your genuine intention?
– Did the person change his or her view or remain obstinate?

SHARING YOUR LIFE

Read the following statements, reflect, then discuss:

– Why are people so prone to judge from mere externals?
– Why do so many people find it so hard to accept new evidence once they have made up their mind?

– Why is it so hard to accept greatness in the ordinary?
– Why could the Jews not accept Jesus' verbalization of his internal identity, "I am the bread that came down from heaven"?
– Why did the Jews keep on harping about Jesus' external identity?

KNOWING OUR FAITH

Read, reflect, and dialogue about John 6:41–51.

Point out and discuss:

– The big contrast between where Jesus was coming from and where his listeners were coming from.
– Jesus was speaking from his inner identity, his divine dimension.
– The Jews were speaking from Jesus' external identity, his human dimension.
– The Jews, because they saw and believed only in the external (the human) in Jesus, rejected the internal (the divine) and hence in rejecting Jesus rejected eternal life.
– As long as the Jews were complaining or murmuring they could not be disposed to hear what Jesus was really saying.
– The Jews resisted the "drawing by the Father" because of lack of faith.
– The manna in the desert was physical food for the body. What Jesus is giving is spiritual food bonding the person to the Father.

MAKING THE FAITH OUR OWN

Read the following statements, reflect, then discuss:

– The Jews judged Jesus on externals only. They could not see how a poor ordinary carpenter, "whose father and mother we know," could be a special messenger from God. Where do you stand in this regard?
– Do you believe that when Jesus said, "I am the bread that came down from heaven," he was revealing his divine identity?
– Do you believe Jesus is truly man and truly God?
– Do you believe that Jesus is really present in the Eucharist?
– As the divinity of Jesus was hidden and manifested in his humanity, so the whole Jesus, human and divine,

is hidden in the consecrated bread and wine, the
Holy Eucharist. Does this belief fill you with awe and
reverence?
- Do you believe Jesus' words: "The bread that I shall
give is my flesh, for the life of the world"?

LIVING OUR FAITH

Read the following statements, reflect, then discuss:

- Will you make sure to participate every Sunday in the
eucharistic liturgy?
- Will you receive Holy Communion with reverence?
- (For catechumens) Will you diligently participate in
the liturgy of the word in order to prepare yourselves
for the Eucharist?
- Will you make an effort not to judge from externals
only?
- With whom will you share this good news?

PRAYER

Most of us are not called to do extraordinary things but
to do ordinary things extraordinarily well.

Responsorial Psalm

Psalm 34

℞.   Taste and see that the Lord is good.

I will bless the Lord at all times,
his praise always on my lips;
in the Lord my soul shall make its boast.
The humble shall hear and be glad. ℞.
Glorify the Lord with me.
Together let us praise his name.
I sought the Lord and he answered me;
from all my terrors he set me free. ℞.
Look toward him and be radiant;
let your faces not be abashed.
This poor man called; the Lord heard him
and rescued him from all his distress. ℞.
The angel of the Lord is encamped
around those who revere him, to rescue them.
Taste and see that the Lord is good.
He is happy who seeks refuge in him. ℞.

Spend some time in socializing and informal discussion.

*Pastoral and Doctrinal Issues: Humanity and Divinity
of Christ, Eucharistic Presence, Liturgy and Spirituality*

Fr. Michael Koch

Twentieth Sunday in Ordinary Time

Proverbs 9:1–6
Ephesians 5:15–20
John 6:51–58

BASIC MESSAGE: THE EUCHARIST—THE NECESSITY OF COMMUNION

The catechist calls the catechumens (and sponsors) together and invites them to sit in a circle. He or she greets them and begins the session.

GATHERING PRAYER

Let us pray. (silence)

O Lord our God, we hunger and thirst for union with you. Without you we are nothing, nothing but emptiness wandering in the desert. We bow before you in gratitude for giving us your Son Jesus. Jesus in turn gives us his flesh and blood to be our bread of life. Help us, Lord, to recognize your presence in the Eucharist and eat you in Communion. Through this faith-filled act you lead us to eternal life. We make our prayer in the name of Jesus, our Lord. Amen.

LOOKING AT LIFE

- Recall an experience in your life where you had a deep desire to be intimate or one with a person whom you loved. This may be a spouse, a friend or Jesus.
- Describe the experience, the feeling of longing.
- Do you feel nurtured by this communion?
- What happens to you when you experience this nurturing?
- What would happen to you if this communion was destroyed?

SHARING YOUR LIFE

Read the following statements, reflect, then discuss:

- Why do you have this desire for union with another?
- Why does such a union nurture you?
- Why are many people afraid of such a close union?

- Why is communion necessary for life?
- Why are you happy and at peace when you enjoy such communion?
- Why did Jesus desire to give himself as living bread to be eaten?

KNOWING OUR FAITH

Read, reflect, and dialogue about John 6:51–58

Point out and discuss:

- Jesus describes himself as the bread of life.
- Jesus identifies "the bread of life" with his flesh and blood.
- The "living bread" equals "the body and blood of the Lord."
- The Jews argue among themselves. The Jews continue to understand what Jesus says on a different level than what Jesus means.
- When Jesus says, "For my flesh is real food and my blood is real drink. He who eats my flesh and drinks my blood lives in me and I live in him," he is referring to his whole self. The Jews understand Jesus' teaching in a cannibalistic sense.
- For the Jews blood stands for life. Blood was never eaten; it belonged to God. For a Jew to consume blood was unthinkable, yet Jesus is saying that unless you consume life, you cannot have life.
- The bread our ancestors ate (manna) was earthly bread; it gave only temporary physical life.
- The bread which Jesus gives (himself) is spiritual bread; he gives eternal spiritual life.
- If you want life, you must come and sit at that table where you can eat that broken bread and drink that poured-out wine which somehow, by the grace of God, brings you into contact with the love and the life of Jesus Christ.
- John has no account of the Last Supper.

MAKING THE FAITH OUR OWN

Read the following statements, reflect, then discuss:

- Do you believe that Communion with Jesus is necessary for Christian and eternal life?
- Do you believe that whenever a Catholic Eucharist is

celebrated, the bread and wine become the body and blood of Jesus, that Jesus himself is present?
- Do you believe that after Communion in a eucharistic liturgy, Jesus is present in a new way in all those who have partaken in Communion?
- Do you believe that Jesus nourishes us in Communion?
- What do you believe about Communion in our sister churches?

LIVING OUR FAITH

Read the following statements, reflect, then discuss:

- Will you do all you can to prepare yourself to worthily commune with Jesus in the Eucharist?
- Are you able to truly rejoice in the teaching of Jesus, as understood in the Catholic Church?
- Will you engage in ecumenical healing?
- Does the dismissal, before the liturgy of the Eucharist, make your heart grow fonder?
- Will you spend time praying about this sacred matter?

PRAYER

Responsorial Psalm

Psalm 34

℞.   Taste and see that the Lord is good.

I will bless the Lord at all times,
his praise always on my lips;
in the Lord my soul shall make its boast.
The humble shall hear and be glad. ℞.
Revere the Lord, you his saints.
They lack nothing, those who revere him.
Strong lions suffer want and go hungry
but those who seek the Lord lack no blessing.
    ℞.
Come, children, and hear me,
Who is he who longs for life
and many days, to enjoy his prosperity? ℞.
Then keep your tongue from evil
and your lips from speaking deceit.
Turn aside from evil and do good;
seek and strive after peace. ℞.

Spend some time in socializing and informal discussion.

Pastoral and Doctrinal Issues: Eucharist, Prayer, Ecumenism

Fr. Michael Koch

Twenty-First Sunday in Ordinary Time

Joshua 24:1–2, 15–17, 18
Ephesians 5:21–32
John 6:60–69

BASIC MESSAGE: THE EUCHARIST—CHALLENGE TO FAITH

The catechist calls the catechumens (and sponsors) together and invites them to sit in a circle. He or she greets them and begins the session.

GATHERING PRAYER

Let us pray. (silence)

O Lord our God, with folded arms we stand puzzled before your mystery. Your profound teaching is beyond our understanding. With disbelief and criticism we judge your revelation. Heavenly Father, open our minds and soften our wills. Help us to accept you without understanding, eat you with trust, and, with our arms open to you, be led to eternal life. We make our prayer in the name of Jesus our Lord. Amen.

LOOKING AT LIFE

– Recall some of the teachings of the Church which the media and many others have trouble with, e.g., birth control, abortion, divorce, celibacy, ordination of women, etc.
– How do you feel toward these teachings?
– What do you think of these teachings after you have examined both sides?
– Is there a materialistic and spiritual way of looking at these questions?
– To what do these teachings challenge you?
– What kind of faith is required to accept these teachings?

SHARING YOUR LIFE

Read the following statements, reflect, then discuss:

– Why are the media and so many others so puzzled by these teachings?

– Why do so many say, "This is intolerable language. How could anyone accept it?"
– Why do so many people leave and no longer walk with the Church?
– Why is it so hard to accept something which we cannot easily analyze and understand?
– Why did Jesus not back down on his teaching, "I am the bread of life"?

KNOWING OUR FAITH

Read, reflect, and dialogue about John 6:60–69.

Point out and discuss:

– "This is intolerable language. How could anyone accept it?"
– The complaining of Jesus' followers.
– The allusion to the ascension, "What if you should see the Son of Man ascend to where he was before?"
– "It is the spirit that gives life; the flesh has nothing to offer." Flesh here does not refer to eucharistic flesh, but mere material flesh.
– "Many of his disciples left him and stopped going with him." They left for several reasons.

   (a) There was defection. Some saw Jesus, in challenging the authorities, on his way to disaster. They were getting out in time. Others came to get something from Jesus. When it came time to suffer for him they quit.
   (b) There was deterioration. This is the gradual deterioration of some in their relationship to Jesus. Judas was a prime example.

– In time ideals, enthusiasm, dreams and loyalties weakened and disappeared.
– The loyal response of the Twelve, verbalized by Peter. Peter was as bewildered and puzzled as anyone else. He also did not understand. Peter, because he loved Jesus, accepted his teaching. There was nowhere else to go.

MAKING THE FAITH OUR OWN

Read the following statements, reflect, then discuss:

– How well can you accept the eucharistic teaching of

Jesus? Can you believe without understanding?
- If you do not accept the teaching of Jesus, do you have somewhere else to go?
- Do you believe the teaching of the Church, even if you do not agree or understand?
- Do you believe that the teaching of the Church today about the Eucharist is congruent with the teaching of Jesus?

LIVING OUR FAITH

Read the following statements, reflect, then discuss and make a decision:

- Read and enjoy Joshua 24:1–2, 15–17, 18.
- Are you able to say with Joshua, "As for me and my house, we will serve the Lord"?
- Will you make an effort to study the teaching of the Church and see why particular positions are held?
- With whom will you share your beliefs?

PRAYER

"Faith opens the door to understanding, unbelief closes it."

(St. Augustine of Hippo)

"Belief is a truth held in the mind. Faith is a fire in the heart."

Responsorial Psalm

Psalm 34

℞.　　　　　Taste and see that the Lord is good.

I will bless the Lord all times,
his praise always on my lips;
in the Lord my soul shall make its boast.
The humble shall hear and be glad. ℞.
The Lord turns his face against the wicked
to destroy their remembrance from the earth.
The Lord turns his eyes to the just
and his ears to their appeal. ℞.
They call and the Lord hears
and rescues them in all their distress.
The Lord is close to the broken-hearted;
those whose spirit is crushed he will save. ℞.
Many are the trials of the just man
but from them all the Lord will rescue him.
He will keep guard over all his bones,
not one of his bones shall be broken. ℞.
Evil brings death to the wicked;
those who hate the good are doomed.
The Lord ransoms the souls of his servants.

Those who hide in him shall not be condemned. ℞.

Spend some time in socializing and informal discussion.

Pastoral and Doctrinal Issues: Dogma, Eucharist, Relationship with the Lord and Moral Decision-Making, Why People Leave the Church and Why People Return to the Church

Fr. Michael Koch

Twenty-Second Sunday in Ordinary Time

Deuteronomy 4:1–2, 6–8
James 1:17–18, 21–22, 27
Mark 7:1–8, 14–15, 21–23

BASIC MESSAGE: EXTERNAL PRACTICES AND INTERNAL FAITH

The catechist calls the catechumens (and sponsors) together and invites them to sit in a circle. He or she greets them and begins the session.

GATHERING PRAYER

Let us pray. (silence)

O Lord our God, we marvel at your creation. Everything we observe grows from inside out, plants, animals and humans. Anything plastered on from the outside is artificial. Jesus has clearly taught us that good and evil come from within us, from the heart. Help us, Lord, to drink deeply of your word, so that we may undergo internal conversion, and then manifest your goodness in human flesh. We make our prayer in the name of Jesus our Lord and Savior. Amen.

LOOKING AT LIFE

– Recall an event where there was more concern over an external law or practice than internal faith and love—e.g., going to Mass when one is too sick to get out of bed, because "I haven't missed Mass in twenty years"; smiling at and greeting someone upon whom you secretly wish evil; fear of missing one of nine First Fridays, but never going to Mass on Sundays; still going to bed with your teddy bear when you are twenty years old.
– How did you get started following this external law, rite or ritual?
– For how long have you been doing this external practice?
– Do you know how this law, rite or ritual got started?
– If you have not outgrown this external practice, do you plan to change?
– Do you understand the role of habit in this practice?

– What does this contradiction do to your personal integrity?
– Would you like to jettison some of your external behavior?

SHARING YOUR LIFE

Read the following statements, reflect, then discuss:

– External laws, rites and rituals (personal or religious) in their beginning are usually an expression of some internal spirit or value. As one goes on in life one usually outgrows these laws, rites and rituals. Why is it so difficult to let go of these external practices even if they are meaningless and outdated?
– Why is it important to know the origin of these laws, rites and rituals?
– Why does habit play such an important role?
– Why is it important to know something of the psychology of fixation?
– Why did Jesus reprimand the Pharisees and scribes about their external practices?

KNOWING OUR FAITH

Read, reflect, and dialogue about Mark 7:1–8, 14–15, 21–23. Point out and discuss:

– The scene between the Pharisees and scribes, Jesus and his disciples.
– The Jewish purification rituals, including the washing of hands, sprinkling, and the washing of different dishes and utensils.
– The disgust that the Pharisees and scribes felt toward Jesus for allowing his disciples to ignore these "traditions of the elders."
– The strong language of Jesus calling the Pharisees and scribes hypocrites.
– The words of Isaiah quoted by Jesus: "This people honors me only with lip-service, while their hearts are far from me. The worship they offer me is worthless, the doctrines they teach are only human regulations."
– Jesus points out to the Pharisees and scribes that they have forgotten the essentials because they are so preoccupied with the peripheral: "You put aside the commandments of God to cling to human traditions."

- Jesus teaches that cleanliness comes from the heart, i.e., what comes out of a man, not what goes into a man. "For it is from within, from men's hearts, that evil intentions emerge."
- The various evil things mentioned which come from within, from the heart of man or women: "Fornication, theft, murder, adultery, avarice, malice, deceit, indecency, envy, slander, pride, folly."

MAKING THE FAITH OUR OWN

Read the following statements, reflect, then discuss:

- Where are you at in regard to your own personal integrity?
- Do you believe that external religious practices without internal conviction are worthless?
- Do you believe that external religious practices with internal conviction but far removed from Jesus, his teaching, and the core of Christianity are also worthless?
- Do you believe that evil like good comes from the heart, grows there and finally manifests itself externally?
- Do you believe that authentic teaching and external practices can penetrate the heart and change it into a new heart which in turn is externalized?

LIVING OUR FAITH

Read the following statements, reflect, then discuss and make a decision:

- Will you make an effort to find out which teachings in the Church are essentially Christian and which are Church regulations which can be changed from time to time?
- If some practices in the Church are not authentically Christian, will you help to change them?
- Will you examine your own life and see what religious practices you need to jettison to make you more authentically Christian?
- When will you start this work?
- Who will help you to be a more authentic Christian?

PRAYER

Responsorial Psalm

Psalm 15

℟.   Lord, who shall be admitted to your tent?

Lord, who shall dwell on your holy mountain?

He who walks without fault;
he who acts with justice
and speaks the truth from his heart;
he who does not slander with his tongue. ℟.
He who does no wrong to his brother,
who casts no slur on his neighbor,
who holds the godless in disdain,
but honors those who fear the Lord. ℟.
He who takes no interest on a loan
and accepts no bribes against the innocent,
such a man will stand firm for ever. ℟.

You might close with one of the following hymns or some other hymn:

"The House Built on the Rock," Glory and Praise #200.

"They'll Know We Are Christians," Catholic Book of Worship II #694.

Spend some time in socializing and informal discussion.

Pastoral and Dogmatic Issues: Christian Growth, Spirituality, Church Laws and Religious Practices, Rites and Rituals, Church Authority, Dissent, Tradition

Fr. Michael Koch

Twenty-Third Sunday in Ordinary Time

Isaiah 35:4–7
James 2:1–5
Mark 7:31–37

BASIC MESSAGE: HEALED TO HEAR AND PROCLAIM

The catechist calls the catechumens (and sponsors) together and invites them to sit in a circle. He or she greets them and begins the session.

GATHERING PRAYER

Let us pray. (silence)

O Lord our God, you are the marvelous inventor of human communication. You gave us mouths with which to speak and ears with which to listen and learn. Through such communication we can share ourselves with others. Through some defect of tongue or ear, many people are left out of many aspects of human community. Heal them, Lord, of their handicap. Heal us, O Lord, who are spiritually deaf, so that we may hear your holy word and then proclaim it with enthusiasm. We make our prayer in the name of Jesus our Lord. Amen.

LOOKING AT LIFE

– Recall some experience in your life that had to do with deaf persons. Amplify and share that experience.
– How did you feel in the presence of this deaf person or persons?
– How well were these people able to speak?
– What was the quality of your communication with them?
– Describe how you think they felt in a social gathering?
– How do you think these handicapped could be helped?
– How are these handicapped helping us?

SHARING OUR LIFE

Read the following statements, reflect, then discuss:

– Why is it difficult for a person to speak correctly when he or she cannot hear or hear correctly?
– Why do so many people embarrassingly turn away from a person who is deaf?
– Why are people usually more blunt with the deaf than with other handicapped persons?
– Why was Jesus so compassionate toward the deaf man with a speech impediment?

KNOWING OUR FAITH

Read, reflect, and dialogue about Mark 7:31–37.

Point out and discuss:

– The journey of Jesus is from Tyre, by way of Sidon toward the Sea of Galilee through the Decapolis region. "By way of Sidon" means going north to get to the south.
– The sensitivity of Jesus toward the deaf man who was brought to him.

  • The positive response of Jesus toward the deaf man.
  • Jesus takes the man aside and in private cures him, to spare him embarrassment.

– The sacramental manner of Jesus' healing. He used words, actions and materials.

  • Spittle in those days was believed to have a curative quality.
  • Looking up to heaven implies that the healing was coming from God.
  • The organs to be healed, the ears and the tongue, were touched.

– The surprise and gratitude of the newly healed man.
– The Palestinian Church, which interpreted Jesus in terms of the eschatological prophet-servant, wrote up the story as a fulfillment of Isaiah 35.

Read the First Reading, Isaiah 35:4–7.

– The Hellenistic Church, which interpreted Jesus in terms of the wonder-worker or divine man, preserved the foreign word "Ephphatha." This was to emphasize Jesus' mysterious power, the touching to emphasize physical healing.
– The place of the story in this narrative is to symbolize what is happening to the disciples. The disciples are still deaf to the teaching of Jesus. Only later at Caesa-

rea Philippi did it dawn on them who Jesus really was, as expressed by Peter's profession of faith.

MAKING THE FAITH OUR OWN

Read the following statements, reflect, then discuss:

- How do you relate to the deaf or other handicapped people?
- Do you believe you can learn patience from dealing with the handicapped?
- Do you believe that Jesus cured the deaf man because of compassion?
- Do you believe St. Mark placed this pericope in this narrative to symbolize the deafness the apostles still had in regard to who Jesus really was?
- Are you filled with admiration and love toward Jesus?

LIVING OUR FAITH

Read the following statements, reflect, then discuss and make a decision:

- Will you make an effort to be more open and helpful toward the handicapped, especially the deaf?
- Will you share with others the marvels of the Lord Jesus?
- Will you spend more time in prayer of praise and thanksgiving?
- Will you be more open toward Jesus, so that he can remove whatever deafness prevents you from really hearing the word of God?
- Will you and your sponsor go and visit some people in an institution for the handicapped?

PRAYER

Responsorial Psalm

Psalm 146

℞.   My soul, give praise to the Lord.

Or: Alleluia.

It is the Lord who keeps faith for ever,
who is just to those who are oppressed.
It is he who gives bread to the hungry,
the Lord, who sets prisoners free. ℞.
It is the Lord who gives sight to the blind,
who raises up those who are bowed down,
the Lord, who protects the stranger
and upholds the widow and orphan. ℞.
It is the Lord who loves the just
but thwarts the path of the wicked.

The Lord will reign for ever,
Sion's God, from age to age. Alleluia. ℞.

You may wish to end your session by singing, "New Life," #124 Glory and Praise Hymnal. (#672 Catholic Book of Worship II)

Spend some time in socializing and informal discussion.

Doctrinal and Pastoral Issues: Healing, Prejudice, Miracles and Compassion to the Handicapped, Discipleship, Revelation

Fr. Michael Koch

Introduction to the Twenty-Fourth Sunday in Ordinary Time through Christ the King

The question of how to develop a series of lessons using the lectionary during Ordinary Time is often a concern for catechists. This section is an example of how such a flow may be planned.

The planning developed along four principles. First there was the idea that in reading a Gospel somewhat continuously we do begin to understand the particular concern that the Gospel author was addressing. For this section, the Gospel of Mark was read from chapters 8 through 12 inclusive. The continuous reading found in Scripture rather than the weekly selection found in the lectionary provided the chance to see the author's own development. Two things became clear about this section of Mark. Jesus was on the journey to Jerusalem to die, and the disciples were confused about the cost of discipleship.

The second planning point was to ask how the catechist personally might be confused about the cost of discipleship and not know how to apply the discoveries in the Gospel author's theme to his or her personal life.

The third point was to note the Church season, feasts and civil calendar. In this case, Mark appears during the autumn. The Church calendar notes the feasts of All Saints, All Souls and Christ the King, as well as saints like Francis of Assisi. The civil calendar holds celebrations such as Halloween and Thanksgiving, as well as the hype for Christmas shopping.

The fourth point was to consider the catechumens. What were the pressures of their particular lifestyle? What were their confusions concerning discipleship?

Having brought together all these considerations, a couple of key issues stood out. One was the materialism in Christmas shopping. Connected with this issue was a whole spectrum of concerns around social justice and economics. Perhaps the bishops' pastoral on economics could be used as background for the lectionary. However, another issue is also appealing. The autumn is a time when nature itself seems to prepare us for considering death. Jesus was on his way to die and the disciples were hesitant to go along. Also the other Scripture readings become more and more apocalyptic toward the end of the cycle. Certainly the issue of death is one which raises in us the same feelings of resistance it raised with the original disciples. Besides, the American society has generally been called a death-denying

culture. All considered, with the final point being what would most touch the lives of the catechumens, the decision was made to focus the cost of discipleship around the issue of death for the first eight sessions. Taking the cue from the Gospel, the last three sessions would be a transition from Mark into Advent time.

The format used for each session has five movements: centering and prayer, a focus for the day's session, Scripture reflection, a process for further learning and sharing, and closing prayer. The same flow has been maintained throughout all the sessions to enable the catechumens to flow with a rhythm.

The sessions begin with a time of centering and prayer. The intent is create a sense of the holy wherein the group may feel enough trust to sincerely look at the issue of death. The quiet, meditative music of Taizé was chosen to aid this atmosphere. Each prayer session ends with the sign of the cross, a mark of a Christian's death and glory. Note the use of new imagery. This is an attempt to break open new understandings of God's name.

Following prayer is a section entitled "Focus." This section is to orient you the reader to perspectives and objectives of the particular session. Likewise, it is suggested that you orient the catechumenate community at the beginning of their session.

The third part is Scripture reflection which begins with the reading of the Gospel. The Gospel is always read at least twice and surrounded by silence. The repetition and the silence help to engage the heart in the listening rather than the thirsty mind. The suggestions on how to further the group's reflection are based on the belief that only a word or phrase from the entirety of the Gospel will be at the core of what each person needs to hear on any one day. As with all of this, these are only suggestions for you to discover how you work best. Adapt! Adapt! Adapt!

A process for further learning and sharing is the fourth movement. Again with this section, these are only suggestions for your own creative design. The idea here is to mix the giving of information with the catechumen's own work of discovering how it touches his or her life today.

The session closes with prayer. These prayer forms were chosen to introduce the catechumens to three psalms and the Liturgy of the Hours. The three psalms, 116, 33 and 146, were chosen because they are responsorial psalms which appear during this season. You may wish to make copies of them or use the text as they are found in Scripture. In praying the psalms, pray them antiphonally—either side to side or with men taking one verse and women the next.

At the end of each session is a list of doctrinal and pastoral issues. By no means is this list exhaustive. Use this creativity to enhance your own. God will bless your work.

Twenty-Fourth Sunday in Ordinary Time

Isaiah 50:4–9
James 2:14–18
Mark 8:27–35

CENTERING

Invite the community to enter the silence, close their eyes and become aware of their breathing. Slow the breath and establish an even pace inhaling and exhaling. Take deep breaths as if you were filling a balloon in your stomach. As the rhythm of breathing becomes more restful, invite people to image God's love filling them as they inhale and tension releasing as they exhale. Rest with the breathing and imaging for a few minutes. When you are ready to move on simply ask the group to bring their awareness back to the room and slowly open their eyes as they are ready.

PRAYER

Song: "Crucem Tuam," *Music From Taizé*,
          G.I.A. Publications, Inc.

Leader: Lord Jesus,
            once again we hear you say
            that we must take up our cross
            and follow you.
            As we gather in trust and love,
            we seek the courage to fearlessly look
            at our lives and the cross you present us.
            We are yours.
            And in confidence, we sign ourselves in
                your name
            (making the sign of the cross),
            Creator, Redeemer and Sanctifier.

All: Amen.

FOCUS

In today's Gospel, Jesus and the disciples set out on their way to Jerusalem. Jesus knew that this was a journey to death. However, the disciples continue to miss the message. They are confused and at times angry over Jesus' insistence that he must die. Not unlike us, they do not want to consider Jesus' message about dying.

Facing one's death usually transforms one's living. When we begin to look at our lives in the light of our death, we often begin to realize the difference between evaluating ourselves by other people's standards and God's.

Over the next eight sessions, we will challenge ourselves to look death in the eye. We will begin by considering the deaths of those close to us. Hopefully in the next weeks we can befriend death. The disciples came to understand that the only "real" death was the death to sin. Once that death was overcome, then the second death was but a small step on the way home.

As we prepare to hear again God's word, let us re-enter the silence.

SCRIPTURE REFLECTION

1. The Gospel is read once, followed by a minute of silence, and then read again.

2. Following the second reading, the question is asked: What word or phrase from this Gospel struck you? Without discussion, share the word or phrase with the group.

3. Open your journals. Take a few minutes to write how the word or phrase you shared relates to your idea of dying. What feelings does the word or phrase bring up for you in connection with death?

4. Have a general sharing on what each person wrote. (Short Break)

PROCESS

1. Consider your closest experience of death, the loss of someone you cared for deeply. Write in your journal the story of your response to this person's death. What were your feelings as you realized the person was dying? How did your feelings and thoughts change from the first moment of realization through the time of death, the funeral and afterward. What has this death experience taught you? How are you feeling right now as you think about death?

2. Once the writing is completed, take a walk with

your sponsor or another catechumen. Share the story of what you wrote at whatever level of disclosure is comfortable. Have your partner also share their story. Return in about twenty-five minutes.

3. As group regathers, bring them to a moment of shared silence. Then open the sharing around the question: What has this death experience taught you?

4. Summarize the sharings and learnings in light of the Gospel. Speak to the varied response of the disciples to Jesus' message. Especially, highlight Peter's concern and Jesus' strong response.

5. Ask catechumens and sponsors to be even more sensitive with each other over the next weeks. The issue of death often opens up deep feelings and resistances in us. The mutual support of catechumen and sponsor is crucial during this time. Have catechumens and sponsors commit to at least speak by phone with each other within three days.

PRAYER

Song: "Crucem Tuam," *Music From Taizé,*
                G.I.A. Publications, Inc.

Psalm 116

Intercessions (from Psalter Week IV) followed by spontaneous ones.

Concluding Prayer: from Liturgy of the Hours, Sunday of the Twenty-Fourth Week.

Doctrinal and Pastoral Issues: Christology, Suffering Servant, Paschal Mystery, Faith and Good Works, Death and Dying

Alexander J. Shaia

Twenty-Fifth Sunday in Ordinary Time

Wisdom 2:12, 17–20
James 3:16—4:3
Mark 9:30–37

CENTERING

Invite people to enter the silence, join their hands and close their eyes. Slow the breath and establish an even pace. Image inhaling God's love and exhaling all tension or anxiety.

Ask each person to be love for the one's left hand they are holding. Image God's love moving through themselves to the other person. After a few minutes, have them switch their focus to the person whose right hand they are holding. After a few more minutes, ask them to just rest in this circle of love, allowing love to flow into them from their right hand and from them through their left. To close the meditation, invite people to slowly open their eyes as they are ready to do so.

PRAYER

Song: "Ubi Caritas," *Music from Taizé,* G.I.A. Publications, Inc.

Leader: Loving Father,
we are now for a moment
that circle of love you wish us to be.
Yet we are aware how easily
jealousy and competition break us apart.
As we listen to your Word in our midst this day,
grant us the grace and perseverance to heal division
and rise from our death in sin.
We ask this (making sign of cross) in the Name of the One who creates,
the One who loves
and the One who Sanctifies.

All: Amen.

FOCUS

Mark portrays how easy it was for the original disciples to become jealous of each other. Jesus answers this brokenness by reminding them of their call to serve. However, he goes further by speaking of such service as a death. In the end, Jesus seems to compare a Christian's welcome of such a death to the type of welcome one would give a small child. For the disciples this was a large challenge. I imagine the challenge for us is just as great. Keeping in our hearts the love of this community along with our own brokenness and divisions, let us listen again to this day's Gospel.

SCRIPTURE REFLECTION

1. The Gospel is read once, followed by a minute of silence. Then the Gospel is read a second time.

2. Following the second reading, the question is posed: Which word or phrase seemed to be said directly to your life today?

3. Without discussion, simply go around the group, having each person share his or her word or phrase.

4. Open your journals. Take a few minutes to write: If your life ended today, how would you evaluate yourself in light of the word or phrase you shared?

5. Share with the group a sense of what you wrote.

(Short Break)

PROCESS

1. Turn to a clean sheet in your journals. Draw a very large circle on the sheet. Place an X on the circle at a spot of your choosing. This X signifies both the moment of your birth and the moment of your death. Travel clockwise around the circle from the X. Mark the spot where you are in your life today in relation to the moment of your birth/death.

2. Ask yourself: Did you place your present mark near or far from the birth/death moment? How does it feel to consider the time between now and your birth/death? Have you ever considered birth and death as the same moment before? What does it feel like for you?

3. Consider that your life is now over. All that you are

ever going to do in this life has already been done. In your journal, write a eulogy about yourself. Write the eulogy as if you were another person looking at your life. Speak of both your virtues and your vices.

4. After you have finished writing sit quietly with your sponsor or another catechumen and share the eulogy. Both persons in the pair have the opportunity to share.

5. Come back together in the large group. Take a moment to note your feelings about imaging one's eulogy and funeral.

6. In the large group, share your learnings and experience from this exercise.

7. Have the catechist summarize the group's learnings. Speak to how death often changes our perspective on life. So much of what seems important just appears to melt away. Jealousy and strife which may have loomed large now just appear as minor sidepaths. Each of us is simply a person walking home. Look at what you have written and shared today. What new priority do you have for the coming week? Note it in your journal. Share it with your sponsor.

PRAYER

Song: "Ubi Caritas," *Music From Taizé*, G.I.A. Publications, Inc.

Psalm 116

Intercessions (from Psalter Week I) followed by spontaneous ones.

Concluding Prayer: from Liturgy of the Hours, Sunday of the Twenty-Fifth Week.

Doctrinal and Pastoral Issues: Stewardship, Ministry, Servant Leadership, Death and Fear of Death

Alexander J. Shaia

Twenty-Sixth Sunday in Ordinary Time

Numbers 11:25–29
James 5:1–6
Mark 9:38–43, 45, 47–48

God's reign fall with our tradition's attempt to make sense of life and life beyond. As we listen to God's word this morning, let us open ourselves to our own beliefs about the next life.

CENTERING

Invite the group to enter the silence, close their eyes and become aware of their breathing. Inhale God's love. Exhale all tension and anxiety. Image a bright light about a foot over your head. Allow the light to come into the top of your head and slowly move down through your body until the light reaches your toes. Image the light moving on into the earth. Allow the earth's energy to move up through you. See this energy as if you were a tree growing back to God's light. Rest in this flow: God's light pouring down and creation's energy moving up. As people are ready, invite them to open their eyes.

PRAYER

Song:　　"Jubilate Deo," *Music From Taizé,* G.I.A. Publications, Inc.

Leader:　O God, Creator of the universe,
　　　　　your light and grace pour through us.
　　　　　We give you thanks and praise.
　　　　　We yearn for the day when our whole self
　　　　　may join with all of creation in singing your praise.
　　　　　We pray that your will may be done this day
　　　　　as we again mark ourselves (making sign of cross)
　　　　　in the name of the One who blesses,
　　　　　the One who is anointed,
　　　　　and the One who binds all together.

All:　　 Amen.

FOCUS

Mark's Gospel today speaks of a place called Gehenna which is far from God's reign. Throughout the Christian tradition, people have used different images to portray the sense of an afterlife. The image of Gehenna and

SCRIPTURE REFLECTION

1. The Gospel is read once followed by a minute of silence. Then the Gospel is read a second time.

2. Ask each person to look at a copy of the Gospel. In the journal ask each person to make two columns. Down one column place all the phrases from the Gospel which confront, challenge or frighten you. Down the second column place the phrases which comfort or affirm you.

3. Share with the group what you placed under each column.

4. Visualize what you believe about the afterlife. How many places are there? What is each one like? Who is in each one? Is there more than one? What happens there? What does a usual day there look like? How are people selected to be in each place? Who does the selection? Primarily, where have your images of afterlife come from: parents? teachers? Scripture? Note your responses in your journal.

5. Share your visualization with the large group.

(Short Break)

PROCESS

1 . Give a presentation on past and current images of the afterlife found in Christian tradition. Note the transition from the static and concrete images of heaven, purgatory, and hell to a more fluid and present moment concept of God's reign right now in our lives. In a present moment sense, speak of Gehenna as a place in our lives right now where we experience the unquenchable fires.

You may wish to go even further and begin to image heaven and Gehenna as attitudes in the midst of everyday living. One image may see heaven as an attitude of acceptance and non-attachment to possessions. Gehenna, by contrast, may be seen as an attitude of addiction. How hard it is to change our addictive patterns. In fact, we may come to rely on our addictions to the point where we do not believe we could live without them. In the Gospel, Jesus expresses this notion by speaking of the need to even separate from our hands, feet or eyes. We recoil in horror! He cannot be serious. Certainly, Jesus did not mean for us to do physical harm to ourselves. However, death calls us to leave all behind.

2a. Have the catechumens reconsider their images of the afterlife. How are they being challenged? What new imagery are they wishing to explore? What are their questions? Where are they feeling uncomfortable?

b. Have a sharing with the group on the word "addiction" and what it means to them. After hearing their definitions, pose the question: If you were to discover you had a terminal illness this week, what would be the hardest things or people to consider leaving behind? Have each person create his or her own list in their journal. Ask for a sharing on the top three things listed. For the coming week, take your top three items into prayer. Meditate on the line: "Your will be done." Ask for the Lord's grace to not be possessive of these top three things. Ask that you may be open to the Lord's design, whatever that is.

PRAYER

Song: "Jubilate Deo," *Music From Taizé*, G.I.A. Publications, Inc.

Psalm 116

Intercessions (Psalter Week II) followed by spontaneous ones.

Concluding Prayer: from Liturgy of the Hours, Sunday of the Twenty-Sixth Week.

Doctrinal and Pastoral Issues: Ecumenism, Social Justice, Materialism, Bishops' Pastoral on the Economy, Afterlife, Heaven and Hell, Eschatology

Alexander J. Shaia

Twenty-Seventh Sunday in Ordinary Time

Genesis 2:18–24
Hebrews 2:9–11
Mark 10:2–16

CENTERING

Invite the group to enter the silence, close their eyes and slow their breathing. Allow the community to simply be in silence for a few minutes.

PRAYER

Song: "Ubi Caritas," *Music From Taizé*, G.I.A. Publications, Inc.

Leader: All-embracing and generous Lord,
we give you praise for healing and binding
our wounds.
So often we use the gifts you have given us
to bring division and hurt into the human
family.
We gather today to once again contemplate
your sacred word.
May our prayer and work bring forth in us
the grace of forgiveness
and the courage to create oneness from division.
We mark ourselves in your name (making
sign of the cross),
the all-embracing, the loving
and the wise Lord of our life.

All: Amen.

FOCUS

In today's Gospel, the Pharisees seek to test Jesus. They are attempting to create division and discord through the use of their intellect and judging mind. Yet Jesus counters again with the image of how God's reign is a place without divisions and separations between people. For a second time, Jesus holds up the child as the attitude for living in God's reign. As we listen to the word, let us open our hearts to our own inner child.

SCRIPTURE REFLECTION

1. The Gospel is read once followed by a minute of silence. Then the Gospel is read a second time.

2. Ask the group: Which word or phrase struck you in this hearing of the word? Have each person share their word with no discussion.

3. Open your journals. Write the word shared with the group in your journal. Be quiet with the word for a minute. Allow the word to bring up for you a hurtful, dividing situation you are presently in. Note the situation in your journal.

PROCESS

1. Set the scene for the community. Speak about how the image of divorce can be seen in a much wider context than that which may happen between a husband and wife. Ask the group to share the feelings and sense of the word "divorce" as it may apply in their everyday life.

2. Ask each person to choose one situation to work with today. The situation may be the one noted at the end of Scripture reflection or it could have to do with a relationship which has been hurt by the addictions spoken of last week.

3. Have each person write a letter. All should address the letter to the person whom they have hurt or who has hurt them. The form of the letter is as follows. The letter is composed of five sections. Each section is one paragraph. Ask the people to write the letter moving through the sequence in order. In the first paragraph express your anger toward the person or situation. In the second section, move on to write of your hurt and sadness. The third part expresses your fears and insecurities. In the fourth section write of your own sense of responsibility and guilt in the situation. The last and fifth section allows you to express your love, forgiveness or understanding toward the person.

4. After finishing your letter, take a walk with your sponsor or another catechumen. Have each person share what happened for them in the writing of the letter. During this sharing, have one partner share

while the other is present through listening. Then switch roles.

5. When the large group is reconvened, ask for a sharing of the experience. What did writing the letter feel like for you? What are you learning?

6. Give a presentation on the five stages of loss. The stages were popularized by Elisabeth Kübler-Ross. Her work emphasized these steps as part of the letting go as one physically dies. However, it is now understood that these steps comprise the process with any loss experience. Briefly, speak to the five movements: denial, anger, bargaining, depression and acceptance. Also make the connection with how our inner child may help or hinder our movement through these stages. The positive inner child lives in the spontaneous now, neither holding onto the past nor anticipating the future. On the other hand, the hurt inner child is possessive and full of tantrums. What additional images may your community come up with for the positive and hurt inner child?

7a. Pose the questions: How have you experienced the loss/divorce process in your own life? How is the catechumenate a loss experience for you? Have you experienced the five stages in part or whole? What stage do you see yourself in now? Are you moving or stuck?

b. What types of things does your inner child like? When and how do you feel playful and spontaneous? How can you can get yourself into that creative space when you get down?

PRAYER

Song: "Ubi Caritas," *Music From Taizé*, G.I.A. Publications, Inc.

Psalm 116

Intercession from Psalter Week III followed by catechist imposing hands on each catechumen, praying for healing in the loss experience of each or praying for the loving inner child.

Concluding Prayer: from Liturgy of the Hours, Sunday of the Twenty-Seventh Week.

Doctrinal and Pastoral Issues: Theology of Marriage, Christian and Jewish Perspectives on Marriage, Divorce and Annulments in the Church, Process of Death and Dying, Separations and Endings

Alexander J. Shaia

Twenty-Eighth Sunday in Ordinary Time

Wisdom 7:7–11
Hebrews 4:12–13
Mark 10:17–30

One of the guests might be asked beforehand to do one of the readings.

PRAYER

Song: "Veni Sancte Spiritus," *Music From Taizé,* G.I.A. Publications, Inc.

Leader: (The people continue to sing softly as the passage from Wisdom is read. As the passage concludes, the singing again rises.)

FOCUS

Last Sunday we entered our own experience of loss and separation. And today we hear Peter exclaim, "We have put everything aside to follow you." As humans we are great pack rats; when we leave one thing behind, we tend to pick up another. This morning we have with us a guest (guests), who would like to share a very special journey. A short time ago, they discovered that they have a life threatening illness. They are here with us this morning to share their story and experiences of everyday life. (To arrange for a terminally ill person, contact a local hospice group or a pastoral care unit in a hospital. If you are not able to have someone in person, consider an audio or video tape. Hospice groups usually have a selection which they use in training. A last note: this would be an excellent time to invite an AIDS patient to tell his or her story. The usual resistance which comes up in dealing with this illness is precisely the type of death experience these eight sessions are challenging us to.) As a community truly seeking to know the Lord's wisdom, let us open our hearts to the Scriptures this morning:

SCRIPTURE REFLECTION

Read the Gospel twice with silence between readings.

PROCESS

1. Introduce the guest or guests.

2. Ask them to simply tell their story, to speak of how they came to know of their illness and the spiritual journey as they live with the possibilities. What are the cycle of feelings they find? What has happened with their families, and friends? Do people tend to shy away from them? What do they want from those around them? How can we help?

(Short Break)

3. Open up for sharing and questions among the community with the guest(s).

4. Ask catechumens to record and reflect on this experience in their journals and with their sponsors in the coming week.

PRAYER

Song: "Veni Sancte Spiritus," *Music From Taizé,* G.I.A. Publications, Inc.

Psalm 33

Intercession (Psalter Week IV) followed by spontaneous intercessions.

Ask community to lay hands on the guest and pray that all which separates one from God's will be removed.

Concluding Prayer: from Liturgy of the Hours, Sunday of the Twenty-Eighth Week.

Doctrinal and Pastoral Issues: Materialism, Social Justice, Stewardship, Illness and Healing

Alexander J. Shaia

Twenty-Ninth Sunday in Ordinary Time

Isaiah 53:10–11
Hebrews 4:14–16
Mark 10:35–45

PRAYER

Song: "How Blessed Are You," *Music From Taizé,* G.I.A. Publications, Inc.

Leader: O most strong and generous Lord,
we draw together today,
aware of our need for you.
Like the disciples,
thoughts of glory and prestige
are never far from our acts of service.
By our prayer and work,
convict our hearts
to the lowly and hidden ways
we may truly give you praise.
Once again we commit ourselves to the
cross
(making sign of the cross)
in the name of the Father, Son and Holy
Spirit.

All: Amen.

FOCUS

The Gospel of Mark continues to remind us how different service is in the Christian sense. First, we serve others not for our own glory but for God's. We are not the creators of love but rather love's servant. Today, we have with us some volunteers who work with the dying as a way to serve love. As we asked ourselves last week, what do the terminally ill have to teach us about living? This week we ask what service teaches us about the letting go and dying to self. (Contact hospice services or persons in pastoral care to the sick to be guests.)

SCRIPTURE REFLECTION

Read the Gospel twice with silence between readings. One of the guests might be asked beforehand to do one of the readings.

PROCESS

1. Introduce the guests.

2. Ask the guests to share how they felt called to the work they do, what their work actually entails, and how this service teaches them about themselves and their God.

(Short Break)

3. Invite sharing and questions from the community.

4. Ask the catechumens to record and reflect on this experience in their journals and with their sponsors during the coming week. How are you called to embrace the Gospel readings—in your work, family, neighborhood relationships? Share this with sponsor or small group.

PRAYER

Song: "How Blessed Are You," *Music From Taizé,* G.I.A. Publications, Inc.

Psalm 33

Intercessions (Psalter Week I) followed by spontaneous intercessions.

Ask community to lay hands on guests and pray for their ministry and for the people they serve.

Concluding Prayer: from Liturgy of the Hours, Sunday of the Twenty-Ninth Week

Doctrinal and Pastoral Issues: Church Hierarchy, Ministry of the Faithful, Servant Leadership

Alexander J. Shaia

Thirtieth Sunday in Ordinary Time

Jeremiah 31:7–9
Hebrews 5:1–6
Mark 10:46–52

PRAYER

Leader: O Divine Lover and Healer,
we today, like the blind Bartimaeus of old,
cry out, "Have pity on us."
Give us the courage to throw off our
cloaks.
Remove from us all that binds and holds us
from walking with you.
We take up your cross as our staff,
and sign ourselves
(making the sign of the cross)
in the name of the One who sustains,
protects and liberates.

All: Amen.

Song: "Laudate Dominum," *Music From Taizé,*
G.I.A. Publications, Inc.

FOCUS

In today's Gospel, Jesus leaves Jericho on his way to Jerusalem. Death draws closer. The crowds gather around to watch. In the midst of what almost is a circus atmosphere, Jesus remains centered and true to his mission. In the face of death, which role do we play: the crowd? the disciples? Bartimaeus?

Over the last few weeks, we have considered the stories of those who are conscious of their dying and of those who walk with the dying. Today, we wish to once again consider our own death and the healing our faith offers us and our families. As we prepare for our work, let us listen to the faith and healing of Bartimaeus.

SCRIPTURE REFLECTION

1. Read the Gospel twice with a moment of silence in between.

2. As you reflect back over the events of your life the past week, which person do you most identify with in the Scripture: the crowd? the disciples? Jesus? Bartimaeus?

3. Briefly note in your journal which character fits your life this past week, and explain why.

4. Share with the group.

(Short Break)

PROCESS

1. Give a presentation on the rites of Christian burial. Cover all the options one has in planning wakes, prayer services, Mass of the Resurrection, and graveside prayers. Have handouts available. Prepare a worksheet for people to follow in putting together their services.

2. If time permits, or perhaps in another session, a funeral home director could speak on planning needed from their perspective.

3. For the week to come, ask participants to outline the type of services they would like and to choose the Scriptures for those services. Further ask them to decide on the details of the funeral: Coffin or cremation? Waked in church or elsewhere? Flowers or memorials? If memorials, which ones?

4. Have catechumen and sponsor share their planning with each other before the next session. All should bring their completed plans with them to the next session.

5. Further Suggestion: Discuss the Feasts of All Saints and All Souls. This is a good time to visit the graves of deceased family and friends. If weather permits, take the time to clean around the gravesite or do planting if it is the appropriate season. You might read aloud to the deceased his or her favorite Scripture or poem, etc. Or you might read to the deceased your own favorite Scripture etc. Talk to those who have gone before. Their body is no longer here, yet we know they live.

PRAYER

Song: "Laudate Dominum," *Music From Taizé,* G.I.A. Publications, Inc.

Psalm 33

Intercessions (Psalter Week II) followed by spontaneous intercessions.

Concluding Prayer: from Liturgy of the Hours, Sunday of the Thirtieth Week.

Doctrinal and Pastoral Issues: The Priesthood of Jesus, Healing, New Testament Miracles, Pastoral Care of the Sick, Communion of Saints, Christian Burial and All Souls

Alexander J. Shaia

Thirty-First Sunday in Ordinary Time

Deuteronomy 6:2–6
Hebrews 7:23–28
Mark 12:28–34

PRAYER

Song: "Crucem Tuam," *Music From Taizé,* G.I.A. Publications, Inc.

Leader: Let us take a few minutes in quiet
to give thanks to the Lord
for Sister Death
who teaches us how to love each other
and to love the Lord
with all our heart and strength.

Song: "Crucem Tuam."

FOCUS

For the past seven session we have looked at the many faces of death. We have attempted to understand death as part of the path of Christian discipleship. No doubt, we like the original disciples will find this coming to love Sister Death a lifelong task. Yet with all of our strength and the Lord's grace may we continue our walk to Jerusalem. In the midst of the journey today, let us pause to once again hear God's word in our midst.

SCRIPTURE REFLECTION

1. Read the Gospel twice with silence between readings.

2. After the second reading, ask for a sharing on which word or phrase stood out for them. Have them share the word without discussion.

3. Then ask for a sharing on how the word they chose connects with the feelings they experienced this past week in planning their funeral services.

(Short Break)

PROCESS

1. Spend time alone reviewing your journal and remembrances from the past seven weeks. Look back to that first eulogy you wrote. Compare the feelings of that to doing your funeral services this past week. Ask yourself: How have I grown? How am I different than I was two months ago? How have I been challenged? What's the one thing I really want to do or remember from this experience? Write your responses in your journal.

2. Share with the group your sense of growth and where you still need to grow more.

PRAYER

Song: "Crucem Tuam."

Psalm 33

Intercessions (Psalter Week III) followed by spontaneous intercessions.

Concluding Prayer: from Liturgy of the Hours, Sunday of the Thirty-First Week.

Doctrinal and Pastoral Issues: The Hebrew and Christian Covenants, Social Justice Issues, Bishops' Pastoral on the Economy, Funeral Rite

Alexander J. Shaia

Thirty-Second Sunday in Ordinary Time

1 Kings 17:10–16
Hebrews 9:24–28
Mark 12:38–44

PRAYER

Song: "How Blessed Are You," *Music From Taizé,* G.I.A. Publications, Inc.

Leader: Gracious and just Lord,
you know our hearts and thoughts.
You call us to be a people
who give from our want
more than from our surplus.
Yet we so often play the scribe.
Help us this day to trust more in your
providence.
Commit us this day to praise you
(making the sign of the cross)
in the name of the poor, the widowed and
the orphaned.

All: Amen.

FOCUS

The Gospel catches us today in a familiar situation. So often we become involved in gift-giving for many reasons other than to praise and thank the Lord. Soon we will be in the midst of the most hectic season of gift-giving. Let us take the time today to scrutinize our own reasons for giving to others and giving to God.

SCRIPTURE REFLECTION

1. Read the Gospel twice with silence between the readings.

2. Form four small groups. Give each group one of the following characters from today's Gospel: the scribe, the crowd, Jesus and the widow.

3. Ask each small group to picture their particular character in our present day Christmas shopping season. Describe the scribe as he or she is seen today. Describe the crowd, the widow, and Jesus. Each group's presentation of their character may be presented as a skit or in some story form.

4. Each group presents and the total group shares.

(Short Break)

PROCESS

1. Give a presentation on the principles of Christian stewardship. In essence we are called to give from our want, not simply from our surplus. Relate this principle to the Christmas season. In the United States alone, Christmas is a thirty billion dollar industry. Some describe our Christmas giving as one scribe gifting another, while the widows look on. Discuss this image. Pose these questions to the group: To whom do you give gifts at Christmas? Why? How do you gauge your expenses? Which people are your highest priority in gift giving? Why? (For further material on this topic, see *Unplug the Christmas Machine*, by Jo Robinson and Jean Coppock Staeheli, William Morrow and Company, Inc., New York, 1982.)

2. In the four small groups, discuss the above questions.

3. Bring the small group discussions to a total group sharing.

4. In journals, write the two main ideas or principles you wish to govern your gift giving this season.

5. For the next session, ask participants to review the past Church year and their reading of Mark. Have them choose a favorite Markan passage to bring to the next session.

PRAYER

Song: "How Blessed Are You."

Psalm 146

Intercessions (Psalter Week IV) followed by spontaneous intercessions.

Concluding Prayer from Liturgy of the Hours, Sunday of the Thirty-Second Week.

Doctrinal and Pastoral Issues: Old and New Testament Images of Priesthood, Christmas, Stewardship, Economics, Social Justice

Alexander J. Shaia

Thirty-Third Sunday in Ordinary Time

Daniel 12:1–3
Hebrews 10:11–14,18
Mark 13:24–32

PRAYER

(Begin with a centering exercise. Ask the community to enter the silence and slow their breathing. As the calm grows, softly begin the song.)

Song: "Stay With Us," *Music From Taizé, Volume II*, G.I.A. Publications, Inc.

Leader: (Ask the community to continue to hum the song as the Gospel is read. The Gospel is read once, slowly. Following the reading, invite the community to sit quietly and reflect on the thoughts and feelings which the reading brought up for them. After this time of silence begin the song once again.) As the song concludes, the leader says:

O Most Gentle One,
we also recognize you in power and might.
We know you are the Lord
of all time and every season.
With you, we recall our year:
we remember the cold and darkness of last winter,
the light and warmth of the spring,
the heat and fruits of summertime,
the cool and colors of fall.
The cycle is complete; darkness falls again.
And we pray with confidence: Be with us, Lord.
In praise of your holy name
we mark ourselves with your creation
(making the sign of the cross),
Father Sky, Mother Earth, and Spirit Universe.

All: Amen.

FOCUS

Though the Church year does not end until next Sunday, today is the last time we read from the Gospel of Mark. As we say farewell to Mark for three years, let us take time to reflect over this year and what his Gospel has come to mean for us.

PROCESS

1. Ask each person to share his or her favorite passage from Mark. Which Sunday of the Church year was it proclaimed? What was he or she feeling or experiencing at that time? How does the passage speak to him or her today?

2. In general, how would you sum up for yourself the message of Mark? What has been the image of Jesus and discipleship portrayed in Mark? Have a general discussion and sharing.

PRAYER

Instrumental of "Stay With Us."

Psalm 146

Invitation for each person to reverence the Scriptures which are turned open to Gospel of Mark. (A person may kiss the book, place hands on it, simply hold it, etc.) Once each person has reverenced and said "farewell" to Mark, the leader reads the line from today's Gospel: "The heavens and earth will pass away, but my words will not pass." After reading the line, the Gospel book is gently and solemnly closed.

Song: "Stay With Us."

Doctrinal and Pastoral Issues: Eschatology, Day of Judgment, Apocalyptic Literature, Gospel of Mark

Alexander J. Shaia

Christic the King

Daniel 7:13–14
Revelation 1:5–8
John 18:33–37

PRAYER

Song: "Crucem Tuam," *Music From Taizé,*
          G.I.A. Publications, Inc.

Leader: Lord of the universe,
          we proclaim you king.
          We eagerly await your coming
          amidst trumpets and shouts of glory.
          Yet, year after year, you appear
          as one oppressed, unloved and forgotten.
          Lord, you surprise us.
          We look constantly for glory,
          and you show us a lonely and neglected
              road.
          We pray that as the darkness of winter de-
              scends,
          we may once again come to depend upon
              your light,
          and travel the forgotten path of your truth.
          In praise of your reign,
          we mark ourselves in the name
          (making the sign of the cross)
          of the oppressed, the forgotten and the un-
              loved.

All: Amen.

FOCUS

The Feast of Christ the King begins the last week of the Church year. Next Sunday we enter Advent. For Americans, the Feast of Christ the King and Thanksgiving often fall within the same week. As a result we may tend to confuse the two images. We may tend to think of our Thanksgiving dinner as the banquet for which we so easily name our God a king. However the picture of kingship found in today's Gospel is not the one of thanks around a full table. Christ appears before Pilate as one who is oppressed, forgotten and unloved. Yet in the midst of such loss and despisal, Jesus speaks with

confidence and authority. As we listen to the Gospel today, let us examine our own hearts. Do we only name the Lord "King" in the midst of a banquet feast? How grateful are our hearts when God's truth leads us down the narrow road?

SCRIPTURE REFLECTION

1. Read the Gospel twice with silence between readings.

2. Ask the people to meditate on the word "truth." Have them take a moment to write in their journals a definition for truth.

3. Share the definitions. Have someone also read the definitions as found in a dictionary. What are the common ideas? What are the differences?

4. Bring the discussion back to the Gospel passage. What is the meaning of the word "truth" as Jesus uses it? What is the truth that he is testifying to?

(Short Break)

PROCESS

1. Have the group name all the places or countries in the world where Christians are not free to worship or spread the good news. Put each place's name on a piece of paper or poster board. Hang the names all around the meeting space.

2. Discuss the hardships Christians face in those countries. If possible invite someone with first-hand experience of religious persecution to share their story with the group.

3. However, bring the discussion back home. Other countries may have external persecutions, but Americans have internal hardships with being a Christian and Catholic. Have them name in their journals the personal hardships they face in being Catholic with friends, spouses, family, and work associates. Discuss what was written in their journals.

4. To close, have the group return to their journals.

This week what will it cost you to testify to the truth? How truly thankful are you for that cost?

PRAYER

Psalm 146.

Intercessions from Liturgy of the Hours for Christ the King.

Spontaneous Intercessions.

Concluding Prayer from Liturgy of the Hours for Christ the King.

Song: "Jubilate Deo," *Music From Taizé,* G.I.A. Publications, Inc.

Doctrinal and Pastoral Issues: Christology, Apocalyptic Literature, Advent, God's Reign, Day of Judgment

Alexander J. Shaia

HOLY DAYS

Mary and the Saints

By Eugene A. LaVerdiere

Besides all the other feasts and solemnities which we have already seen, the liturgical year includes two great feasts of our Lady and the Feast of All Saints. For this last, the Gospel reading is Matthew 5:1–12, the beatitudes.

The beatitudes (Mt 5:1–12) introduce Jesus' great discourse on the mount, in which Matthew gathered many sayings of Jesus into a great synthesis of Christian living. The Sermon on the Mount is the law of Christian discipleship. The mountain which Jesus ascends to interpret the old law and present the Christian way of life is not so much geographical as theological, the place where revelation is given, as had been the case at Sinai.

The beatitudes present Jesus' challenging vision in a form characteristic of wisdom literature: "Blessed are . . .for they shall." Note, however, that for the poor in spirit (5:3) and those who are persecuted for righteousness' sake (5:10), we read: "Blessed are . . .for theirs is," since the reign of God has already broken into the world in the life and teaching of Jesus. The reason the poor in spirit, those who mourn, etc., are blessed is not that they are poor in spirit or because they mourn, but because they have been granted the kingdom of God and they shall be comforted. The good news is proclaimed to the poor. The form of the last beatitude is very different. In it, Jesus speaks directly to the persecuted community of Matthew. The other beatitudes must have formed a rhetorical whole framed by "Theirs is the kingdom of God" (5:3, 10) before its addition.

The feasts of Mary are that of the Immaculate Conception, which comes on December 8, during Advent, and that of the Assumption, which we celebrate on August 15, during Ordinary Time. The readings for these feasts are from Luke's prologue.

The Promise

With the Feast of the Immaculate Conception we celebrate the story of God's promise of salvation, from the first covenant to the fulfillment of the covenant in Christ. The story is epitomized by the person of Mary through whom God's life and word became flesh. Mary also embodies the vocation of the Church and of every Christian.

The reading for the feast is Luke 1:26–38, the story of Gabriel's annunciation that Mary would be the Mother of the Son of God. Touched by grace, she was open to the Holy Spirit and accepted to be the servant of the Lord. In such a life and commitment, there is no sin. The Church is called to the same selfless service and to bring forth the life of God into the world. Unlike Mary, we are not sinless, but we do have her as an ideal expression of what humanity ought to be. Mary is the vision of humanity's fulfillment in the reign of God. As such she stretches our hopes beyond the horizon of our personal lives and beyond history itself.

The Fulfillment

With the Feast of the Assumption we celebrate the story of how God's promise is fulfilled over and over again throughout history. It is because we have seen the promise fulfilled so often that the promise is a source of hope for us. The story of fulfillment, like the story of the promise, is epitomized in the person of Mary, whom Elizabeth greeted in the name of the entire Old Testament as well as in our own name as the Mother of the Lord.

The reading for the feast is Luke 1:39–56 which includes the Magnificat, Mary's song of praise, in which her rejoicing sings of how God is glorified in what has been done through her person. Her song is also the prayer of the Christian fulfillment. All that we pray for in the Lord's prayer is celebrated in anticipation as already fulfilled. No longer need we pray that God's name be hallowed. His name is hallowed. His reign is established in the reversal of worldly values. The lowly have been raised up and the mighty toppled from their thrones, and the hungry have been filled with good things. Thus it is that in the person of Mary we celebrate both the promise and the fulfillment of life and history.

Introduction to the Assumption, Immaculate Conception and All Saints Day

The sessions for these feasts are arranged as follows:

Opening Prayer
Reflection
Integration
Closing Prayer

In each session there are a number of reflection and integration sections. Note that these sessions are for use with catechumens rather than the elect.

The opening prayer begins with a song chosen from familiar liturgical music. These hymns may be listened to reflectively or sung together if a musician is available. The leader then prays the opening prayer. The closing prayer usually revolves around a meditative reading of the Gospel of the day. Various ways are sug-gested to enhance the environment for prayer. The catechist should also be mindful of the need to vary the group's posture while at prayer.

The method for this section is one of reflection and integration. The catechist is called to lead the group in reflecting first on some aspect of their experience, then on the Scriptures. After each reflection, the integration section poses questions for reflection or discussion. The method is thus based on a dialogue between the catechist and the catechumens. The catechist should be careful to allow time for quiet reflection when posing the integration questions. At times, a small group discussion or exercise is called for as a way of responding to the questions. Note too that there are a variety of questions from which the most appropriate may be selected.

Feast of the Assumption

August 15

Revelation 11:19; 12:1–6, 10
1 Corinthians 15:20–26
Luke 1:39–56

OPENING PRAYER

Opening Song

"Lift Up Your Hearts," (*Glory and Praise*, NALR, or similar song of praise)

Leader: Happy are they who believe the promises of the Lord will be fulfilled.

All: Happy are they who believe the promises of the Lord will be fulfilled.

Leader: For God has called us out of darkness into light.

All: Happy are they who believe the promises of the Lord will be fulfilled.

Leader: And God has chosen us as special and holy.

All: Happy are they who believe the promises of the Lord will be fulfilled.

Leader: Truly god has blessed us with the hope of our future.

All: Happy are they who believe the promises of the Lord will be fulfilled.

Leader: Let us remember each other's needs: (spontaneous prayer)

All: Happy are they who believe the promises of the Lord will be fulfilled.

Leader: Let us pray.
Good and gracious God,
happy indeed are we who believe
that all you have promised us will be ours.
Give us the wisdom to see more clearly
your guidance and support in these days.
Give us tongues to sing out and proclaim
  your goodness
everywhere we go.
Give us the conviction, like Mary your servant,

to entrust our lives into your hands.
We make this prayer in the name of Jesus,
who is both Redeemer and Brother,
through the power of your Spirit. Amen.

REFLECTION

(Material for leader to develop)

"The sun will come out tomorrow; bet your bottom dollar that tomorrow, there'll be sun." So goes the song "Tomorrow" from the Broadway musical *Annie*. Sometimes we live only for tomorrow, placing our hope and trust in the many tomorrows that lie before us. We dream dreams and plan our lives out. For many of us, today is only bearable because there is a tomorrow for us. And just maybe that tomorrow will make things different.

Tomorrow can be a vision of hope. But more often than we would like to admit, tomorrow becomes an escape. Scarlet O'Hara from *Gone with the Wind* captures the sentiment in her closing words: "I just can't think about it now; it'll drive me crazy. I'll think about it tomorrow. For tomorrow is another day." Tomorrow can become the motivation to "close up shop" today and not care, not take action, not respond, bury our head in the sand, become immobile.

INTEGRATION

(Choose appropriate exercise/discussion questions)

1. Share some experiences when you were waiting for "tomorrow." Was there a sense of anticipation? of wonder? of excitement?

2. Discuss why some people might be truly longing for tomorrow, such as victims of war who wait for the relief tomorrow may bring, or the starving who pray tomorrow may bring food.

3. What are some concrete ways in which tomorrow can be an escape?

4. Try and remember some "escapes" into tomorrow. What seemed to be driving you? What were you

hoping for? Were you satisfied when tomorrow came?

REFLECTION CONTINUES

The celebration of the Feast of the Assumption is a celebration of tomorrow, God's tomorrow: the full and final kingdom of God. The kingdom of God is God's reign of compassion, justice, peace, love. Inaugurated in the person and life of Jesus, the Christ, the kingdom will be fully realized when all creation is drawn up into the fullness of God's embrace of love, i.e., when all creation has allowed itself to experience the gratutitous gift of God's love which transforms and redeems.

INTEGRATION

(Choose appropriate exercise/discussion questions):

1. Share with each other the important parts of Jesus' message that you think make a difference. List these qualities. Do they have anything to do with the kingdom of God?

REFLECTION CONTINUES

Choosing to live with the kingdom of God as one's vision means to live God's tomorrow today. The kingdom of God is at hand! It is not choosing to stand back and let life go by with the hope that someday God will come and take us away from it all. Rather, it is a call to be immersed in life now, to truly live life now, to be about God's values now so that all creation will be touched by God's values now. And the depth of this challenge reaches out to all people, to social institutions, to all of creation. God's kingdom is not a private possession we hold onto. It is not a private privilege you or I hope to have fully someday. God's kingdom is the community of God's people gathered together. This is present in root form today as the new creation, and this has profound social implications. Mary's canticle of praise in today's Gospel bears witness to the call to justice. This beautiful hymn, patterned after Hannah's song in 1 Samuel 2:1–10, is a proclamation of God's unending love and compassion which calls us to justice and fellowship today because we have been touched by God.

INTEGRATION

(Choose appropriate exercise/discussion questions)

1. Recall a time when the vision of tomorrow strength-

ened you at that time. How did that affect how you lived then? Did you desire the vision of tomorrow any differently after that?

2. What are some of the excuses we use to avoid confronting evil and injustice? How often is tomorrow one of them (i.e., I'll help them tomorrow)?

REFLECTION CONTINUES

Mary's assumption is a symbol of our hope that we too will be raised to glory with God. This feast celebrates Mary who shares our destiny, our future. She touches our deepest longings and desires for completion and fulfillment in God. All of this is brought together for us in the resurrection of Jesus, the Christ. The focus is God's activity, not Mary. God has raised Jesus from the dead. Mary, because of her obedience to God by living in fidelity to God's continual call in her life, now shares in the fullness of God's presence. Mary becomes the symbol of all we will be in Christ. (Cf. Corinthians text)

Talk of resurrection raises the important notion of the body. Is the resurrection a "spiritual" matter, and hence the "soul" is raised? Mary's assumption offers an important clarification to the discussion of the resurrection. The tradition holds that Mary was assumed "body and soul," i.e., one complete person. Salvation is for the whole person. Hence, Mary's assumption becomes an affirmation of the worth and goodness of the material. We are called upon to examine our vision of our bodies, our sense of material goods, our use of resources. The doctrine of the resurrection affirms that "all will be made new," i.e., we will be raised in our transformed bodies (this is not the corpse). Jesus has redeemed us fully: the whole person and not only the "spiritual" dimension.

INTEGRATION

(Choose appropriate exercise/discussion questions)

1. How do you view your body? What are some images or words which describe your body to you? How might you appreciate your body more?

2. Discuss the importance of being balanced, of moving toward wholeness on all levels: emotionally, physically, psychologically, intellectually, spiritually, etc. Take a brief inventory on how faithful you are to your whole person, i.e., how do I care for myself and how do I not care for myself? Choose life this day.

CLOSING PRAYER

Leader: Let us pray.
Creator God,
it is you who are our beginning and our
end.
You are the source of life, and to you all
life is drawn.
Help us recognize the deep hunger we
have for you.
Give us the strength and courage needed
to allow ourselves
to listen deeply to your word proclaimed.
And transform our hearts by this same
Word
so we might be men and women of conviction and justice.
May we sing out in praise of you as did
Mary as she prayed:

All: My soul proclaims the greatness of the
Lord . . .
(continue with the Canticle of Mary)

*Doctrinal and Pastoral Issues: Eschatology, Justice and
Peace, Resurrection, Assumption*

Thomas H. Morris

(Reprinted from BREAKING OPEN THE WORD OF GOD, CYCLE A)

Feast of all Saints

November 1

Revelation 7:2–3, 9–14
1 John 3:1–3
Matthew 5:1–12

OPENING PRAYER

Song

"For All the Saints" (or similar song) (Traditional melody)

Recite the psalm response of the day (Psalm 24) with the antiphon "We Praise You, O Lord" (Dameans) between strophes.

REFLECTION

(Material for leader to develop)

Heroes and heroines—everyone has them. In fact, the contemporary cry is that we don't have enough heroes and heroines to meet the new demands of our times. Yet for many of us, we grew up with our heroes and heroines right there by our side. We knew them from literature, or from the silver screen, or from government. Sometimes our models were local town folk, maybe even someone in our family. But more often than not, our heroes and heroines were people we had not met but who touched us and inspired us. Be they a Hemingway, a Hepburn, a Roosevelt, a Garbo or even a Linus van Pelt, heroes and heroines helped form our lives, gave us vision.

Sometimes we make our heroes and heroines unreachable, untouchable, and hence unreal. We create their story to be larger than the person—and we lose touch with the special quality such a person brings to our lives: their own expression of humanity. If we are not careful, our heroes and heroines become our new gods: we fill them with such mystery and awe that we catch ourselves saying things like: "Oh, I worship the ground he walks on" or "I simply adore her." Then our heroes and heroines become distorted and we lose sight of their valuable contribution to human living: the fidelity with which they lived life and used their gifts for the creation of a more human world. But if we allow our

heroes and heroines to be human, to experience pain and doubt, to make mistakes, then we can appreciate them more fully, see them more clearly, and be inspired more profoundly because they chose to live life from their gifts.

INTEGRATION

(Choose appropriate exercise/discussion questions)

1. Name some of your childhood heroes and heroines. Why were they important to you? How have your heroes and heroines changed since your childhood? What makes the difference now?

2. What can happen when we idolize our heroes and heroines? What happens to us because of this?

REFLECTION CONTINUES

Today's great feast is about heroes and heroines. Today we celebrate the many men and women who chose to live life from their gifts in response to a call from God, a call each of us is given. The Church sets them aside and holds them as models of Christian life. And this is so not because they led extraordinary lives (though the popular tales about the saints seem to suggest this), but rather because in their very ordinary lives they lived faithfully the Gospel way of life. They struggled and sinned and sought forgiveness; they prayed and experienced darkness and reached out for light; they embraced the cross and allowed God to transform them. They were like you and me, ordinary people who believed that the cross of Jesus Christ made all the difference. And it did.

INTEGRATION

(Choose appropriate exercise/discussion questions)

1. Do you have a favorite saint? Tell your favorite story about this saint. Why is he or she special to you?

2. Can you relate to your favorite saints as friends, fam-

ily, neighbors, or do you behold them from afar and gaze at them?

REFLECTION CONTINUES

We are called to be saints, to be holy. But how can we become holy? How can we make a difference? Today's Gospel spells out the way of life for those who choose to follow Jesus. The Beatitudes reflect a new code of living. And what rises as fundamental is not so much the actions we take (or don't take) but the attitude which grounds these actions. We all know people who are charitable for the praise they can get, and people who are just because their profit is at stake, and people who are helpful because they want you to repay their kindness back a hundredfold. And perhaps these people are us. But the Beatitudes point to a different way of living life, different attitudes which form and direct our actions.

INTEGRATION

1. Reread today's Gospel slowly. In small groups, discuss the various attitudes which the text invites us to develop. Restate the text for contemporary men and women using these attitudes.

2. How can we live from these Beatitudes? How do you undersand purity of heart (single-heartedness, to desire one thing: God and God's will, to see all creation as part of God's will, to focus on the way of life Jesus models, etc.)?

3. How do the Beatitudes relate to God's vision?

REFLECTION CONTINUES

"Oh, when the saints go marching in, when the saints go marching in. How I want to be in that number, when the saints go marching in." Yes, we do want to be part of that number, and we can. Today we celebrate not only the great men and women of our tradition who lived in fidelity to the Gospel call, who lived the attitudes of the Beatitude life, but we also celebrate our destiny, our heritage, our own way of living life. We are invited to reflect on the quality of our lives, the patterns we have chosen, and ask the hard questions. Then we too will be counted among those "who have survived the great period of trial; they have washed their robes and made them white in the blood of the Lamb" (Rev 7:14).

INTEGRATION

1. What does it mean for me to be a saint? How can I live a holy life while still being involved in my work, family, career? What will make the important "difference" in all of this?

CLOSING PRAYER

Leader: Good and gracious God,
with great love and devotion we celebrate
our sisters and brothers who have witnessed to your love.
We thank you for them and for the life
they have led.
We are grateful that we have known some
of them
as family, friends, colleagues, members of
our community.
May we continue to be inspired and empowered
by their way of life of self-sacrificing love.

Litany of Saints: sung response: "Pray for us."

(Be careful not to drag the litany. It is meant to be a mantra chant, and should move gracefully and crisply)

Holy Mary, Mother of God . . .
St. Peter and St. Paul . . .
St. Mary Magdalene . . .
St. Stephen . . .
St. Perpetua . . .

(continue with names of catechumens and
other saints you wish to mention)

St. Elizabeth Ann Seton . . .
Pope John XXIII . . .
Dorothy Day . . .
Thomas Merton . . .
All holy men and women of God . . .

Close with exchange of peace.

Doctrinal and Pastoral Issues: Communion of Saints, Intercession, Beatitudes

Thomas H. Morris

(Reprinted from BREAKING OPEN THE WORD OF GOD, CYCLE A)

Feast of the Immaculate Conception

December 8

Genesis 3:9–15, 20
Ephesians 1:3–6, 11–12
Luke 1:26–38

OPENING PRAYER

Opening Song

"Glory and Praise to Our God" (or similar praise song)

Leader: Let us give thanks to our God.

All: For God's love endures forever!

Leader: Let us sing praise to the One who has loved us.

All: For God's love endures forever!

Leader: Let us rest in confidence in God's providence.

All: For God's love endures forever!

Leader: Let us remember the needs of each other (silence).

All: For God's love endures forever!

Leader: Let us pray . . .
Good and gracious God,
we gather to break open your word
so that we might be nourished and fed.
Open our hearts and minds
that we may gently receive the gift of this day.
Help us to ponder the wonder of your servant, Mary,
as her life models for us the call to obedience.
We make this prayer
in the name of Jesus,
who is both Redeemer and Brother,
through the power of the Spirit. Amen.

REFLECTION

(Material for leader to develop)

Beginnings. Beginnings seem to intrigue most of us.

People are often in search of their roots, their family tree, the foundations of a certain group or society. Beginnings attract us because they seem to contain some hidden wisdom, some simple insight as to the direction or goal of a person, family or event.

INTEGRATION

(Choose appropriate exercise/discussion questions) (Allow time for quiet reflection and small group sharing)

1. Tell a story about the beginnings of your family.

2. Why do you think people are so intrigued by their beginnings?

3. Why do you think having a sense of history is important for knowing yourself?

REFLECTION CONTINUES

The celebration of the Feast of the Immaculate Conception is a celebration of beginnings. Through Mary, God manifests the triumph of grace; the natural order is now the order of a graced nature. God surrounds Mary with the gift of God's love or grace; this is God's free choice and initiative. Mary stands as symbol of the relationship God also offers each of us: from the very beginning we have been surrounded with God's love, immersed in God's love so much so that God's love is indeed at the very core of our person. We were created as God's loved ones, "holy and blameless: to be full of love."

INTEGRATION

(Choose appropriate exercise/discussion questions)

1. Spend a few moments in silence. Create for yourself a sense of being in the womb. Create for yourself a sense of life within you. What would that experience be like? Envision this child (you) covered with bright light, feeling very good and warm, feeling welcomed and cared for. How do you think this will affect the child?

2. Reflect on stories you remember about yourself as a baby. Remember times when people loved you, cared for you. In this remembering is God's initial caring for you as you are.

REFLECTION CONTINUES

This feast also questions our awareness of our free choice to refuse life in God's love, to choose the reality of sin. It would be naive to think we live faithfully in relationship with God, choosing love as the center of our lives. We see the forces of dehumanization and degradation around us, and we need to humbly acknowledge our personal involvement in such destructive patterns of living. This is original sin: the reality that we are born into a world in which exists evil. We are not born evil and yet we find ourselves caught in the web of violence and destruction.

INTEGRATION

(Choose appropriate exercise/discussion questions)

1. What does sin look like? Try to create images that describe sin.

2. Have you ever felt "caught up" in a group experience, such as a pep rally or a football game? Describe the feeling. Can you remember similar experiences which were unhealthy, such as being caught up in a gossip circle, or other forms of violence? Describe the experience.

REFLECTION CONTINUES

The closing line of the Genesis texts links us with our Gospel account. Eve was named the mother of the living, a sign of hope of the ultimate victory of God's grace over death. Mary models the life of one who lives in fidelity to the core of a person, the grace-filled center where God is present. Great things happen in Mary because of God. She trusts who she is gifted to be and hence is open to the possibilities of life with God (rather than hiding in fear and shame). Mary is willing to entrust herself to God.

We are back to beginnings, new beginnings. Do we choose being turned in on ourselves, and hence being fearful, shamed, hiding? Or do we choose openness to possibilities? Such openness does not guarantee we will not be troubled or disturbed. But it bespeaks of a posture of life that is willing to listen to God's call, and therefore to be obedient. We can choose isolation and selfishness or we can choose a trust in God that can lead to a healthy sense of indifference, i.e., whatever the outcome, one trusts that God's will is our well-being. The Feast of the Immaculate Conception reminds us of not only Mary's beginnings but our beginnings as well. It is not a celebration of Mary's separation from the rest of us, but rather Mary as rooted in our deepest identity: men and women graced with God's presence at the core of our being. Mary chose to live from her center. What is your choice?

INTEGRATION

(Choose appropriate exercise/discussion questions):

1. Name your gifts. Gifts are not necessarily talents such as singing, or sports. How do you discover your gifts and the gifts of others?

2. Gifts are given for all. Reread the Gospel text slowly. Note where Mary recognizes her giftedness from God. How does she respond? How are you like Mary?

CLOSING PRAYER

Leader: Let us pray.
We praise you, O God who fashioned us
and loved us with an enduring love.
You are the source of our beginnings
and you have gifted us with your very life
    within us.
Give us the courage to look within
to discover the gifts of love you give us.
Help us find that our true beginning
is to start again and again as your children.
We make this prayer in the name of Jesus,
who is both Redeemer and Brother,
through the power of your Spirit. Amen.

Doctrinal and Pastoral Issues: Theology of Grace, Original Sin, Sin, Free Will, Role of Mary, Distinction Between Immaculate Conception and Virgin Birth, Stewardship of Gifts

Thomas H. Morris

(Reprinted from BREAKING OPEN THE WORD OF GOD, CYCLE A)

Additional Catechetical Resources

Listed on this bibliography are additional resources for a catechumenate director. Books listed in the various sections of this text are not necessarily reiterated here. This is a list of additional resources. This list is also in no way meant to be the last word. There are other exceptional materials available. Hopefully, there will be many more developed in the future.

Bausch, William J. *Storytelling: Imagination and Faith.* Twenty-Third Publications, Mystic, CT., 1984.

Bergan, Jacqueline and Schwan, S. Marie. *Forgiveness: A Guide for Prayer.* St. Mary's Press, Winona, 1985.

Coughlin, Kevin. *Finding God in Everyday Life.* Paulist Press, New York, 1980.

DeBoy, James. *Getting Started in Adult Religious Education.* Paulist Press, New York, 1979.

DeMello, Anthony. *Sadhana: A Way to God.* Institute of Jesuit Sources, St. Louis, 1979.

———, *The Song of the Bird.* Image Books, New York, 1984.

Duggan, Robert, Editor. *Conversation and the Catechumenate.* Paulist Press, New York, 1984.

Farrell, Edward. *Celtic Meditations.* Dimension Books, New Jersey, 1976.

Fischer, Kathleen. *The Inner Rainbow: The Imagination in Christian Life.* Paulist Press, New York, 1983.

Forum. Newsletter of the North American Forum on the Catechumenate. Washington, D.C.

Groome, Thomas. *Christian Religious Education.* Harper & Row, New York, 1980.

Halpin, Marlene. *Imagine That.* Wm C. Brown, Dubuque, Iowa, 1982.

Hays, Edward. *Prayers for the Domestic Church.* Forest of Peace, Easton, Kansas, 1979.

Hefling, Charles C. *Why Doctrines?* Cowley Publications.

Hestenes, Roberta. *Using the Bible in Groups.* Westminster Press, Philadelphia, 1983.

Huck, Gabe. *Teach Me to Pray.* Sadlier, New York.

Ivory, Tom. *Looking at Our Faith.* Sadlier, New York.

Link, Mark. *Breakaway.* Argus Communications, Allen, Texas, 1980.

Maloney, George. *Centering on the Lord Jesus: The Whole Person at Prayer.* Michael Glazier, Inc., Delaware, 1982.

McCauley, George. *The Unfinished Image.* Sadlier, New York, 1983.

McMakin, Jacqueline. *Doorways to Christian Growth.* Winston Seabury, 1984.

Palmer, Parker. *To Know as We Are Known: A Spirituality of Education.* Harper & Row, San Francisco, 1983.

Rite of Christian Initiation of Adults. USCC, Washington, D.C.

Share the Word. Paulist Evangelization Center, Washington, D.C.

Simons, George F. *Keeping Your Personal Journal.* Paulist Press, New York, 1978.

Smith, Gregory Michael. *The Fire in Their Eyes.* Paulist Press, New York, 1976.

Wallis, Jim. *A Call to Conversion.* Harper & Row, New York, 1981.

Warren, Michael, Editor. *Sourcebook for Modern Catechetics.* St. Mary's Press, Winona, 1983.

CALENDAR: ADVENT TO PENTECOST: 1986–1999

Year	Sunday Cycle	1st Sunday of Advent	1st Sunday of Lent	Easter Sunday	Pentecost
1986–87	A	Nov. 30	Mar. 8	Apr. 19	June 7
1987–88	B	Nov. 29	Feb. 21	Apr. 3	May 22
1988–89	C	Nov. 27	Feb. 12	Mar. 26	May 14
1989–90	A	Dec. 3	Mar. 4	Apr. 15	June 3
1990–91	B	Dec. 2	Feb. 17	Mar. 31	May 19
1991–92	C	Dec. 1	Mar. 8	Apr. 19	June 7
1992–93	A	Nov. 29	Feb. 28	Apr. 11	May 30
1993–94	B	Nov. 28	Feb. 20	Apr. 3	May 22
1994–95	C	Nov. 27	Mar. 5	Apr. 16	June 4
1995–96	A	Dec. 3	Feb. 25	Apr. 7	May 26
1996–97	B	Dec. 1	Feb. 16	Mar. 30	May 18
1997–98	C	Nov. 27	Mar. 1	Apr. 12	May 31
1998–99	A	Nov. 29	Feb. 21	Apr. 4	May 23

Contributors

Kathleen Brown is currently a member of the staff at the North American Forum on the Catechumenate. She received her Master's in Theology from St. Paul University in Ottawa, Canada. Ms. Brown was formerly the Adult Education Coordinator and Catechumenate Director for a parish in Tempe, Arizona.

Ellen Bush, CSC is a team member for the North American Forum on the Catechumenate and is currently working in Latin America. She formerly was Coordinator for Adult Development and Liturgy for the Diocese of Boise, Idaho. Her pastoral ministry also includes work in Colorado and in Southern California. She holds a Master's in Theology from the University of Notre Dame.

John T. Butler is Director of Parish Services for the Archdiocese of Washington, D.C. He holds a degree in counseling and is presently studying at Washington Theological Union for his Master's in Theological Studies. For the past five years he has been a team member for the North American Forum on the Catechumenate and is currently a member of their steering committee.

Clare M. Colella is Director of Electronic Communications for the Diocese of San Bernardino. She formerly was Director of the Office of Sacramental Formation there and continues to serve them as resource person, as well as being on her parish catechumenate team. For several years she served on the Board of the North American Forum on the Catechumenate. Mrs. Colella holds a Master's in Religious Education from Seattle University.

Rev. James B. Dunning, of the Diocese of Seattle, is currently President of the North American Forum on the Catechumenate and consultant in parish renewal and formation. Father Dunning is a recipient of the John XXIII Award for Contribution to Continuing Education of Priests. He is the author of *New Wine, New Wineskins: Exploring the Rite of Christian Initiation of Adults* and *Ministries: Sharing God's Gifts.*

Rev. Michael J. Koch is pastor of St. Philip Neri Church in Saskatoon, Canada. He received his education at the University of Saskatchewan and St. Joseph Seminary, Edmonton. He also studied at the University of San Francisco and in Jerusalem. Father Koch is a member of the steering committee of the North American Forum on the Catechumenate.

Rev. Eugene A. LaVerdiere, SSS is the editor of *Emmanuel* magazine and an associate editor of *The Bible Today.* He holds a doctorate in New Testament and Early Christian Literature from the University of Chicago. Father LaVerdiere is the author of many books as well as audio and video cassettes. His most recent books include *The New Testament in the Life of the Church* and *When We Pray* (both Ave Maria Press).

Elizabeth S. Lilly is the Liturgy Coordinator and Director of the Catechumenate in St. William Parish, Los Altos, California. She holds a Master's in the History of Art from the University of California, Berkeley. She is a member of the Diocesan Committee on the RCIA, Diocese of Monterey.

Thomas H. Morris is Director of Religious Education at St. Mary of the Mills Parish, Laurel, Maryland, where he also directs the catechumenate program. He holds a Master's in Theology from the Washington Theological Union and is completing doctoral studies in Christian Spirituality at The Catholic University of America.

Karen Hinman Powell is Executive Director of the North American Forum on the Catechumenate and consultant for parishes on the Rite of Christian Initiation of Adults and Adult Formation. Past experience includes work with three parish catechumenates in Mississippi, Maryland, and Virginia. She is the author of *How To Form A Catechumenate Team* (Liturgy Training Publications) and co-editor of *Breaking Open the Word of God* for Cycle A. She holds a M.Div. degree from the Jesuit School of Theology in Chicago.

Alexander J. Shaia is currently the Director of the RCIA for a parish in the Bay Area of California. He has had many years of experience in catechetical work and the catechumenate process. His work spans the national and diocesan levels, as well as parish ministry. He holds Master's degrees in Religious Education and Counseling.

Joseph P. Sinwell is Diocesan Director of Religious Education, Diocese of Providence, and Co-Director of the Rhode Island Catechumenate. He is a founding member of the North American Forum on the Catechumenate and currently serves on its executive committee as treasurer. He holds Master's degrees in Religious Education and Agency Counseling and is a candidate for a Doctor of Ministry degree at St. Mary's University, Baltimore. Mr. Sinwell is co-editor of *Breaking Open the Word of God,* Cycle A.